Carmen ~~Cann~~ was ~~......~~ ~~.......~~ ...ne to the UK in 1960. A book p~~.......~~ ~~........~~ ~~.......~~)72 and ten years later became m~~.......~~ ~~.......~~ ~~...~~ & Windus. She is the author of *Bad Fai~~.......~~ ~~....ry of~~ Family and Fatherland*, which was shortlisted for the Samuel Johnson prize. She lives in London.

~~.....~~ **n Tóibín** was born in Ireland in 1955. He is the author of six ~~nov~~els including *The Master*, which won the Los Angeles Times ~~Boo~~k Prize for Fiction, the International IMPAC Dublin Literary ~~Aw~~ard and the Prix Medicis étranger. He has also written short ~~stor~~ies, a play and several works of non-fiction. He lives in Dublin.

THE
MODERN LIBRARY

Carmen Callil and Colm Tóibín

RUNNING PRESS
PHILADELPHIA · LONDON

ROBINSON

Constable & Robinson Ltd
3 The Lanchesters
162 Fulham Palace Road
London W6 9ER
www.constablerobinson.com

First published in the UK by Picador, 1999

This paperback edition published in the UK by Robinson,
an imprint of Constable & Robinson, 2011

A copy of the British Library Cataloguing in Publication Data is available from the British Library

UK ISBN 978-1-84901-676-6

1 3 5 7 9 10 8 6 4 2

First published in the United States in 2011 by Running Press Book Publishers.
All rights reserved under the Pan-American and International Copyright Conventions

9 8 7 6 5 4 3 2 1

Digit on the right indicates the number of this printing

US Library of Congress Control number: 2010940976
US ISBN 978-0-7624-4276-8

Running Press Book Publishers
2300 Chestnut Street
Philadelphia, PA 19103-4371

Visit us on the web!
www.runningpress.com

Typeset by TW Typesetting, Plymouth, Devon

Printed and bound in the UK

Contents

Contents

For Peter Straus

Introduction

Books such as this often come with a daunting or gloomy introduction in which the condition of the novel is put under a microscope. Is the novel read? Is the novel dead? Has anything worthy been written since Austen, Dickens, Melville, Joyce? How can the novel compete with satellite and cable television, video, films, CD roms, the internet, sport, rock music and other forms of what is known as mass culture? We live today, in the famously miserable words of the American critic Harold Bloom, in the 'Age of Resentment' in which 'devoted and solitary readers are now necessarily beleaguered': culture is in irretrievable decline, the romance of reading gone for ever. We think otherwise. Merchants of cultural doom are hostile to change. We are not: we embrace it, were brought up with it, wallow in it rather, fighting political correctness with one paw, and gloomy ideologies with the other.

For the novel survives and flourishes: there are more bookshops than ever before, and wider choice; late twentieth-century marketing methods have been skilfully used by publishers; novels continue to be a source for film, television and the theatre. As anyone who has worked in the business of publishing, or who has been published, however fretfully, knows, the second fifty years of this century – the years we two have lived through – have been a period as sublime and exciting as any other for the novel. The mass market paperback came into its own during these fifty years. Books have benefited from a revolution in publishing and printing and selling methods; the computer has waved a magic wand over most publishing processes; authors have more rights, and many, if still too few, earn more money.

Enthusiasm is the driving force of this book. Its purpose is to celebrate the writers we have loved best, and to proselytize on behalf of their novels: sources of entertainment and enjoyment as satisfying as any Hollywood movie, football match, computer game or rock video. We recommend these novels, not for their academic interest, or their illustration of the theory of the death of the author (an invention, in Carmen Callil's opinion, of academic literary critics

1

with not enough to do to pass the time of day), but for precisely the opposite reason, for their illustration of the very life of the author, the power of the live voice, the passion to tell a story, invent characters and find a form.

The Modern Movement in literature – as represented by, say, Eliot, Joyce, Pound and Woolf has been seen as a great revolution which swept everything else away, or, on the other hand, as an insurrection, a rebellion, which seemed like a revolution until everything went back to the state it was in before the insurgents began. The novels written in English over the last fifty years manage to illustrate both of these theories.

Novels have appeared: William Gaddis's *The Recognitions*, for example, or Alasdair Gray's *Lanark* or Thomas Pynchon's *Gravity's Rainbow* or Angela Carter's *Wise Children* or Iain Sinclair's *Downriver* – which take their bearings from Joyce and Woolf, which remain massively ambitious and complex, in which language and form are fluid and under pressure, in which notions of characters, dialogue, plot, action are open to question.

But other novels have appeared alongside them, such as John Steinbeck's *East of Eden* or Anita Brookner's *Family and Friends* or Sam Hanna Bell's *December Bride* or Patrick Hamilton's *The West Pier* or Elizabeth Jenkins's *The Tortoise and the Hare* or Margaret Laurence's *A Jest of God*, which seem to take their bearing from a much earlier tradition, which treat character and plot and dialogue as not open to question at all, and insist successfully on an earlier narrative style, a system in which things are slowly revealed and objects in the landscape are described in some detail.

And then there is a third way in which novelists have worked – and this is the most common. They have attended to all the lessons which Joyce and Woolf taught about language and form and especially voice and tone, but they have refused to abandon completely lessons learned from other novelists who adhered to more traditional methods. Thus the revolution did not cause the destruction of the novel in which character and voice and plot play a non-revolutionary role; instead, it refined the idea of character and voice and plot, it made novelists more self-conscious, more careful, and the language of the novel more precise, snappier and richer. Thus the battle between Modernism and tradition has been enabling and useful for the individual talent and the individual reader: it allows us not to take sides, but to reap the rewards of what is various and multi-faceted.

Over the past fifty years the map of the novel has changed. There are countries where English is seen as both a plague inflicted on the population and at the same time as a language which they have come to possess more sonorously than the English themselves. In this way, we have studied the novel in English, and not the English novel. And so, here is a choice from India, Pakistan, New Zealand, England, Ireland, Scotland, the USA, Australia, Canada, Africa, the Caribbean, Hong Kong and more.

An example of the joy to be found in this worldwide flowering of the novel in English is the sheer pleasure of coming across, say, the fiction of modern India, in which all the familiar narrative genius of the traditional novel – the eighteenth-century confessional novel, the nineteenth-century Dickensian novel – is completely transformed into a vehicle for dramatizing the sprawl, variety and sense of infinite possibility which is modern India. At the other end of the scale, the Scottish novel in the 1980s and 1990s has become a sharp weapon in the battle for Scottish identity and autonomy.

The period from 1950 is characterized by a change in those who wrote and read fiction too. Women have moved to the centre of the novel, so that if you look at the list which we have made today and compare it with an equivalent list from the first half of the century, the new power of women as writers is obvious, though the tradition in which they write is not new at all. Anyone who has read the work of Jane Austen and looks then at the work of Penelope Fitzgerald, Ivy Compton-Burnett, Elizabeth Taylor, Elizabeth Jolley, Beryl Bainbridge will notice a definite continuity of tone and theme, and the abiding presence of wit. The silent history of certain human experiences was made public for the first time in a number of influential novels – not only by women, but by writers from parts of the world which had never produced writers before. And these became vital for people, not only as books which they enjoyed, but as books which changed their lives – Toni Morrison's *Beloved*,

3

Doris Lessing's *The Golden Notebook*, Chinua Achebe's *Things Fall Apart*, Frank Hardy's *Power Without Glory*, John McGahern's *Amongst Women*.

Another reason for this book is to represent the novelist as a person who performs a function essential to the soul of every community: the secret conscience of the tribe. Some of us live in societies in which our governments support and celebrate sportsmen and sportswomen, film stars, opera singers and pop singers and ignore more or less completely their writers. This is particularly true of England and the USA where the gap between those who are aware of their literary inheritance and those who are not is uncomfortably large. Other countries are different. In societies such as Ireland or Scotland, as we have already said, the novel has come to fill in certain gaps, spaces between the public and the private, and the novelist – whether he or she likes it or not – has seemed to strengthen a fragile identity. In Nigeria, the novelist has become a dangerous opposition to those in power. In Canada, they produce only geniuses. In other societies where whole communities have been marginalized and impoverished, the novel has yet to enter its heroic phase.

On the other hand, the way the novel has developed has not always been appreciated by the publishing industry. Publishers in London or New York, still the two centres of power in English language publishing, continue to display very little interest in the writers of, say, Australia or India. There are the Whites and Maloufs and the Mistrys and Desais, of course, but in Britain and the United States it is hard to find the books of Elizabeth Jolley or Jessica Anderson, and much of Narayan is out of print. With the continuing demise of the power of the editor within publishing, there is even less chance that the true richness of English-language fiction will be internationally known. We have used bookshops and scholars all over the world to help us track down hidden treasures, and it seems to us amazing, having done this work, that writers such as Eugene McCabe, Frank Sargeson, Alistair MacLeod and Bapsi Sidwha have not won the international fame that they deserve. They belong to an international secret canon which this book seeks to disclose.

4

What we have noticed and appreciated in these books is the sense of the individual voice at work and sometimes at play, the individual will, the individual choice, the individual talent, the direct relationship between the writer and the reader. (No wonder governments are suspicious of writers.) But there are fascinating national myths and mores, aspects of heritage and history, to which many writers subscribe.

It is, of course, not possible to talk about a National Style for novelists, but some themes have endured: from the Indian novels chosen here you will learn a great deal about Partition, the British Raj, the caste system, the influence of mass poverty and religion on India; there are a good number of novels in this list about racial tension in the United States (Morrison, Baldwin, Harper Lee, Styron, Pete Dexter, Doctorow); other Americans, men only, attempt a sweeping, ambitious history, as though no other version existed (Pynchon, DeLillo, McCarthy, Heller, Mailer); other Americans manage to dramatize the individual's isolation, eccentricity and sense of not being part of the official version (Flannery O'Connor, Cheever, Marilynne Robinson, Salinger, Edmund White, Plath, Easton Ellis). In Africa, the conflict between colonized and colonizer remains a theme which no one can escape. In Ireland, the Troubles haunt some contemporary writing, but then other writers (Beckett, Roddy Doyle, John Banville) refuse to deal with them, and their work becomes all the richer and stranger for that. In Britain, the rise of Margaret Thatcher (Mrs Torture in Salman Rushdie's phrase) has animated a number of novelists (Martin Amis, Angela Carter, Jonathan Coe, Alasdair Gray), and the class system has provided novelists with much material (Pat Barker, Elizabeth Jenkins, Agatha Christie, Maureen Duffy, Bruce Chatwin, L. P. Hartley). In England novelists have also played with a storytelling tradition, producing novels that have a solidity and beauty (Alan Hollinghurst, Julian Barnes, Anthony Powell, Sylvia Townsend Warner). In Australia, the creation of the new nation itself, the arrival of the whites and their efforts to make a society out of that vast country, and to come to terms with its original inhabitants, has been a large theme. It is impossible to make generalizations about Canada: the connection between Michael Ondaatje, Alice Munro,

Mavis Gallant, Margaret Atwood, Robertson Davies, Mordecai Richler, Alistair MacLeod and Margaret Laurence is only that they are writers whom everyone should read.

This idea of a national inheritance is complicated by the great migrations of the nineteenth and twentieth centuries. Was Brian Moore Irish or Canadian? Is Amy Tan American or Chinese? Is V. S. Naipaul Trinidadian or English? Is Oscar Hijuelos Cuban or American? The answer is all are both.

While we differ in our response to literary theory – one of us is hostile to it, the other cannot have enough of it – we were as one in our determination to ignore the distinction between so-called popular fiction and literary fiction (also so-called). This false distinction which is prevalent in literary prizes, in academia and in our educational mores, has been responsible for the treacherous suggestion that reading is a chore, and that the best writing is always difficult and obscure.

For us, the debate as to whether *Interview with the Vampire* is of greater intrinsic merit than *Oscar and Lucinda* is irrelevant, because any decision on the subject – and a decision can be made – alters not at all the fact that both are splendid feats of the human imagination, explains nothing of the pleasure experienced as the novelists' words lock into the reader's imagination, but simply reveals a great deal about those arguing. The critical dividing line between popular and literary also ignores the reader and the writer, who rarely contemplate the novel in this way.

There are novelists, of course, who are not interested in the reaction of their readers, who would write for a seagull if that bird praised such a novelist's self-absorptions. We have, generally, avoided them effortlessly. Not altogether, of course, because some, albeit few, are great writers who have created complex and difficult novels, which require concentration but are worth it.

We chose these books together on the basis that the idea of two people disputing – hotly at times, not at all on other occasions – is always preferable to one person laying down the law. We come from different places. Both of us come from the Free World, i.e. neither of us is English or American, and we have not the slightest interest in political correctness. We have different prejudices and preferences. Any list such as this is entirely personal, but in every choice we've looked for the same quality – a certain (or sometimes even an uncertain) genius in the work, a certain (always certain) excitement in the reading, and a feeling that you would love to hand this book to someone else to read. Most of us, these days, are almost imprisoned by choice, as anyone examining the fiction shelves of a large bookshop will notice. We have used our prejudices and preferences to cut a path through this rich jungle, using as our final point of judgement that touch of genius and sense of excitement which connect Patrick White with Ruth Rendell, Georgette Heyer with Don DeLillo, Daphne du Maurier with Katherine Anne Porter, J. D. Salinger with Irvine Welsh.

A large part of the list is common to both of us; some choices, while admired by both, more passionately belong to one or the other. In only two cases we could not agree: V. S. Naipaul and Saul Bellow have two entries, not because we consider them greater than any of the other novelists we have chosen, but because one of us considered *A Bend in the River* and *Herzog* to be the masterworks of Naipaul and Bellow, while the other disliked *Herzog* but argued passionately for Bellow's *The Adventures of Augie March* and could not feel *A Bend in the River* to be the equal of *A House for Mr Biswas*. For the rest, and for arguably greater writers, only one entry was necessary. It was often difficult to decide which work by a single writer to include: in the case of Nabokov, for example, between *Ada*, *Pnin*, *Pale Fire* or *Lolita*; in the case of Nadine Gordimer between *The Conservationist*, *July's People* and *Burgher's Daughter*. We also chose to ignore the ghetto into which short stories are often placed.

Only books published in 1950 or afterwards and only books written in English qualified. We have included some collections of stories but mainly novels. We have included trilogies and single books from trilogies. There are no translations except those done by the author. We did not consider novels which were written in the earlier half of the century, but not published, for various reasons, until the second half. (These include E. M. Forster's *Maurice*, Hemingway's *The Garden of Eden* and Flann O'Brien's *The Third Policeman*.) Many of the novelists we have chosen flourished also in the earlier half of the century – Faulkner, Waugh, Lehmann, du Maurier, Welty, Hemingway, Agatha Christie, P. G. Wodehouse, Patrick Hamilton, Graham Greene, Elizabeth Bowen: we hope to send readers back to earlier years and so trace an enduring tradition.

Why 194 choices, and not 200 as in the title of the book? As we chose and wrote, and agreed and disagreed, we came across novels, often famous novels, which we did not appreciate: Tolkien's *Lord of the Rings* for instance, science fiction and fantasy novels, and most historical novels. We read and rejected them knowing that even two omnivorous readers cannot represent every taste. Indignation, as well as pleasure, will, we hope, be among the first reactions to this book. We are well aware of our omissions, and want the reader to spot them. This is a book which requires action on the part of the reader, and so six novels have been chosen by the book-reading public and added to this book for all future editions.

We have chosen these novels for readers, readers of every age and taste, for those who have never read a novel before and for experts who want to quarrel with our choice; for school students and undergraduates, grandfathers, priests and nuns, Antarctic explorers. There are short novels and long novels, each kind providing a different kind of pleasure. A twelve-year-old could read Harper Lee's *To Kill A Mockingbird*, a ninety-year-old Anne Tyler's *Breathing Lessons* and be very happy; Thomas Flanagan's historical masterpiece *The Year of the French* and Thomas Harris's startling *Red Dragon* offer other pleasures, as indeed do Hubert Selby Jr's *Last Exit to Brooklyn* and William Burroughs' *Naked Lunch*.

For surrealists, there is Henry Green and Ivy Compton-Burnett, for romantics Rosamond Lehmann, Louis de Bernières and Sybille Bedford, for wits Muriel Spark, J. G. Farrell, for murder fiends Agatha Christie and Elmore Leonard, Carl Hiaasen and Donna Tartt, Roy Heath and P. D. James, not to speak of Bret Easton Ellis; for Cold War fanatics there is Graham Greene and Don DeLillo; for lovers of Dickens and Eliot there is Mistry, Byatt, Smiley, Storey. There are many crime novels and thrillers. Some of the greatest writers of the period are represented by their short stories – V. S. Prichett, Alice Munro, Mavis Gallant, Mary Lavin, Raymond Carver.

Most exciting was the discovery that some novels loved first twenty or thirty years ago have improved with age. For instance, Olivia Manning's Balkan trilogy, B. S. Johnson's *The Unfortunates*, Evelyn Waugh's Sword of Honour trilogy, John O'Hara's *From the Terrace* feel ready for reassessment. However good we thought them before, they seem finer now.

There were no quotas for men, women or race in choosing these books. The only constraint on our choice was the lack of availability of books from certain countries. Otherwise, we began and ended with open minds, and the books we chose are here because we loved them.

We both have memories from childhood and adolescence of being wrapped up in books. Books were a way of escaping the world, and also of entering it in a way that was more intense; a way of discovering feeling; a working out of how to live. Both of us were constantly reminded, as we did our research, of moments from childhood and adolescence – finding a book we hadn't read or had forgotten, and after a few pages, suddenly being enclosed, cocooned, absorbed and totally involved in its world; finding ourselves anxious and dispossessed until we took it up again.

Books were happiness. We were brought up in places where reading was a passion and a joy. It still is for us. And so here they are: books which we offer wholeheartedly to the reader as you would give to a friend going on a journey; 194 examples of the best novels and stories in English published during the last half of the twentieth century.

How to use this book
All entries are alphabetical under the name of the author. Sometimes we have chosen a novel within a sequence, sometimes the sequence itself: the full work is detailed in both cases.

A note on this edition
Our readers, all over the world, sent us thousands of entries for the final six titles for this book. The four most popular are included

here. In order of popularity they read as follows: Sebastian Faulks' *Birdsong*, Charles Frazier's *Cold Mountain*, John Fowles' *The Magus* – which beat his *French Lieutenant's Woman* by a whisker – and Vikram Seth's *A Suitable Boy*.

We used our rights as authors to choose the last two: William Maxwell's *So Long, See You Tomorrow* because it was a grave omission and authorial mistake of ours in the hardback edition, and Helen Garner's *The Children's Bach* because she topped the poll outside the world of British and American writers, who seem to dominate our readers' tastes.

List of titles in order of publication

1950   **A Murder is Announced** Agatha Christie
Nothing Henry Green
Power Without Glory Frank Hardy
The Grand Sophy Georgette Heyer

1951   **December Bride** Sam Hanna Bell
My Cousin Rachel Daphne du Maurier
The West Pier Patrick Hamilton
The Ballad of the Sad Café Carson McCullers
A Dance to the Music of Time (1951–75) Anthony Powell
The Catcher in the Rye J. D. Salinger

1952   **Invisible Man** Ralph Ellison
The Old Man and the Sea Ernest Hemingway
The Natural Bernard Malamud
The Financial Expert R. K. Narayan
Wise Blood Flannery O'Connor
East of Eden John Steinbeck
The Sword of Honour Trilogy (1952–61) Evelyn Waugh

1953   **Private Life of an Indian Prince** Mulk Raj Anand
Go Tell it on the Mountain James Baldwin
The Adventures of Augie March Saul Bellow
The Long Good-Bye Raymond Chandler
The Go-Between L. P. Hartley
The Echoing Grove Rosamond Lehmann
The Palm-Wine Drinkard Amos Tutuola

1954   **Lucky Jim** Kingsley Amis
Lord of the Flies William Golding
The Tortoise and the Hare Elizabeth Jenkins
The Flint Anchor Sylvia Townsend Warner

1955   **The Molloy Trilogy** (1955–58) Samuel Beckett
The Recognitions William Gaddis
The Talented Mr Ripley Patricia Highsmith
Lolita Vladimir Nabokov

1956   **A Legacy** Sybille Bedford
Train to Pakistan Khushwant Singh

1957   **Owls Do Cry** Janet Frame
On the Road Jack Kerouac
Angel Elizabeth Taylor
The Fountain Overflows Rebecca West

1958   **Things Fall Apart** Chinua Achebe
Anecdotes of Destiny Isak Dinesen
From the Terrace John O'Hara
Saturday Night and Sunday Morning Alan Sillitoe

1959   **Naked Lunch** William Burroughs
A Heritage and its History Ivy Compton-Burnett
The Little Disturbances of Man Grace Paley

1960   **To Kill a Mockingbird** Harper Lee
The Balkan Trilogy (1960–65) Olivia Manning
The Rabbit Quartet (1960–90) John Updike
Jeeves in the Offing P. G. Wodehouse
(US: *How Right You Are, Jeeves*)

1961   **Catch-22** Joseph Heller
A House for Mr Biswas V. S. Naipaul
The Prime of Miss Jean Brodie Muriel Spark
Riders in the Chariot Patrick White

1962   **That's How it Was** Maureen Duffy
The Reivers William Faulkner

The Golden Notebook Doris Lessing
The Lonely Girl Edna O'Brien
(renamed *Girl with Green Eyes* 1964)
Ship of Fools Katherine Anne Porter

1963   **The Little Girls** Elizabeth Bowen
        The Spy Who Came in from the Cold John Le Carré
        The Group Mary McCarthy
        The Bell Jar Sylvia Plath

1964   **Herzog** Saul Bellow
        Heartland Wilson Harris
        Last Exit to Brooklyn Hubert Selby Jr.

1965   **Memoirs of a Peon** Frank Sargeson
        The Interpreters Wole Soyinka

1966   **The Magus** John Fowles
        A Jest of God Margaret Laurence
        Wide Sargasso Sea Jean Rhys
        The Jewel in the Crown Paul Scott
        Cotters' England Christina Stead
        (US: *Dark Places of the Heart* 1967)

1967   **The Confessions of Nat Turner** William Styron
        A Grain of Wheat Ngugi Wa Thiong'o

1968   **In the Heart of the Heart of the Country** William H.
        Gass
        The Nice and the Good Iris Murdoch

1969   **The Unfortunates** B. S. Johnson
        Happiness Mary Lavin
        The Godfather Mario Puzo

13

| 1970 | **Fifth Business** Robertson Davies |
| | **Master and Commander** Patrick O'Brian |

1970   **Fifth Business** Robertson Davies
              Master and Commander Patrick O'Brian

1971   **The Day of the Jackal** Frederick Forsyth
              St Urbain's Horseman Mordecai Richler
              Black List, Section H Francis Stuart

1972   **The Optimist's Daughter** Eudora Welty

1973   **The Siege of Krishnapur** J. G. Farrell
              Gravity's Rainbow Thomas Pynchon

1975   **Ragtime** E. L. Doctorow
              Heat and Dust Ruth Prawer Jhabvala
              Changing Places David Lodge

1976   **The Lost Salt Gift of Blood** Alistair MacLeod
              Interview with the Vampire Anne Rice
              Saville David Storey

1977   **Injury Time** Beryl Bainbridge
              Falconer John Cheever
              A Book of Common Prayer Joan Didion
              The Ice Age Margaret Drabble

1978   **Tirra Lirra by the River** Jessica Anderson
              Plumb Maurice Gee
              The Human Factor Graham Greene
              The Murderer Roy A. K. Heath
              The Cement Garden Ian McEwan

1979   **The Year of the French** Thomas Flanagan
              From the Fifteenth District Mavis Gallant
              Burger's Daughter Nadine Gordimer
              Sleepless Nights Elizabeth Hardwick
              The Executioner's Song Norman Mailer
              A Bend in the River V. S. Naipaul

1980   **Earthly Powers** Anthony Burgess
          The Transit of Venus Shirley Hazzard
          Riddley Walker Russell Hoban
          Lamb Bernard MacLaverty
          So Long, See You Tomorrow William Maxwell
          Housekeeping Marilynne Robinson
          A Confederacy of Dunces John Kennedy Toole
          Puffball Fay Weldon

1981   **Lanark** Alasdair Gray
          Red Dragon Thomas Harris
          Midnight's Children Salman Rushdie
          A Flag for Sunrise Robert Stone

1982   **On the Black Hill** Bruce Chatwin
          Schindler's Ark Thomas Keneally
          (US: *Schindler's List*)
          The Color Purple Alice Walker
          A Boy's Own Story Edmund White

1984   **Money** Martin Amis
          Empire of the Sun J. G. Ballard
          Flaubert's Parrot Julian Barnes
          In Custody Anita Desai
          The Children's Bach Helen Garner
          Nation of Fools Balraj Khanna
          Machine Dreams Jayne Anne Phillips

1985   **Family and Friends** Anita Brookner
          Blood Meridian Cormac McCarthy
          Lonesome Dove Larry McMurtry
          Black Robe Brian Moore
          Oranges Are Not the Only Fruit Jeanette Winterson

1986   **The Sportswriter** Richard Ford
          An Artist of the Floating World Kazuo Ishiguro

A Summons to Memphis Peter Taylor
A Dark-Adapted Eye Barbara Vine (Ruth Rendell)

1987   **Ellen Foster** Kaye Gibbons
           Double Whammy Carl Hiaasen
           Misery Stephen King
           Beloved Toni Morrison
           In the Skin of a Lion Michael Ondaatje
           The Other Garden Francis Wyndham

1988   **Oscar and Lucinda** Peter Carey
           Where I'm Calling From Raymond Carver
           Paris Trout Pete Dexter
           The Sugar Mother Elizabeth Jolley
           Forty-Seventeen Frank Moorhouse
           Ice-Candy-Man Bapsi Sidhwa
           Breathing Lessons Anne Tyler
           The Bonfire of the Vanities Tom Wolfe

1989   **The Book of Evidence** John Banville
           The Mambo Kings Play Songs of Love Oscar Hijuelos
           The Joy Luck Club Amy Tan

1990   **Possession** A. S. Byatt
           Age of Iron J. M. Coetzee
           A Home at the End of the World Michael Cunningham
           The Snapper Roddy Doyle
           Get Shorty Elmore Leonard
           Amongst Women John McGahern
           The Great World David Malouf
           Friend of My Youth Alice Munro

1991   **The Regeneration Trilogy** (1991–95) Pat Barker
           Wise Children Angela Carter
           A Strange and Sublime Address Amit Chaudhuri

American Psycho Bret Easton Ellis
The Redundancy of Courage Timothy Mo
Mating Norman Rush
Downriver Iain Sinclair
A Thousand Acres Jane Smiley
Reading Turgenev William Trevor
Cloudstreet Tim Winton

1992　**Death and Nightingales** Eugene McCabe
The Butcher Boy Patrick McCabe
The Secret History Donna Tartt

1993　**The Virgin Suicides** Jeffrey Eugenides
Birdsong Sebastian Faulks
A River Sutra Gita Mehta
The Shipping News E. Annie Proulx
My Idea of Fun Will Self
A Suitable Boy Vikram Seth
Trainspotting Irvine Welsh

1994　**What a Carve Up!** Jonathan Coe
(US: *The Winshaw Legacy*)
Captain Corelli's Mandolin Louis de Bernières
(US: *Corelli's Mandolin*)
The Folding Star Alan Hollinghurst
Original Sin P. D. James
How Late it Was, How Late James Kelman

1995　**The Tortilla Curtain** T. Coraghessan Boyle
The Blue Flower Penelope Fitzgerald
A Fine Balance Rohinton Mistry

1996　**Alias Grace** Margaret Atwood
Asylum Patrick McGrath
Last Orders Graham Swift
The Night in Question Tobias Wolff

1997   **Quarantine** Jim Crace
Underworld Don DeLillo
Cold Mountain Charles Frazier
American Pastoral Philip Roth

1998   **The Lady From Guatemala** V. S. Pritchett

Chinua Achebe 1930–

1958   *Things Fall Apart*

This short novel, written in short chapters, tells the story of the end of one era of civilization in a remote part of Nigeria, and the beginning of colonialism and Christianity. Achebe's touch is so light, however, and his skill with character and pacing so brilliant, and his sense of detail and nuance so delightful, that you barely realize as you turn the pages that you are being steeped in the atmosphere of a crucial moment in history. The novel focuses on the character of Okonkwo, strong, stubborn and hard-working, locked into the traditions he has inherited. It tells the story of his wives and his children, village life, local traditions, including the story of a boy who is taken from another village as retribution; he comes to live with Okonkwo's family, and slowly Okonkwo grows to love him, but the reader knows that he will eventually have to be sacrificed. The scene where he is killed is magnificently stark, almost unbearable to read. It is clear now that Okonkwo's strength is a sort of weakness. The arrival of the English is seen first as a small, insignificant event, and there are moments towards the end of the book where Achebe presents what the reader knows will be a tragedy with a mixture of irony, sadness and a sort of anger. When this novel was first presented to Heinemann, the reader wrote 'the best first novel since the war'. Forty years later, it is still the best first novel since the war.

Chinua Achebe was born in eastern Nigeria and divides his time between Nigeria and the USA. *Things Fall Apart* has sold over two million copies and been translated into thirty languages. It is the first book of the Africa trilogy; the others are *No Longer at Ease* (1960) and *Arrow of God* (1964). He was awarded the Man Booker International Prize in 2007.

Age in year of publication: twenty-eight.

Kingsley Amis 1922–1995

1954 *Lucky Jim*

This is the story of Jim Dixon, who finds himself lecturing in Medieval History in a provincial university. Jim's prospects are grim; he knows hardly anything about his subject. His real skills are making funny faces behind people's backs and disguising his complete contempt for those around him (especially his dreadful boss) – but the second of these fails him when he meets Bertrand, his boss's bearded and pretentious artist son. Jim is half in love with mad Margaret who teaches at the university; she throws him out of her room when 'he made a movement not only quite unambiguous, but, even perhaps, rather insolently frank'. In one set scene the boss gives a really awful party, and our hero manages to burn the bedclothes.

The writing is constantly funny; Dixon's ability to cause calamity all around him and then make things much worse, his mixture of innocence and pure malice, make you laugh out loud and follow his antics and his fate with amusement and great interest. Amis is brilliant at stringing out a joke, at twisting and turning the plot, and at never making Jim either ridiculous or stupid, but somehow right to get drunk when he does, or put on funny voices, or curse his boss, or hate the Middle Ages and an appalling student called Michie. The comedy is brilliantly sustained in the book, and the conflicts well articulated, so that the narrative becomes a picture of the post-war age when a new generation – the Jims of this world – grew up having no respect for their elders and betters.

Kingsley Amis was born in South London and taught at the University of Swansea and then Cambridge before settling again in London. He was the author of more than twenty works of fiction. *Lucky Jim* was filmed in 1958. He won the Booker Prize for *The Old Devils* in 1986.

Age in year of publication: thirty-two.

Martin Amis 1949–

1984   *Money*

John Self is one of those young men who sprang up in Thatcher's England in the 1980s, savouring money and using it like tomato sauce. A thirty-five-year-old director of TV commercials, Self is about to make his first real movie. With his devotion to alcohol and nicotine, pornography and video nasties, and sufficient fast food to ensure his hideous pot belly a life of its own, it's only money keeping the wolves of excess from Self's door. He jets between New York and London encountering a misbegotten collection of narcissistic and exquisitely named stars – Butch Beausoleil, Caduta Massi, Spunk Davis – panting alternately after his English girlfriend Selina Street and his American muse Martina Twain.

Self's story is a corrosive moral tale about England's recent past – 'The skies are so ashamed. The trees in the squares hang their heads, the evening paper in its cage is ashamed.' With the mordant thud and rhythm of his startling prose, Martin Amis beats the greed and venality of that decade into submission. The verbal rainstorm that Amis pours through Self's repellent mouth – the dialogue acid, perfectly pitched – is a rousing example of the Amis style which has made his work in general and *Money* in particular so important to his contemporaries, and so splenetic a mirror of late twentieth-century England.

Martin Amis was born in Oxford and lives in London. Amongst his most influential novels are the West London trio beginning with *Money*, and followed by *London Fields* (1989) and *The Information* (1996).

Age in year of publication: thirty-five.

Mulk Raj Anand 1905–2004

1953   *Private Life of an Indian Prince*

In 1947, the year of Indian independence from Britain, there were five hundred and sixty-two Indian princedoms. These princes were gradually stripped of their power and Anand, the great Indian chronicler of the humble poor, turned his attention to these 'poor rich'. Anand's fictional prince, the Maharaja Ashok Kumar, is one of those who preferred to believe Queen Victoria's pledge – reaffirmed by subsequent British governments – that their rights would be protected in an independent India. Foolish man. Scion of a long line of equally foolish Maharajas of Sham Fur, Ashok is a charmer, but decadent, spoilt and politically incompetent. Having rid himself of two Maharanees, he is ruled by the whims and hysterics of his mistress, the spellbinding Ganga Dasi. He lives in disintegrating times: his greed and improvidence have led his subjects towards revolt; his assertion of independence is anachronistic and useless. There remains only his sexual obsession, and this survives betrayal and madness to take on an integrity of its own. Anand is a master of character and circumstance, and he recounts his prince's story with a powerful mixture of psychological understanding, perverse humour and political insight. This is one of the best descriptions of sexual obsession: it is rare to find a portrait of a man bewitched, which is at once so ironic and lyrical, so profoundly affecting.

Mulk Raj Anand was born in Peshawar and after many years in England, returned to India at the end of the Second World War. *Untouchable* (1935) and *Coolie* (1936) are amongst his famous novels.

Age in year of publication: forty-eight.

Jessica Anderson 1916–2010

1978   *Tirra Lirra by the River*

'Tirra Lirra' was the song Sir Lancelot sang as he rode by the river on his way to Camelot. Nora Porteous discovers this in a book of her father's, who died when she was six. Camelot becomes a region of her mind, a retreat for her artist's imagination from the dismal gentility of Australian suburbia. Seventy years later, after adult life in Sydney and London, Nora returns to the now empty family home and stretches her memory not only to recall, but to understand the past. In seven flashbacks she contemplates her marriage to the repulsive Colin – 'Look, just lie still, will you? That's all you have to do'; her artistic life as a skilled dressmaker and embroiderer; her female life – love, the lack of it, the presence of it in unexpected places, the trauma of an illegal abortion, acutely rendered. Jessica Anderson transforms this superficially simple story of an eighty-year-old woman's quest for a sense of self into a fine novel. Often laconic, and very often funny, her intuitive understanding of the reek of futility that seeps through most people's lives produces a telling account of the nobility of the everyday. Nora, 'a woman of no consequence', becomes a heroine in one of the very few novels in which an old woman is such a memorable character.

Jessica Anderson was born in Queensland and lived in Sydney. She also wrote short stories, and her novel *The Impersonators* (1980) was highly praised. *Tirra Lirra by the River* won the 1978 Miles Franklin Award.

Age in year of publication: sixty-two.

Margaret Atwood 1939–

1996   *Alias Grace*

Grace Marks was imprisoned in 1843 as an accomplice to the murder of her employer Thomas Kinnear and his mistress, the housekeeper Nancy. Grace is a mysterious person, young, defenceless, not at all stupid, given to the odd remark that keeps her watchers guessing. Her sentence of death is commuted to life imprisonment, at which point she becomes fair game for the doctors and do-gooders who wish to analyse good and evil and women in general, and Grace in particular.

Muffled ambivalences surround Grace, her life, her minders and her betters. The medical absurdities the professionals perpetrate, and the potent contribution of sex, greed and ambition, illuminate the manners of those times, and contrast piteously with the wretched condition of the lower orders in eighteenth-century Canada – as everywhere else.

Alias Grace has the sharp flavour of Margaret Atwood's formidable intelligence; her ability to control form and structure is always remarkable. Within her easy mastery of social realism she accommodates serious matters, crucial ideas. The battle for power represented by enigmatic sexual encounters shows men manipulating women, and vice versa, in all the ways that flourished then and linger now. Reading this novel is both a gleeful and an exciting experience, because Grace herself is the perfect subject for Margaret Atwood's talents, embroidering intricate patterns of mystery, wit and paradox on the rough fabric of her story.

Margaret Atwood was born in Ottawa and lives in Toronto. Among her internationally successful novels are *Surfacing* (1972), *The Handmaid's Tale* (1986), *Cat's Eye* (1989) and *The Blind Assassin* which won the Man Booker Prize in 2000. She is also a poet and critic.

Age in year of publication: fifty-seven.

24

Beryl Bainbridge 1934–2010

1977 *Injury Time*

Simpson thought 'how unfair it was that the nicer moments of life – a few drinks under the belt, good food, a pretty woman seated opposite – were invariably spent in the company of one's wife'. This selflessness sets the scene for *Injury Time*, in which Simpson and his wife Muriel trot off to have dinner with Binny, Simpson's mistress of several years, and with Edward, Simpson's accountant. This is Binny's first public dinner party; Edward has a wife, Helen, whose presence is always felt. All of them are in the injury time of life; little do they know that they are also about to enter the last chance saloon. Into Binny's party, a dinner party from hell, erupts a gaggle of gunmen. Marriages and affairs, topsy-turvy before, disintegrate in the chaos that follows. One of Bainbridge's specialities is her close inspection of women who are in love with useless men, generally also of dubious physical attraction. Binny is one of Bainbridge's happiest creations, and Edward a prince of poltroons. There is a wonderful boldness about the works of Beryl Bainbridge, ably assisted by her conjuror's timing and an enviable ear for the way people talk. Sentimentality withers under her ironic, detached gaze, but canniness and black comedy flourish, as does laughter in this wily account of the ungovernable precariousness of love.

Beryl Bainbridge was born in Liverpool and lived in London. *The Bottle-Factory Outing* (1974) won the Guardian Fiction Prize, *Injury Time* the 1977 Whitbread Novel Award, and *Every Man for Himself* the 1996 Whitbread Novel Award.

Age in year of publication: forty-three.

James Baldwin 1924–1987

1953 *Go Tell it on the Mountain*

This is a great novel about restriction and freedom, the urge to control versus the urge to love, the battle within each person between pride and vulnerability, weakness and religious zeal. It is written with a superb rhythmic energy and flow; the rich cadences in the prose are light and effortless. It tells the story of young John Grimes, who is sensitive, clever and religious; we watch the world of fraught family life and serious sexual temptation through his eyes, much as we do through Stephen's in James Joyce's *A Portrait of the Artist*. But then the novel moves into the consciousness of three older members of the family: his aunt, who is dying; the man he believes is his father, a preacher in Harlem; and his mother. The portraits of the older members of the family are full of complexity and heart-rending loss and regret. Both his stepfather and his mother are hauntingly aware of a deep sensuality in themselves, much more fundamental than any religious feeling. Their stories give you a sense of the weight which John must carry, how his family and his religious heritage are burdens rather than gifts. Baldwin has a brilliant range of sympathy, an ability to create an intriguing and memorable web of relationships and stories. This, his first novel, remains one of the great books about family and religious bonds.

James Baldwin was born in New York. His other novels include *Giovanni's Room* (1956) and *Another Country* (1962). He was also an influential essayist and polemicist. He lived for many years in France.

Age in year of publication: twenty-nine.

J. G. Ballard 1930–2009

1984   *Empire of the Sun*

'"It might be a bit strange," Jim admitted, finishing the last of the weevils.' Jim is eleven in 1941, lost in Shanghai when Pearl Harbor and invasion by the Japanese separate him from his parents. He spends the war in an internment camp and on death marches. Straightening his tattered blazer, a *Just William* kind of boy, he uses every means in his power – servility, deviousness, expert scrounging, ferocious negotiations for food – to survive through years of starvation, disease and physical disintegration, described mesmerically by Ballard in a novel which is one of the truly great novels about war.

As Jim gets hungrier, his open sores festering, the words Ballard chooses to describe the horrific last days of the war in Shanghai become brighter and brighter, almost incandescent. In his words of fire, the sun, the light, the sky, the beams in the air become as translucent as the human beings disintegrating into death in front of Jim. Ballard's description of the chaos of war, the way men and women look as they wither from starvation, the way minds behave as they keep their bodies company, moves brilliantly through small human events – minutely recorded and heartwrenchingly moving – to take on large meaning. War is a young Japanese kamikaze pilot flying to death, unnoticed, unremembered; war is suicide, nothing more.

J. G. Ballard was born in Shanghai, came to England in 1946 and lived in Teddington, Middlesex. This autobiographical novel has a sequel, *The Kindness of Women* (1991). A prolific and apocalyptic novelist, Ballard was also widely acclaimed for his many science fiction novels which explore 'inner space'.

Age in year of publication: fifty-four.

John Banville 1945–

1989   *The Book of Evidence*

John Banville is one of the best prose stylists writing in English now. His tone is aloof and mandarin, subversive and slyly comic; the voice in his work is close to that of the Beckett of the Molloy trilogy and the Nabokov of *Lolita* and *Ada*. His second novel, *Birchwood* (1973), represents a watershed in contemporary Irish writing: it is a novel in which history becomes a rich black comedy full of land agitation and Gothic characters, and a sense of bewilderment at the nature of the universe fills the pages.

The Book of Evidence, however, is the book where his skills as a stylist and his macabre vision come best together. It is written as a speech from the dock by one Freddie Montgomery – Banville loves playing with posh Anglo-Irish identities – who tells the story of how he came to murder a servant girl in a big house. Banville clearly relishes the voice he has created – versions of the same Freddie appear in *Ghosts* (1991) and *Athena* (1993) – which deals in perfectly crafted sentences and images, and has a narrative thrust which is dark and utterly free of guilt. Banville also loves the idea of invention, and enjoys playing with notions of evil. In this novel, all this comes together with a murder story which is moving, gripping and totally absorbing.

John Banville was born in Wexford, Ireland, and now lives in Dublin. He has published eleven works of fiction. *The Book of Evidence* won the Guiness Peat Aviation Award in 1989. *The Untouchable* (1997) won the Los Angeles Times Book Prize. *The Sea* (2005) won the Man Booker Prize. He has also written a series of crime novels under a pseudonym Benjamin Black.

Age in year of publication: forty-four.

Pat Barker 1943–

1991–1995   The Regeneration Trilogy

Regeneration (1991), *The Eye in the Door* (1993), *The Ghost Road* (1995)

This is a rich and complex retelling of the story of British combatants in the First World War. It uses as a focus and centre the work of a real (as opposed to fictional) character, Dr William Rivers, whose job it is to deal with men who have been traumatized by their time in the trenches at a period when little was known about trauma. Other real characters appear in the books, notably Siegfried Sassoon and Robert Graves.

The trilogy also dramatizes the life and times of one Billy Prior, a triumphantly buoyant and brilliant creation, working class but an officer, and bisexual. The opening of the second volume has one of the best descriptions ever of sex between men. The third, which is plainly written, using short scenes and a large number of subplots, deals with divisions within the characters themselves, including the doctors, and within the governing ideologies. Ideas of bravery, fear, recovery, madness, the unconscious, masculinity, friendship, leadership, pacifism and the class system, to name but a few, are examined in terms that are deceptively simple.

Barker is in full control of her material: she understands her characters and their dilemmas, she has an enormous sympathy with people, and an astonishing range. These three books establish her as one of the most talented English novelists of her time.

Pat Barker was born in Thornaby-on-Tees and lives in Durham. *Regeneration* was made into a film by Gillies Mackinnon; *The Eye in the Door* won the Guardian Fiction Prize; *The Ghost Road* won the Booker Prize.

Age in years these books were published: forty-eight – fifty-two.

Julian Barnes 1946–

1984   *Flaubert's Parrot*

In this book Julian Barnes turns his attention to the great French writer Gustave Flaubert (1821–1880), author of *Madame Bovary*. The result is a novel like no other, in which Barnes himself jostles with Flaubert and with the narrator of the novel, a fussy sadsack called Dr Braithwaite, for centre stage. Braithwaite is a widower; his wife has committed suicide – she was unfaithful to him. Flaubert advances and retreats before our eyes: in France, in Damascus where he eats dromedary, on trains, at home, in love or not as the case may be, unfaithful, syphilitic, affectionate, writing with a stuffed parrot on his desk.

Braithwaite's biographical pursuit of Flaubert alternates between the ponderous, the comic and the revealing – 'Louise is puzzlingly unable to grasp that Gustave Flaubert can love her without ever wanting to see her' – presenting us with an intriguing if elusive Flaubert, a man who issues *pensées* which crack the heart. Behind both Flaubert and Braithwaite lurks Barnes himself, playful and astute, his encyclopedic intelligence always surprising the reader into laughter or astonishment. *Flaubert's Parrot* is a novel to be read again and again for its sardonic wit and biographical eccentricities, for the precision of Barnes's use of language and for its enigmas. It is, as was Flaubert's parrot, 'a fluttering, elusive emblem of the writer's voice'.

Julian Barnes was born in Leicester and lives in London. A prizewinner in England, France and Germany, among his other acclaimed novels are *A History of the World in 10½ Chapters* (1989), *Talking it Over* (1991), *England, England* (1998) and *Arthur and George* (2005).

Age in year of publication: thirty-eight.

Samuel Beckett 1906–1989

1955–1958   The Molloy Trilogy

Molloy (1955), Malone Dies (1956), The Unnameable (1958)

Samuel Beckett's trilogy, published first in French in the early 1950s, and then translated by the author (with Patrick Bowles as a collaborator on *Molloy*) and published in English some years later, remains his monumental achievement in prose fiction, although some of his later short prose fiction is magnificent.

Beckett is concerned in his prose, and in his plays, to deal once and for all with the idea of narrative and character and plot. His characters think and remember, but this does not help them; they are sure that Being is a sour joke inflicted on them. They know they are alive because their bodies tell them so, and they are constantly humiliated by their bodies. The drama is between action and inaction, between the possibility that the next sentence will lead us nowhere, or further back, or forward into a joke, or a snarl, or a nightmare, or a terrible darkness. Some of the writing – the sentence construction, the rhythms, the pacing and timing, the voice – is exquisitely beautiful, not a word out of place, but at the same time every word out of place, every word (and, indeed, action and memory) open to constant interpretation, revaluation, negation. The tone in the last volume becomes more dense and difficult, and at times more simple and stark. 'This silence they are always talking about, from which supposedly he came, to which he will return when his act is over, he doesn't know what it is, nor what he is meant to do, in order to deserve it.'

Samuel Beckett was born in Ireland. He lived most of his life in France. He won the Nobel Prize in Literature in 1969.

Age in years these books were published: forty-nine–fifty-two.

Sybille Bedford 1911–2006

1956   *A Legacy*

'I spent the first nine years of my life in Germany, bundled to and fro between two houses.' This is the voice of seven-year-old Francesca, recounting the story of the life of her father and his two German families before the beginning of the First World War.

The first are the von Feldens, Bavarian Catholic barons in Baden in southern Germany, culturally more French than German. The story of her uncle, Johannes von Felden, forced into the German army, and of how his fate affects his three brothers, is one which Bedford uses to shocking effect to reveal the chasm between old Bavaria and the brutality of northern militaristic Prussian ways. The other family are the Merzes, Jewish upper bourgeoisie, living in Berlin on money made from banking and trade. The lives and marriages of these two dynasties provide the rococo structure of this history, always presaging German terrors to come.

A Legacy is unique. Sybille Bedford's recollections of the houses, travels, animals and eccentricities of these excessively wealthy people are perfectly matched with her style, which is elegant, evocative, even dispassionate. The quizzical tone of this novel, too, is entirely individual. Sybille Bedford takes us within the bosom of these families, teasing them out of hiding, providing a witty elegy to – and a celebration of – a world long gone, and in English little recorded.

Sybille Bedford was born in Charlottenburg, Germany, and lived in London. Biographer, novelist and travel writer, she drew on the experiences of her family for this famous novel.

Age in year of publication: forty-five.

Sam Hanna Bell 1909–1990

1951 *December Bride*

In the second half of the century, a few writers continued to work as though the modern movement in fiction – Joyce, Woolf, Faulkner – and the Industrial Revolution had never existed, as though they were still living in the eighteenth century. Yet there is a strange beauty and intensity about some of these books, as though the authors were well aware that they were working against the grain, telling old-fashioned stories with a dark Freudian self-consciousness.

December Bride is set on the coast of County Antrim in Northern Ireland in a small, tightly knit Presbyterian community. After their father's death in a drowning accident, two brothers, Hamilton and Frank, continue to employ Sarah Gomartin and her mother as servants. When the mother leaves, Sarah stays on, and to the horror of those around her she begins to consort with both brothers; no one knows which of them is the father of her children. She is an immensely selfish and bigoted woman – her hatred of a local Catholic family is extraordinary – but there's a sort of innocence about her in the book, and her involvement with the brothers is so lovingly described, so slow and uneasy in its development, that she becomes oddly sympathetic, her independence and stubbornness seem like gifts. There are scenes towards the end of the book, when the new generation has grown up, that are heartbreaking. The writing is plain, deliberate and flawless. This is a book which everyone interested in modern fiction should read: it shows what can still be done.

Sam Hanna Bell was born in Scotland and brought up in Northern Ireland. He worked for more than twenty years as a producer for BBC Radio in Belfast. His other books include *Summer Loanen* (1943), *A Man Flourishing* (1973) and *Across the Narrow Sea* (1987).

Age in year of publication: forty-two.

(1) Saul Bellow 1915–2005

1953   *The Adventures of Augie March*

Bellow's Augie March is born into immigrant Jewish poverty in Chicago, before the Depression. Augie is on a mythical quest to discover 'the lessons and theory of power' but everywhere he finds greed and lies, until acquired wisdom reveals that the greedy and the prevaricators, including his good self, are not to be despised.

This is a picaresque masterpiece, issuing forth the words and thoughts of Augie March in Bellow's marvellous language, roiling from the gut, strong and vivid. Augie's pilgrimage begins with his tattered childhood with his mother, his retarded brother George and his labyrinthine older brother Simon, each of them 'drafted untimely into hardships'. Proceeding through a variety of dubious jobs and precarious adventures – wonderful street theatre involving the riff-raff, rich and poor, of Bellow's Dickensian humanity – Augie best loves women, the flesh of them, their pernickety brokering for power. Augie chooses Thea, Mimi, Lucy, Stella and more, trailing through abortions, falcon training, each portion of female anatomy closely observed. 'Guillaume's girl friend . . . was a great work of ripple-assed luxury with an immense mozzarella bust . . .'

This novel is a hymn to city life, suffused with eagerness and delight. Bellow's pulsing use of words is controlled by the simplicity Augie constantly insists upon, and so this novel avoids the Jewish sentimentality and convoluted clamour which become tiresome in Bellow's later works. This is a *Great Expectations* or *David Copperfield* set in Chicago, full of a sense of longing – a longing for family, for love: the greatest and most universal of all themes in fiction.

Saul Bellow was born in Canada and lived in Boston. Among his famous novels are *Seize the Day* (1947), *Henderson the Rain King* (1959) and *Humboldt's Gift* (1975), which won the Pulitzer Prize. Both *The Adventures of Augie March* and *Herzog* won National Book Awards. He was awarded the Nobel Prize in Literature in 1976.

Age in year of publication: thirty-eight.

(2) Saul Bellow 1915–2005

1964 *Herzog*

Herzog is Bellow's most accomplished novel in which ideas are presented fluently without damaging the characters or the sense of life in the narrative. It has a marvellous first sentence: 'If I am out of my mind, it's all right with me, thought Moses Herzog.'

He is indeed out of his mind, and he has many good reasons to be so. One, his mind is too well stocked, he knows too much, he has read too much Western philosophy and it weighs him down. Two, his wife has behaved appallingly, has run off with his friend; 'run off' may not, however, be the appropriate term since his friend has only one leg. Three, he is oversexed for a man of his age. Four, his whole family history and the emotion surrounding it exasperate him and make him sad. And these are only four examples.

Moses Herzog will not lie down; his despair is made all the worse by the fact that it is rich in comedy. He writes letters to elderly relatives, to the President, to the *New York Times*, to many dead philosophers. He is deeply worried about the future of civilization, but he is easily distracted by jealousy, further bouts of madness, lust and memories of childhood, not to speak of guilt and hatred, and by his new girlfriend, the wonderful Ramona. The novel possesses an extraordinary narrative energy. Herzog and those close to him take on a life of their own in the book, and the ideas about the future of civilization which obsess him are woven carefully and skilfully into the story of his disintegration.

Age in year of publication: forty-nine.

Elizabeth Bowen 1899–1973

1963   *The Little Girls*

The title of this novel is ironic. Whatever their age, the three girls in question are in spirit anything but little. Diana-Dinah (Dicey), Clare (Mumbo) and Sheila (Sheikie) emit that fiery power certain women have, which they get from smelting whatever gifts circumstances have given them, however shoddy, into monumental wills of iron. In 1914 the girls are at school together at St Agatha's in Kent. Fifty years later, Dinah begins to fret for her old friends and she advertises for them; Mumbo and Sheikie surface. These bare bones convey nothing of the rich flesh of this novel, splendidly droll both in its dialogue and in the testy, ironic tone of Bowen's writing. She is given to short, devastating sentences and she applies them to places and persons: her account of the streets and 'flaccid gates' and crumbling dogs of the houses of southern England is incomparable. But the real treasure of this novel is its excavation of the meaning of memory, the meaning of time passing, Bowen's attempt to catch the very moment when it does. That she succeeds turns this brisk comedy into an extraordinary piece of work: clever, beautifully written, a novel which grasps in words and images and laughter that comic despair which comes from the acceptance of life as something which can be only half seen, half known, half understood.

Elizabeth Bowen was born in Ireland and lived both there and in England. *The Death of the Heart* (1938) and *The Heat of the Day* (1949) are two of her most praised novels.

Age in year of publication: sixty-four.

T. Coraghessan Boyle 1948–

1995   *The Tortilla Curtain*

T. Coraghessan Boyle is one of the funniest, sharpest, most original novelists in the United States now. He is interested in the advanced humour inherent in advanced capitalism; America is the vast, dark comedy to which he is wide awake.

The Tortilla Curtain tells the story of two Californian families. The first, led by the nature-loving Delaney, is white and rich and less liberal as the days go by and illegal Mexicans haunt the horizon. The second family is Mexican and illegal and open to every possible calamity known to the human race – fire, flood, robbery, hunger, rape, poison, to name but a few. Delaney's wife Kyra is one of the most vile people in contemporary literature, and as the book proceeds Delaney starts to join her.

The plot may sound deterministic and crude, as chapters alternate between the ghastly rich and the *simpatico* poor, but the writing and pacing of the book are too clever for that, and the characters too deeply felt and carefully drawn. The book is, however, very political indeed, startlingly so in a time when hardly any American writing is political; it makes you loathe white middle-class Californians, and this must surely be a good thing.

T. Coraghessan Boyle was born in Peekshill, New York, and is the son of Irish immigrants. His other novels include *Water Music* (1981), *East is East* (1990) and *The Road to Wellville* (1993).

Age in year of publication: forty-seven.

Anita Brookner 1928–

1985 *Family and Friends*

In this tart comedy of manners Anita Brookner uses family photographs – wedding photographs – to tell the story of the Dorns, a well-off London family with wistful echoes of a middle-European milieu left behind. There is the matriarch Sofka and her four children: Frederick, her pride and joy; Betty, the favourite daughter; Mimi, the gentle one; and Alfred, the sacrificial lamb. In their world of comfort and coffee, brandy and marzipan cake, an 'air of family unity serves to disguise unforgivable facts'. Some of these are that Frederick and Betty – two of Brookner's most artful monsters – are heartless and self-serving, manipulators of family arrangements which seem superficially innocent, but which flicker with unexplored deceits and vanities.

Family and Friends includes some of Anita Brookner's finest writing – and some of her most trenchant. Her fiction is noted for its subtlety and technical skill but this can be deceptive, and has indeed deceived the odd ghetto of English critics who greet her novels with delighted misunderstanding. Elsewhere it is recognized that, in ambush behind her classically beautiful prose, rooted in her territory of small lives, is a devilry that works on her stories like lemon zest. *Family and Friends*, in Alfred's final revenge, provides a finale so delicate and precise that you can almost see the keen eye of the author slowly blinking at you.

Anita Brookner, the daughter of Polish parents, was born and educated in London, where she lives. Her fourth novel, *Hôtel du Lac*, won the 1984 Booker Prize.

Age in year of publication: fifty-seven.

Anthony Burgess 1917–1993

1980   *Earthly Powers*

Anthony Burgess wrote a thousand words a day – journalism, reviews, criticism, autobiography, verse, short stories, novels. He never repeated himself. He wrote science fiction and a thriller, he wrote *A Clockwork Orange* (1962), he wrote novels about Shakespeare, Christopher Marlowe and Beethoven, and many comic novels.

His most ambitious novel and the work in which he combines his comic talent, his sense of history and his nose for a good story is *Earthly Powers*. It is narrated by one Kenneth Toomey, an octogenarian celebrity writer, a cross between Burgess himself, Somerset Maugham and Graham Greene, a man capable of producing the following first sentence: 'It was the afternoon of my eighty-first birthday, and I was in bed with my catamite when Ali announced that the archbishop had come to see me.' The archbishop wants to talk about Carlo, Toomey's brother-in-law who became Pope and could work miracles. The novel explores the cruelty of the century watched through Toomey's decadent and world-weary eyes. It is a gripping, exhilarating and often melodramatic book which plays with ideas of good and evil, and combines moments from history – the Holocaust, the death of the followers of Jim Jones, changes in the Catholic Church – with strong characters and moments of pure theatre.

Anthony Burgess was the pseudonym of John Anthony Burgess Wilson. He was born in Manchester of a Catholic family and lived for many years in Monaco. He was also a composer. In 1984 he produced a book which listed his ninety-nine favourite novels. People suspected this was the hundredth.

Age in year of publication: sixty-three.

William Burroughs 1914–1998

1959   *Naked Lunch*

This is a novel of dreams and nightmares, hallucinations and sudden moments of crystal clarity. Nothing connects, except an uncompromising tone, an attitude, and the constant presence of the body in all its ugly manifestations, and the state, or organized society, in all its brutality. This is not to forget the narrator's relish in offering further images of pure disgust, setting scenes of cruelty and violence and drug-induced craziness and laughing at the good of it all. If there is a pregnancy, then there will be a bloody miscarriage; if there are teeth, then they will fall out; if there is a passenger plane, then someone is chopping the floor out of the lavatory. Blood, semen, pus, gangrene, venereal diseases, all types of drugs, belches, farts, hangings, shit, toilet paper, condoms, are everywhere. There is some marvellous surgery, including a scene in which a live monkey is sewn into the patient. There are sick jokes about 'niggers' and Jews; there are some good one-liners: 'May all your troubles be little ones, as one child molester says to the other.' The tone is often deadpan, matter of fact, like a movie script; the book is full of a morbid energy and rhythm; the method, which is fast-moving, aleatory and jumbled, holds your attention and makes the novel oddly riveting, relentlessly dark and crazed.

William Burroughs was educated at Harvard. He lived for many years in Central and South America and Morocco. His other books include *Junkie* (1953), *Cities of the Red Night* (1981) and *Queer* (1987).

Age in year of publication: forty-five.

A. S. Byatt 1936–

1990 *Possession*

This feast of a novel, accurately subtitled 'A Romance', is replete with love stories both passionate and fateful, with high comedy, languishing tragedy, poetry, mystery and adventure.

The time is now – and then. Now tells the story of an array of scholars of varying levels of greed or goodwill, anxiety and envy, who pursue the literary and emotional pasts of the Browningesque poet Randolph Henry Ash, and Christabel LaMotte, poet and muse. Then is the story of the Victorian liaison between Ash and LaMotte which is dramatic and obscure, and – as is slowly revealed – thoroughly heartwrenching. The present-day lovers-to-be, Ash research assistant Roland Michell and LaMotte scholar Maud Bailey, are inheritors of and act in counterpoint to the lovers from the past.

A. S. Byatt is remarkable for the abundance and richness of her storytelling gifts. She offers robust drama – and a hundred other pleasures: myth and fairytale mingle with the poetic works of Ash and LaMotte and with journals, letters, mishaps, discoveries and farcical absurdities. *Possession* is a romance and a detective story which combines all the entertaining virtues of popular fiction with those qualities A. S. Byatt shares with George Eliot: prodigious narrative, imaginative energy and intelligence. Reading *Possession* is a mesmerizing experience; it becomes a happy addiction, one of those rare novels that lingers in the mind.

A. S. Byatt was born in Sheffield and lives in London. Amongst her novels, criticism and short stories are the Frederica Quartet: *The Virgin in the Garden* (1978), *Still Life* (1985), *Babel Tower* (1996) and *The Whistling Woman* (2002). *The Children's Book* came out in 2009. *Possession* won the 1990 Booker Prize.

Age in year of publication: fifty-four.

Peter Carey 1943–

1988 *Oscar and Lucinda*

This is a virtuoso performance, an eloquent love story and an epic account of mid-nineteenth century life in England and Australia, interweaving a mercurial adventure story with the intimate, the comic and the fanciful.

Oscar Hopkins is born in Devon, the frail and red-headed son of a fundamentalist member of the Plymouth Brethren: his escape first into Anglicanism and then into gambling takes him to Australia in the 1850s to bring the word of Christ to New South Wales. Lucinda Leplastrier is an orphaned heiress, daughter of an early feminist, and she scandalizes Sydney by wearing rational dress, owning a glass factory and gambling compulsively. One of Carey's triumphs in the novel is to make us care fervently about these two odd misfits; another is to surround them with an explosion of clergymen, glass-blowers, explorers, villains, a profusion of idiosyncratic characters galvanized into vigorous pursuit of the vagaries of chance by Carey's singular genius. Equally admirable is his ferocious caricature of Imperial Britain and of nineteenth-century Australian history, and of the bigotry and intolerance of Christianity, particularly in its extreme Nonconformist modes. But it is Carey's fertile imagination and quirky curiosity about all manner of things that give *Oscar and Lucinda* its special quality. This is a most sympathetic novel, full of ideas, endearing, full of gusto.

Peter Carey was born in Bacchus Marsh in Victoria and now lives in New York. His award-winning novels include *Bliss* (1981), *Illywhacker* (1985) *Jack Maggs* (1997), *Theft* (2003) and *His Illegal Self* (2006). *Oscar and Lucinda* won the 1988 Booker Prize and *True History of the Kelly Gang* won the 2001 Booker Prize.

Age in year of publication: forty-five.

Angela Carter 1940–1992

1991   *Wise Children*

Dora Chance, a seventy-five-year-old ex-hoofer, is the leading lady of *Wise Children*. Clustered round her, as in a Busby Berkeley musical extravaganza, is the theatrical dynasty of Hazards and Chances, artistes and entertainers. Everything comes in twos in this novel. Twins are everywhere, born on both sides of the blanket. Dora and Nora Chance are the illegitimate twin daughters of the great thespian Sir Melchior Hazard. Living in Bard Road, Brixton, they are 'two batty old hags' now, but they were not always thus, and Dora is writing her reminiscences, a garrulous account of their theatrical ups and downs – a 'history of the world in party frocks'. *Wise Children* turns a hundred cartwheels as it introduces its entertainments. One of them is about fathers, known and unknown – for, as Dora says, 'You can't fool a sperm.' Another is a rapturous homage to the theatre of Shakespeare and the bawdy cheer of showbusiness. Most of all, this is a ribald satire on Britain's enduring class system. It speaks for the popular and for the people, celebrating the incivilities and trash culture of those who live with vim and vigour on the wrong side of the tracks.

Angela Carter was a trailblazer. She made British the idea of magical realism and injected her glittering version of it into the work of many of her contemporaries.

Angela Carter was born and lived in London. An admired critic, short-story writer and polemicist, her fiction includes *The Bloody Chamber* (1979) and *Nights at the Circus* (1984).

Age in year of publication: fifty-one.

Raymond Carver 1938–1988

1988   *Where I'm Calling From*

Raymond Carver chose this selection of his stories before he died, a permanent deterrent to the rash of imitators who have since appeared. Fortunately his writing is inimitable.

His voice is that of contemporary America. Carver man is mostly out of work, at home with the vacuum cleaner and the family cat, a bottle too near to hand. Carver woman, with stretch marks, heart of steel and that extra pound of flesh, is keeping herself together with a fixed grin and the nearest beer.

These are gutsy lives full of regret, opportunities lost, luck that should have been just a little better: but there is love too – all the more real because it grows in arid soil. Carver's home patch is modern marriage, of which he is the official recorder: 'Once I woke up in the night to hear Iris grinding her teeth', and 'There was a time when I loved my first wife more than life itself. But now, I hate her guts. I do. How do you explain that?' Only Raymond Carver can. His style, economic, unadorned, emphasizes the tough realities of his domestic themes. He has been called the laureate of the dispossessed and he is, but he packs much more than that into the ten or twenty pages of each of these life-changing stories, a classic of modern American writing.

Raymond Carver was born in Oregon and lived in various cities in America, finally settling in New York. Some of these stories come from his collections *Will You Please Be Quiet, Please?* (1976) and many were used by Robert Altman in the film *Short Cuts.*

Posthumous publication.

Raymond Chandler 1888–1959

1953   *The Long Good-Bye*

Raymond Chandler's original style, the dry humour of his wise-cracking private eye, Philip Marlowe, instantly created a milieu perfectly suited to the ways of the late twentieth-century world. 'I hear voices crying in the night and I go see what's the matter.' Grief is Marlowe's business.

Marlowe is not a trusting man: too much alcohol, too many lies have given him a hide of iron. But he takes to Terry Lennox, a scarred war hero, a drunk, like so many Chandler heroes, who is married to Sylvia, the daughter of a power-obsessed multimillionaire. Brilliantly constructed around the brutal murder of Sylvia Lennox, Marlowe's disillusioned despair is matched by the drunken writer Roger Wade, married to another of Chandler's extraordinary women – these women are always half-crazed, beautiful, angelically so: in Chandler's jungle it's a moot point whether beauty masks good or evil. Chandler's importance and influence are more than a matter of his taut writing style. His genius lies behind the personas of the great Hollywood film stars – Humphrey Bogart, Robert Mitchum, Lauren Bacall, Barbara Stanwyck and others – who portrayed the characters he invented. Chandler's novels originated Hollywood *film noir*, not the other way around. In this, the sixth of his seven Marlowe novels, his immortal private eye engages with murder and betrayal in his meanest and most moving crusade.

Raymond Chandler was born in Chicago, educated in England and lived in California, the setting for most of his work. Other great Marlowe novels are *The Big Sleep* (1939) and *Farewell, My Lovely* (1940).

Age in year of publication: sixty-five.

Bruce Chatwin 1940–1989

1982   *On the Black Hill*

This is a brooding, dark novel which has conscious echoes of Hardy and Lawrence. It opens at the turn of the century on a hill farm in Wales when the twin boys Lewis and Benjamin Jones are born to Mary, who has married beneath her, and Amos, a fiercely independent spirit.

Chatwin makes the love which binds these four people into something taut and hard which maims them and haunts them, and is under constant pressure. The twins behave as one person and can feel each other's pain; Chatwin manages to make their behaviour credible and interesting. The novel is full of detail about farming, weather, animals, nature, furniture, clothes, mood swings, auctions, feuds between neighbours, social changes.

The arrival of the First World War makes Amos even more sour than he is already; one of the twins is forced to join the army, and then Chatwin makes them both even more inwardlooking and strange when the war is over. All the main characters in the book are motivated and controlled by forces which they do not understand, nothing comes easy to them, and the reader becomes totally involved then in the great battles which go on within each of them and between all of them, and between all of them and the world outside. Although this is an old-fashioned family saga, it is not a piece of pastiche. It is a deeply felt and deeply moving novel about complex characters and relationships.

Bruce Chatwin was born in Sheffield and died in the South of France. His other books include *In Patagonia* (1977), *The Songlines* (1987) and *Utz* (1988). *On the Black Hill* (1982) won the Whitbread First Novel Award.

Age in year of publication: forty-two.

Amit Chaudhuri 1962–

1991   *A Strange and Sublime Address*

'Sandeep, meanwhile, had come to the conclusion that the grown-ups were mad, each after his or her own fashion. Simple situations were turned into complex dramatic ones; not until then did everybody feel important and happy.' Sandeep is a small Indian boy, an only child who lives in a Bombay high-rise and in this book makes two long visits to his extended family in Calcutta. The novel tells the story of the atmosphere in the small house where they live. He watches his relatives, their servants and their neighbours, alert to everything – sounds, smells, domestic habits, moods, weather, plants. He is vastly amused by tiny details such as his uncle's car, which breaks down, and his uncle's bustling morning rituals. He loves the women in the family, their clothes and perfumes, their voices. He plays with his cousins.

Chaudhuri writes precisely, carefully, trying to capture in the rhythms of his prose the faded happiness of things, the strange, pure remembered moments. The boy is curious and intelligent, and Chaudhuri is clever enough and talented enough to let his observations stand for a lot, to let what he sees and hears become the drama of the book, rather than twists of fate or plot. There are moments of pure evocative beauty such as the family's visit to the elderly relatives, the presence of a new baby, a rainstorm, Chhotomama's illness, his time in hospital, his recovery.

Amit Chaudhuri was born in Bombay and brought up in Calcutta where he now lives. *A Strange and Sublime Address* (1991) won the Commonwealth Prize for best first book. It was followed in 1993 by *Afternoon Raag*, which won the Encore Award for the best second novel of the year, and *Freedom Song* (1998). *A New World* came out in 2000, *Real Time* in 2002 and *The Immortals* in 2009.

Age in year of publication: twenty-nine.

John Cheever 1912–1982

1977   *Falconer*

John Cheever is best known for his comic and ironic short stories, for his quiet, careful, sometimes satirical, often gently unsettling observation of American suburban life. This novel is not like that at all, although it resembles Cheever's other work in its depiction of isolation and broken families.

In just over two hundred pages Cheever constructs a dark, tough, relentless universe. It is the prison called Falconer in which Farragut has been incarcerated for killing his brother, striking him with a fire iron. The novel is written in stark, clear prose; the darkness of the vision is unlike any work produced by Cheever's American contemporaries. There is a blunt, deadpan edge to the sentences and observations; the absence of daylight is in the prose as much as in the prison. Every scene in the book is set up with a mastery and control: the visit of Farragut's wife would break your heart and chill your bones. It seems that things cannot get any worse until you come to the cat-killing scene, the descriptions of drug addiction, the violence, the sheer quality of the despair.

The novel offered Cheever a way to dramatize his own circumspect homosexuality: the homosexual love affair in the book is remarkable and unexpected for its tenderness, and for the quality of the love and longing between Farragut (who has been heterosexual in the outside world) and Jody, a fellow inmate. This book is a serious work of American fiction and deserves to be better known.

John Cheever was born in Massachusetts. His other novels include *The Wapshot Chronicle* (1957) and *The Wapshot Scandal* (1964). *The Stories of John Cheever* (1978) won a Pulitzer Prize and a US National Book Critics Circle Award.

Age in year of publication: sixty-five.

48

Agatha Christie 1890–1976

1950 *A Murder is Announced*

Of the novelists chosen for this book Agatha Christie is the most popular entertainer. In a hundred languages or more, she provides millions of readers with a view of England complete with afternoon teas, vicars, colonels and a dead body – in the library, in the watersplash, in bed, on trains, at sea and in every innocent seeming English village street.

She created two eccentric detectives – Hercule Poirot, who exercised his little grey cells and fingered his moustache through some of her best novels (*The Murder of Roger Ackroyd*, 1926 and *Murder on the Orient Express*, 1934) – and she wrote brilliant stories in which neither appeared (*Ten Little Niggers*, 1939 and *Death Comes as the End*, 1944). Her second detective, Miss Jane Marple, was Christie's alter ego in the guise of a fluffy, elderly spinster, conservatively opinionated and sharp as a tack beneath her grey curls and woolly mufflers. Miss Marple is the genius at work in *A Murder is Announced* in which, in the wonderfully named village of Chipping Cleghorn, the local newspaper startles its inhabitants with an announcement of the precise date, time and location of a murder; thither wend the village worthies; the murder occurs on time, every clue is presented to us, but as ever only the ingenuity which is the hallmark of a Christie detective story makes the solution, perfectly obvious once revealed, utterly baffling until that moment. She fools us every time.

Agatha Christie was born in Torquay, Devon. The acknowledged Queen of Crime, she published seventy-nine mysteries of which over sixty were novels. Many were, and continue to be, filmed and televised.

Age in year of publication: sixty.

Jonathan Coe 1961–

1994   *What a Carve Up!*
(US: *The Winshaw Legacy*)

This novel is an octoped. First, for those who experienced them, it emits a wonderful blast of indignation about the Thatcher years; secondly, for those spared that experience, it provides a hilarious and potent send-up of any political party driving its people round the bend at any given moment. Thirdly, it is a most satisfactory family saga, telling the story of the Winshaw dynasty, a gaggle of persons of the kind that owned, bought or ran Britain in the 1980s and 1990s.

Fourthly, its hero, Michael, biographer of the Winshaw family, is addictively engaging in the David Copperfield manner, the sort of young man who, sensitive, vaguely inept in a business sense, kind, embodies everything the Thatcher years most hated. Fifthly, Coe is a writer who uses the movies in magical ways, the title itself being a 1960s British film comedy which becomes crucially important as mysteries unfold. Sixthly, this is a mystery story too. Seventhly, Coe laces his satire with compassion, pointing the finger at the blusterers who tell us what to do and at us for our patience in putting up with same. Eighthly, *What a Carve Up!* is an incisive and funny polemic and a perfectly pitched satire that succeeds triumphantly in everything it attempts. Reading it is like watching *Citizen Kane* crossed with *Singing in the Rain:* we are left bouncing with laughter and admiration.

Jonathan Coe was born in Birmingham and lives in London. The author of several novels, including *The House of Sleep* (1997), *The Closed Circle* (1998). He has also written a prize-winning biography of B.S. Johnson *Like A Fiery Elephant* (2004).

Age in year of publication: thirty-three.

J. M. Coetzee 1940–

1990   *Age of Iron*

Three novels by J. M. Coetzee could easily have made this list. They are *Waiting for the Barbarians* (1980), *Life and Times of Michael K* (1983) and *Age of Iron* (1990). Coetzee is a master of tone and colour, subtleties and ironies. His novels are full of echoes of other work – Shakespeare, the Bible, Kafka, Dostoevsky – and are at times harrowing.

Age of Iron demonstrates Coetzee's skill at using voice: Elizabeth Curren, who is dying of cancer in the old South Africa, writes to her daughter, who lives abroad. From the first page, you can feel the tension in her voice, her sense of right and wrong, how frightened she is, how frail and vulnerable.

In Coetzee's work, the public world becomes a sort of darkness, constantly encroaching, threatening to take over. Here we have the drama of the last years of the apartheid regime: riots, schoolchildren on strike, white liberals like our narrator deeply shocked by the savagery of what is going on around them. The sentences are perfect, the tone is relentless and unforgiving, and the sense of despair, both public and private, fills the book with a grief which is almost overwhelming.

J. M. Coetzee was born in Cape Town and now lives in Australia. His novel *Life and Times of Michael K* won the Booker Prize and the Prix Femina étranger in 1983. *Disgrace* won the Booker Prize in 1999. He was awarded the Nobel Prize in Literature in 2003.

Age in year of publication: fifty.

Ivy Compton-Burnett 1884–1969

1959   *A Heritage and its History*

'"I hope Father will drop down dead on his way home," said Ralph Challoner. "I really do hope it."' This ferocious request is customary within the families of Ivy Compton-Burnett's imagination. Simon Challoner longs to inherit the estate of his Uncle Edwin, one of those men who malevolently enters a room just in time to hear ill of himself. Widowed, Edwin marries the young Rhoda, whom Simon impregnates in an idle moment. Edwin accepts the ensuing son as his own, and the distressed Simon, having lost his inheritance, marries Fanny and begets five vocally omnipresent children whom he rears tyrannically, in fear of the workhouse and the orphanage. Simon saves himself and his heritage in a manner so unimaginable that we are left to imagine it.

Written predominantly in dialogue, in devastating conversational exchanges, this high comedy is so biting and acerbic, and so clever, that discussions of potential incest seem much the same as comments on the carving or the state of the nursery. Ivy Compton-Burnett presented her mordant novels of family passions and decay in matchless, clipped prose, revealing beneath the prim surface of English upper middle-class life the presence of sin, the absence of charity and the necessity for suspicion, cunning and revenge – in that order. She is incomparable.

Ivy Compton-Burnett was born in Middlesex and lived in London. Of her nineteen novels, the best-known are *More Women Than Men* (1933), *A House and its Head* (1935) and *Manservant and Maidservant* (1947).

Age in year of publication: seventy-five.

Jim Crace 1946–

1997 *Quarantine*

Sometimes in a writer's life one book seems to crystallize a talent, seems to fulfil all of the promise of the earlier books, seems to deal with themes and obsessions and tones which have appeared before, offering them a new simplicity and seriousness and sense of perfection. Jim Crace's *Quarantine*, which tells the story of Jesus's forty days in the desert, does just this. Crace has always been interested in how society emerges from the primitive, in landscapes which are bleak and deserted, in the intricacies of trading and bonding. His writing has always been stark and poetic, beautifully crafted.

In this novel, Jesus is a chimera, he barely appears. The novel dramatizes his absence and the presence of four other pilgrims in the desert, each carrying a burden of fear and desire. It focuses on Musa, a trader who has been left for dead by his family and who believes that Jesus has healed him; on his wife Miri, who is pregnant; and on their relationships with the pilgrims. The novel is written in a style of calm perfection, full of echoes of W. B. Yeats and Wallace Stevens, with a remarkable number of sentences in iambic pentameter. The physical sense of the desert is superb; Crace's telling of the drama between the characters makes the book the masterpiece that his earlier books had presaged.

Jim Crace was born in north London and lives in Birmingham. His other books include *Continent* (1986), winner of the Whitbread First Novel Award, *The Gift of Stones* (1988) and *Arcadia* (1992). *Quarantine* won the Whitbread Novel Award in 1997, and was followed by *Being Dead* (1999), *The Devil's Larder* (2001), *Six* (2003) and *The Pesthouse* (2007).

Age in year of publication: fifty-one.

Michael Cunningham 1952–

1990   *A Home at the End of the World*

This novel is narrated by four of its characters, and its considerable power and emotional force come from that sense of voice which governs contemporary American fiction. Here the voices of Bobby and Jonathan, old school friends; Alice, Jonathan's mother; and Clare, who befriends both men and has a child with one of them, are compelling and haunting, full of a melancholy effort to make sense of things. There is a luxury in the writing which echoes F. Scott Fitzgerald; the narrative contains beautiful sentences, astonishing moments of insight and disclosure. The first half of the book, especially, has a rich perfection about it; Cunningham is particularly good on family attachments and entanglements. The early relationship between Jonathan and Bobby, their desire for each other, their early sexual encounters, are wonderfully described, and Jonathan's mother's observation of her gay son is superb. ('I knew the bite and meanness of boys was missing from his nature.')

In the end, as in all American fiction, the true hero of the book is America itself: its ability to change; the sudden, bright opportunities it offers to make money, to make friends; the beauty and variety of its landscapes; its ability to tempt us with hope and resolution. This is certainly one of the best American novels of the decade.

Michael Cunningham was born in Los Angeles, and now lives in New York City. *A Home at the End of the World* is his second novel. His fourth novel, *The Hours*, appeared in 1998 and won the Pulitzer Prize. *Specimen Days* appeared in 2005.

Age in year of publication: thirty-eight.

Robertson Davies 1913–1995

1970   *Fifth Business*

'I shall be as brief as I can, for it is not by piling up detail that I hope to achieve my picture, but by putting the emphasis where I think it belongs.' The novel begins with a careful, precise and striking first-person account of a boy growing up in rural Canada in the early years of the century, his sharp intelligence and narrative skills, and perhaps bitter wisdom, cutting through the dark, conservative world of his parents and their village. Our narrator, almost to spite his mother, takes part in the First World War, and his matter-of-fact version of life in the trenches, of his own injuries and time in hospital, is disturbing and convincing.

But this is not a novel about childhood, nor is it a war novel. It is a novel about what happens then, after the drama of childhood and war. It is told in the shadow of four figures from childhood: Boy Staunton, who becomes a millionaire politician; his wife Leola, our narrator's former sweetheart; Mrs Dempster, a minister's wife, who goes mad; her son Paul, who becomes a magician (Davies loved the idea of magic). Our narrator's sensibility makes him a sharp chronicler of the world around him; his interest in saints and religion becomes a secret life. His account of the world and of his own life is rigorously intelligent; its stilted style is in contrast with the deep pain which is buried in the narrative, and the play between the two is often breathtaking and always engrossing.

Robertson Davies was born in Ontario and lived much of his life in Toronto. He published three novel sequences: The Salterton Trilogy, The Deptford Trilogy and The Cornish Trilogy. *Fifth Business* is the first book of The Deptford Trilogy, which was completed with *The Manticore* (1972) and *World of Wonders* (1975).

Age in year of publication: fifty-seven.

Louis de Bernières 1954–

1994   *Captain Corelli's Mandolin*
(US: *Corelli's Mandolin*)

Set on a Greek island during the Second World War, this novel combines narrative sweep, a mixture of tragedy and comedy, a number of extraordinary and lovable characters and the sense of a tightly knit traditional society in a changing world. It almost stands alone in contemporary English fiction for its ability to deal confidently with the outside world, for the warmth of its tone, for its breadth and scope and for its lack of cynicism.

It tells, using methods which remind the reader of both Charles Dickens and Gabriel García Márquez, the story of Dr Iannis and his daughter Pelagia living easily together on Cephalonia in the years before the war. When the Italian army invades the island, the Italian control is half-hearted and almost good-humoured. Dr Iannis and his daughter try to ignore the considerable charms of Captain Corelli, who is billeted with them. The novel moves from Iannis's kitchen to the life of the village to the terrible cruelty of the war. Stories about music, medicine, fishing and horrific events in Greece in the Second World War are placed beside other stories about love and death. The tone moves effortlessly from the very funny to the deeply harrowing once the Germans arrive on the island. The writing is always fluid; the scenes are fast moving and varied and always interesting; the novel is fiercely readable, almost impossible to put down.

Louis de Bernières was born in and lives in London. His other novels include *The Troublesome Offspring of Cardinal Guzman* (1992). *Captain Corelli's Mandolin* won the Commonwealth Writers Prize in 1995.

Age in year of publication: forty.

Don DeLillo 1936–

1997 _Underworld_

The publication of _Underworld_ confirms Don DeLillo, if we needed confirmation, as the most exciting, original and innovative American novelist now working. He has been fascinated by what happens to language, truth and logic during a late phase of capitalism; how a society which grew around dreams of hope, of infinite optimism, deludes itself and is deluded by ritual and images and words. He loves technology, its mystery and glow, its hum and buzz; he is interested in hidden systems and codes, by the poetics of late twentieth-century paranoia.

Underworld, all eight hundred and twenty-seven pages of it, is his epic, his panoramic vision of the United States in his time. It is obsessed with waste and garbage, including the concern of J. Edgar Hoover (who has various walk-on parts in the novel) that protest groups will go through his garbage and put it on public display. The novel is also obsessed with the bomb and the Cold War, and the vast areas of the American imagination which have been filled with images of fear and destruction. In _Underworld_ DeLillo also presents a relaxed version of ordinary life, intimate family relations, memories of childhood, tender love and sexual desire. He places these beside magnificent set scenes about public life and history, and the result is a great monument to the enduring power of the novel.

Don DeLillo, son of Italian immigrants, was born in the Bronx, New York, and still lives in New York City. His novel _White Noise_ won the National Book Award in 1985, and _Libra_ (1988) the Irish Times Literature Prize.

Age in year of publication: sixty-one.

Anita Desai 1937–

1984 *In Custody*

In India, where so many have so little, what is the use, what is the glory of poetry? Anita Desai's answer takes shape in the person of Deven, a teacher of Hindi in a college in Mirepore, a dustbowl town near Delhi. Married to Sarla, a living pillar of pessimism, his real love is poetry, in the old language, Urdu.

Deven is a timid, put-upon soul, bullied by his friend Murad into interviewing the great but reclusive poet Nur. Deven's visits to Delhi to see him turn into a nightmare of farcical episodes in which drink, layabouts, frenzied birds and even more frenzied wives manipulate Deven, forcing him into debt and dishonour. Nur is a splendid creation, lizard-like, rapacious; yet of the two it is Deven who, in his acceptance of the price he has to pay in the service of art, triumphs over the multitudes of self-destructions on offer.

This is a novel with many meanings, many faces. One of the most resonant is that of India itself, with its blazing heat, its preference for individualistic chaos: this is India in the early 1980s on the point of change, during that recent past when the wonders of its history were abandoned and crumbling. Placing this magnificent inheritance in safe custody, Desai exposes the dilemmas of modern India in cool and lyrical prose.

Anita Desai was born in Mussoorie, India, and lives in England and the USA. This novel became a Merchant Ivory film in 1993; other praised novels include *Fire on the Mountain* (1977), *Clear Light of Day* (1980) and *Fasting, Feasting* (1999), which was the runner-up for the Booker Prize.

Age in year of publication: forty-seven.

Pete Dexter 1943–

1988   *Paris Trout*

This is a clearly written, tightly paced novel about the Deep South in the time between the Korean and the Vietnam Wars when racial segregation was absolute, but certain actions against black people – cold-blooded murder of teenagers, for example – would not be condoned by a white jury.

Paris Trout is a moneylender, a small-time banker and a storekeeper. He is tight-lipped and ruthless. He has never paid taxes and he obeys no laws. He has recently married Hanna, an intelligent, sensitive and attractive schoolteacher, and he has made her life a misery. He has also lent money to a black man to buy a car. When the payments are not made he visits the man with a local thug and manages to shoot a young black girl, killing her, and injuring an older woman.

He is brought to trial; Harry Seagraves is his lawyer. Seagraves is a good man, but he is not a hero. He grows to loathe Trout, but he still defends him. He is sure that he can use his clout in the locality to have him released. The novel makes clear that in a society like this no one can afford to behave heroically; most people are prepared to play with the system or be bought. Trout understands this like nobody else. No one's motives are pure except perhaps Hanna Trout's; she remains eloquent and long-suffering and determined to survive. The last hundred pages of the novel are full of unexpected twists and turns; a wonderful addition to the contemporary literature of the South.

Pete Dexter was born in Pontiac, Michigan, and lives in California. *Paris Trout* won the National Book Award in 1988. His other novels include *Brotherly Love* (1992) and *God's Pocket* (1984).

Age in year of publication: forty-five.

Joan Didion 1934–

1977   *A Book of Common Prayer*

A Book of Common Prayer and *Democracy* (1984) are Joan Didion's most powerful works. The style is that of her best journalism: taut, nervous, brilliantly observant and cutting, using constant repetition, searching always for the moment which sums everything up.

A Book of Common Prayer is set in the fictional Central American country of Boca Grande, of which the narrator, Grace Strasser-Mendana, after her husband's death, controls 'fifty-nine point eight per cent of the arable land and about the same percentage of the decision-making process'. She is an anthropologist and scientist, and uses these skills to analyse and describe the story of Charlotte Douglas, who comes to Boca Grande from North America and misunderstands almost everything. The narrator will die, 'very soon (from pancreatic cancer)', she tells us early in the book, and the tone of the narrative has a hardness, an impatience and an urgency, and the sense of someone pushed into making short, sharp observations about people and things. The narrator is at her sharpest when she describes her husband's venal, stupid family, her own wayward son, and of course the musings and antics of Charlotte Douglas. ('Charlotte would call her own story one of passion. I believe I would call it one of delusion.') This is a book which lends itself to constant re-reading – watch how Didion uses single-sentence paragraphs, openings and endings; there is not a word out of place.

Joan Didion was born in California and lives in Berkeley. Her best journalism is included in *Slouching Towards Bethlehem* (1968), *The White Album* (1979) and *Miami* (1987). Her extraordinary memoir of the death of her husband John Gregory Dunne, *The Year of Magical Thinking*, won the National Book Award in 2005.

Age in year of publication: forty-three.

Isak Dinesen 1885–1962

1958   *Anecdotes of Destiny*

'I first began to tell tales to delight the world and make it wiser,' says Isak Dinesen, speaking through Mira Jama, who tells the first of the five tales in this collection.

Isak Dinesen is most famous for her autobiographical account of her life in Kenya, *Out of Africa* (1937), but her fictional work is equally exceptional, and unlike the fiction of anyone else. Though Danish, she generally wrote in English and then translated her work into her native tongue, but this cannot account for the particular quality of her work. Patrician, fantastic, Dinesen's English has unusual beauty and great technical skill. She uses it to explore themes of desire, freedom, artistic endeavour, destiny and the aspirations and inspirations of the human spirit.

In this way the five tales in *Anecdotes of Destiny* are closely connected, and in the writing itself images of angels, birds and, always, the sea, enclose each story. Most famous is 'Babette's Feast', in which Babette, a famous French chef, changes the lives of the members of an obscure and puritanical religious sect living on a Norwegian fjord. In other long stories, 'The Diver', 'Tempests' and 'The Immortal Story', all the influences of the great sources – the *Arabian Nights*, Shakespeare, the Bible – are put to her sophisticated use, creating a fairy-tale world all her own, full of crystal visions and sibylline marvels.

Isak Dinesen was the pen-name of Karen Blixen. She lived in Denmark and in Kenya. *Babette's Feast* was successfully filmed in 1987.

Age in year of publication: seventy-three.

E. L. Doctorow 1931–

1975 *Ragtime*

Ragtime, using stylish sentences and light cadences, tells the secret and unsecret history of the United States at the turn of the century. It is a novel of public drama, murder trials, teeming immigrants, political upheaval, vast wealth, Victorian values and secret longings. It is peopled by Freud and Jung, Houdini and the Archduke Franz Ferdinand, Emma Goldman, Henry Ford ('Henry Ford had once been an ordinary automobile manufacturer. Now he experienced an ecstasy greater and more intense than that vouchsafed to any American before him, not excepting Thomas Jefferson') and J. P. Morgan ('He was a monarch of the invisible, transnational kingdom of capital whose sovereignty was everywhere granted'), but its main protagonists are heroic figures in search of justice in this swiftly changing society.

Doctorow tells these stories with great verve and passion, as though he is inventing a myth of origin for the United States. The story of Coalhouse Walker, the black man whose car is vandalized, is the most powerful and dramatic in the book. (It occurred to Father one day that Coalhouse Walker Jr. didn't know he was a Negro.') The novel's other protagonist, of course, is the privileged narrator himself, whose father has gone on an Arctic expedition, whose uncle's – Mother's Younger Brother – obsessions move right through the novel, whose tone, in its easygoing neutrality and awestruck curiosity, is close to that of the narrator of *The Great Gatsby*.

E. L. Doctorow was born in New York. His other novels include *The Book of Daniel* (1971), *Billy Bathgate* (1988),and *The March* (2005) which won the Pen Faulkner Award and the American National Book Critics Circle Award.

Age in year of publication: forty-four.

Roddy Doyle 1958–

1990   *The Snapper*

The Rabbittes, who appear in *The Commitments* (1987), *The Snapper* and *The Van* (1991), are the first happy family to appear in Irish writing since *The Vicar of Wakefield* (1766). Of these three novels *The Snapper* is probably the most accomplished. *The Snapper* tells the story of Sharon Rabbitte, twenty-year-old daughter of Jimmy and Veronica, who gets pregnant. The father is an unlikely suspect, and Sharon doesn't want anyone to know who it is; the novel follows the course of her pregnancy and the antics of her family and friends.

Doyle captures brilliantly the atmosphere of a working-class Dublin family and community; there is a superb account in the novel of a large family in a small space, all of them shouting different things at the same time on the same page. There is something almost miraculous in this book about the way in which dialogue is manipulated and controlled. The laughter and wisecracks, the drama between individuals and the group, the skilful pacing, make the book incredibly readable. It is also politically sharp in its depiction of an Ireland in which religion and nationalism have lost their power.

Roddy Doyle was born in Dublin and lives there still. He has written five novels and two plays. *The Snapper* was made into a film by Stephen Frears; *The Commitments* was filmed by Alan Parker. *Paddy Clarke Ha Ha Ha* won the Booker Prize in 1993. He has also written two volumes of The Last Round Up: *A Star Called Henry* (1999), and *Oh, Play That Thing!* (2004).

Age in year of publication: thirty-two.

Margaret Drabble 1939–

1977　*The Ice Age*

'A huge icy fist, with large cold fingers, was squeezing and chilling the people of Britain.' This is the 1970s, the decade which followed the flourish of the Swinging Sixties and the Beatles, in which boom and bust and national depression and greed set the scene for the arrival of Thatcher, a punishment for all the sins so splendidly chronicled here.

Margaret Drabble writes in a tradition currently out of fashion – that of Mrs Gaskell and Arnold Bennett, in which social conscience and a social historian's eye control her imagination, making her a fine recorder of the way we live together, and of the moral consequences of same.

Anthony Keating, Drabble's hero, is a perfect Seventies man. He writes songs, he works in television, then throws everything up for property speculation, the quick-buck Seventies virus which infected England, and which in this case gives Keating a heart attack at the age of thirty-eight. Drabble places Keating in a crowded, vivid world. With wife and children, mistress and her children, business colleagues inside and outside prison, danger abroad, danger at home, to a threnody of dead or decrepit dogs, Keating's story is a burst of indignation for a senile Britain. Because Drabble is so skilled a storyteller, *The Ice Age* is full of surprises, full of interest, an immensely absorbing record of a shabby age.

Margaret Drabble was born in Sheffield and lives in London and Dorset. Her body of work includes the trilogy *The Radiant Way* (1987), *A Natural Curiosity* (1989) and *The Gates of Ivory* (1991).

Age in year of publication: thirty-eight.

Maureen Duffy 1933–

1962   *That's How it Was*

There is a nobility about this semi-autobiographical novel. Though it captures a particular time and place of poverty – the East End of London before and during the Second World War – its sense of longing is universal. It is also an unusual addition to the literature of tuberculosis, that disease which infiltrated so many nineteenth- and early twentieth-century families, so often recorded in novels of the time. Most remarkable is the dogged poignancy of its portrait of the love of a child for its mother.

Louey Mahony, one of eight children in a family decimated by TB, falls for an Irishman, Paddy, who leaves her with an illegitimate girl Paddy of her own; the child tells us this story. Poverty and bombing are not the only problems Louey has to face: Louey's TB is of the slow, struggling kind, and Paddy grows up mostly in other people's houses, or, when Louey marries again to give a home to Paddy, with an illiterate stepfamily, peace and money always in short supply. Paddy rages, and escapes, but always her eye is on her mother Louey: resolute, neat as a pin, loving, a good woman who is allotted absolutely nothing by the country she lives in. There is an elegiac quality about this novel, and an anxious yet lyrical strength in Duffy's writing, which fits like a glove the love story she tells.

Maureen Duffy was born in Sussex. She is a poet and biographer, and her fiction includes *The Microcosm* (1966) and *Love Child* (1971).

Age in year of publication: twenty-nine.

Daphne du Maurier 1907–1989

1951   *My Cousin Rachel*

Some of the most satisfying entertainments of the Victorian age were novels such as Mary E. Braddon's *Lady Audley's Secret* and Mrs Henry Wood's *East Lynne*, which sensationally used domestic circumstances as the setting for intrigue, secrets, violence and death.

Daphne du Maurier is the direct descendant of this tradition, and *My Cousin Rachel* a great achievement in this genre. On an estate in Cornwall in the nineteenth century, Ambrose Ashley raises his nephew Philip with servants, dogs, neighbours, tenants – but no women. Ambrose, in Europe, encounters the beautiful Rachel Sangaletti, marries her and in six months is dead, having sent a sequence of troubling letters to Philip accusing Rachel of extravagance – and worse. Philip, the image of his uncle in every way, is possessed by hatred for Rachel until she comes to stay: small, large-eyed, an enchantress, she bewitches Philip entirely.

My Cousin Rachel follows every twist and turn of a heart obsessed; du Maurier's considerable artistry is rooted in her control of hypnotic detail and psychological tension so that even the removal of a vase of flowers takes on a sinister significance. Simultaneously she mocks and reverses our conventional expectations of the sexual desires that drive men and women, always leaving questions in the air. Resolutions unresolved: that was her hallmark, as was providing entertainment of the highest order.

Daphne du Maurier was born in London and lived mostly in Cornwall. Many of her stories – '*The Birds*' (1963) and '*Don't Look Now*' (1938) – and novels were filmed, the most famous being *Rebecca* (1938).

Age in year of publication: forty-four.

Bret Easton Ellis 1964–

1991 *American Psycho*

American Psycho is both a morality tale and a comedy about capitalism and materialism. The abject consumerism of the protagonist and his friends who work on Wall Street, their obsession with brand names, chic restaurants and new trends, and their vicious snobbery are combined with elaborate descriptions of the murdering and dismemberment and torture of women.

The cold, dispassionate tone in which the violence is described has been much misunderstood: the tone of *American Psycho* has the moralistic edge of Swift, suggesting a connection between the obsessive consumerism and right-wing politics of the Reagan years and pathological misogyny. Easton Ellis's crime, perhaps, is to make all this too funny, too readable, too entertaining. His use of lists in the book is inspired, and his sense of New York as the home of the ruling class gives the book a deeply political edge. The book is written in short, titled chapters, like entries in a diary; the narrative is snappy; chapter openings are superbly gripping and interesting. Writing about murdering women in a 'snappy' and 'gripping' style is unlikely to endear the author to many people, but this is an important and disturbing book.

Bret Easton Ellis was born and raised in Los Angeles and lives in New York. His other books are *Less Than Zero* (1985), *The Rules of Attraction* (1987), *The Informers* (1994), *Glamorama* (1998) and *Lunar Park* (2005).

Age in year of publication: twenty-seven.

Ralph Ellison 1914–1994

1952   *Invisible Man*

Like John Bunyan's *The Pilgrim's Progress*, this charismatic novel follows the adventures of a man in search of the meaning of his existence. Our hero lives in the United States, where most people are white: white people can be seen. He is black, part of an amorphous mass, and he comes to see that, black, he is invisible. He tells us his story, and as one event follows another we watch him being led deeper and deeper into a realization of just how angry a black man in America should be.

In his travels as a black man in a white land, his idealism encounters all the temptations of his generation, and as each one comes his way, it is found to be a fraud – 'white' education, Communism and other radical 'isms', gambling, drink, sex, crime, adapting to a white society, fighting white society – all these ploys and distractions are shown to be deadly. Ellison plays with every myth about the black man – rape, for instance – and dismisses each one. He brings this about by concealing his message in a narrative as compelling and engaging as all the great storytelling novels. Picaresque in its vision, and in its insistence, finally, on the necessity for acceptance if not forgiveness, this profound, angry book is one of the great American novels of the post-war period, still resonant today.

Ralph Ellison was born in Oklahoma and lived mostly in the USA. This, his only published novel, won the National Book Award in 1953.

Age in year of publication: thirty-eight.

Jeffrey Eugenides 1960–

1993   *The Virgin Suicides*

Jeffrey Eugenides' novel, *The Virgin Suicides*, is exciting, accomplished and beautifully written. The style is rich, the sentences are carefully modulated, the tone is relaxed and knowing, cynical and humorous, as though F. Scott Fitzgerald and Nabokov and the Coen Brothers had met on the lawns of some grand American suburb.

The novel, narrated by a man in early middle age, tells the story of the five Lisbon sisters, teenagers much sought after by the local youths, who commit suicide in the same year. The narrator becomes a sort of detective, or historian, gathering details about the lives and deaths of the girls, going over and analysing certain encounters with them, or glimpses of them. This is a novel alive with desire, with memories of desire, with fading desire. The mating rituals of white suburban America become, in a superbly controlled narrative, both infinitely sad and infinitely funny. The intensity of the dissection of each detail, as though the antics of the Lisbon family were of immense national importance, gives the novel's dark laughter a manic edge. The novel is full of asides and minor digressions, all of them fascinating and perfectly chosen, some of them funny enough to make you laugh out loud.

Jeffrey Eugenides was born in Detroit and lives in New York. *The Virgin Suicides* was his first novel, his second *Middlesex* (2002) won the Pulitzer Prize.

Age in year of publication: thirty-three.

J. G. Farrell 1935–1979

1973   *The Siege of Krishnapur*

There is, in J. G. Farrell's *The Siege of Krishnapur*, an odd and original mixture of melancholy and hilarity. He is interested in the comic possibilities of the English character abroad as the colonists try to create order from chaos but instead create only further chaos. In *The Siege of Krishnapur* our heroes find themselves in India in the years after the Great Exhibition when the Victorians believed that they could spread progress. The Indians, however, are getting ready to revolt in the Mutiny.

Farrell loves set scenes: the mad sermon during the siege, the fallen white woman to whom no one dare speak, the natives gathering daily on a nearby hill to watch the trouble, love and poetry in a hot climate, knives and forks and spoons in a cannon. There is a sensational argument between two doctors about the cure for cholera; one dies from his own remedy. Farrell's sense of detail never fails him, and his research into Victorian beliefs, or methods of warfare, to give just two examples, offers the novel credibility without overburdening it. He manages a light tone while remaining alert to the weight of his subject; this novel is a brilliantly dark comedy.

J. G. Farrell was born in Liverpool and lived in London until a few months before his death. He was working on his novel *The Hill Station* (1981) when he was drowned off the south coast of Ireland. *The Siege of Krishnapur* won the Booker Prize in 1973. He also wrote *Troubles* (1970), which won the Lost Man Booker Prize in 2010, and *The Singapore Grip* (1978).

Age in year of publication: thirty-eight.

William Faulkner 1897–1962

1962   *The Reivers: A Reminiscence*

This book was written at the end of Faulkner's life, but there is no sign of any loss of energy, or flaws in narrative skill, or waning of sheer enthusiasm. It uses a rambling style full of parentheses and subordinate clauses, as though someone were telling a story and constantly interrupting himself.

It is clear that the story is being told in the early 1960s about events in the early years of the century when old systems of manners and morals and landholding still obtained in the Southern states. Enter a motor car which is purchased by our narrator's grandfather. The narrator is eleven years old, but he is wise even then, and watchful. The car is driven by Boon, his grandfather's black servant, and when all the adults in the family go away for a funeral, our narrator, Boon and a man called Ned travel without permission to Memphis. The roads are appalling, and Ned is not entirely sane. Slowly, we realize that our narrator is telling the story of a few crucial days in his own education, when he mixed with people – including a number of prostitutes – outside his own class, when he witnessed confusion, nights in strange beds, homesickness, possible disaster, a racism which was new to him and an extraordinary amount of highjinks. When he gets home to his ordered upbringing, full of old patrician values, he has changed. The style, however, for all its rambling, has a sharpness and a sophistication, and the reader has a right to feel that as Faulkner lay dying, he must have taken pleasure in creating this novel.

William Faulkner was born in Mississippi and divided his time between there and Hollywood. His novels include *The Sound and the Fury* (1929), *As I Lay Dying* (1930), *Light in August* (1932) and *Absalom, Absalom!* (1936). He was awarded the Nobel Prize in Literature in 1950.

Age in year of publication: sixty-five.

Sebastian Faulks 1953–

1993 *Birdsong*

This novel, one of the most popular of the 1990s, received the most nominations from our readers as their favourite novel of the last fifty years.

An elegiac, romantic work, it is both a heart-breaking evocation of life in the killing fields of the First World War, and a passionate account of an anguished love affair. Faulks interweaves these two central narratives with the love stories of generations of one family, the birth of children, and the power of love, sexual and otherwise, so that hope flutters through the story like the thin but exquisite song of the birds from which this poignant novel takes its name.

Faulks' hero, Stephen Wraysford, is an unwilling survivor: through his sad eyes the agonizing years of battle follow, one after another, and he sees every man with whom he has shared this holocaust blasted to oblivion. Most powerful is the recreation of the underground tunnels which lay beneath the battlefields, constructed at terrible cost, and which Faulks, with consummate skill, presents as an underground Hell, the inevitable punishment for humanity so fruitlessly at war. 'Jack saw part of Turner's face and hair still attached to a piece of skull rolling to a halt where the tunnel narrowed . . . there was an arm with a corporal's strip on it near his feet, but most of the men's bodies had been blown into the moist earth.' And thus Birdsong is also a testament to the millions of men who were slaughtered in the abattoir of Flanders Fields, a reminder to later generations never to forget 'the pity of the past'.

Sebastian Faulks was born in Newbury and lives in London. *Birdsong* was his fourth novel, one of a French trilogy which began with *The Girl at the Lion d'Or* (1989) and concluded with *Charlotte Gray* (1998). His other novels include *On Great Dolphin Street* (2001), *Human Traces* (2005), *Engleby* (2007) and the James Bond novel *Devil May Care* (2008).

Age in year of publication: forty.

Penelope Fitzgerald 1916–2000

1995   *The Blue Flower*

This is a novel about the illogicality of love, and much else: dialectics, philosophy, food, medicine, eighteenth-century surgery (fatal), mathematics and gossip. It fairly hums with absorbing personal and philosophical considerations. The impoverished young nobleman Friedrich (Fritz) von Hardenburg, later known as Novalis, the great eighteenth-century German Romantic poet and philosopher, falls in love with Sophie von Kuhn. She is twelve when Fritz falls in love with her, fifteen when she dies of tuberculosis. Sophie is silly and uninteresting but Fritz's love is not. Embedded in a German world of family and food notable for its unquestioning brutishness – geese, for example, were killed after being plucked alive, twice – Sophie inspires Fritz's writing, philosophy and his Romantic quest, symbolized by his book, *The Blue Flower*. The scene in which Fritz reads the opening chapter of this early work to the uncomprehending Sophie is only one of the episodes in which absurdity and heartbreak cannot be separated.

Penelope Fitzgerald was a writer with an ironic, dry wit, and an exquisite, elliptical prose style. Everything she wrote seemed effortless: her timing, her obliquity, her knowing way of telling us little but implying much. This conciseness nevertheless produced a tumultuous and convincing effect, so that whilst Death stalks its pages, The Blue Flower, crowded with seductive personalities, glows with laughter and fizzles with interest and ideas.

Penelope Fitzgerald was born in Lincoln and lived in London. *The Blue Flower* won the US National Book Critics' Circle Award in 1998. Her other novels include *The Beginning of Spring* (1988), *The Gate of Angels* (1990) and *Offshore*, which won the 1979 Booker Prize. A story collection *The Means of Escape* appeared in 2000 and her selected writings *A House of Air* in 2003.

Age in year of publication: seventy-nine.

Thomas Flanagan 1923–2002

1979   *The Year of the French*

In 1798 the people of County Mayo rose up to join the small force sent by the French Revolutionary government to support Wolfe Tone's United Irishmen in their fight to liberate Ireland from English rule.

To the Irish, the English were 'Big Lords', the absentee landlords, Protestant persecutors; to the English, the Irish were savages, traitors, Catholics. It is a rare writer who can project dispassion into this gruesome relationship. Flanagan does so, his vast knowledge of the period pouring through the voices of a handful of men of the time: we see what happened through their eyes, their passions and suffering. They in turn reveal to us a cast of thousands, so that every sound and vision of 1798 erupts before us – the battles, the beddings, the slaughter, the boozing, the poetry, the hangings, the generals and the English at war, and at their ease.

For the Irish, ease is their music and poetry, which flows through the dramatic pages of this great epic. Even in the thick of battle Thomas Flanagan has a remarkable way of using the particular eloquence of Irish English so that we understand why, two hundred years later, few remember Cornwallis's victory over the rebels at Ballinamuck (the place of the pig), whilst the Irish songs about the year of the French are still sung today.

Thomas Flanagan was born in Connecticut, and lived in both Ireland and America. He won the 1979 US National Book Critics Circle Award for this novel.

Age in year of publication: fifty-six.

Richard Ford 1944–

1986   *The Sportswriter*

Richard Ford has a special ability to create complex moments in his narrative where something difficult – a feeling, a memory, a desire or an action – is explained and understood, and then he allows the explanation not to be enough, he preserves a sense of mystery and strangeness about what his characters feel and how they are motivated.

Frank Bascombe is the narrator of both *The Sportswriter* and *Independence Day* (1995); he lives in New Jersey. His life is, on the face of it, ordinary. He is divorced, he had a child who died, he thinks about women and work, he has friends. Ford surrounds him – both novels take place over a short space of time – with a sort of halo as he meditates on his life and days, tries to come to terms with those around him. He is calm, nothing is exaggerated, the scale of his emotions remains small, and yet – and this is the genius of *The Sportswriter* – his feelings are rendered with such sympathy and complexity, such a sense of wonder and careful, thoughtful prose that he burns his way into the reader's imagination as a modern Everyman. The novel uses time with particular skill: the three days in which it takes place contrasted with a lifetime in flashback and memory. The events of these three days – meetings with close family and friends – are brilliantly and memorably rendered.

Richard Ford was born in Mississippi and has lived in Princeton and Michigan. He has written a number of excellent short stories – collected in *Rock Springs* (1988) *Women with Men* (1997) and *A Multitude of Sins* (2002) – and four important novels: *The Sportswriter*, *Wildlife* (1990), *Independence Day* (1995) and *The Lay of the Land* (2006). *Independence Day* won a Pulitzer Prize in 1996.

Age in year of publication: forty-two.

Frederick Forsyth 1938–

1971   *The Day of the Jackal*

Everybody knows that General de Gaulle died in his bed and all attempts to assassinate him failed. Therefore, any novel which focuses on an attempt to assassinate him must lack one central tension: excitement about the outcome. How is it, then, that this book, almost thirty years old, remains powerful and exciting?

It is written in the style of investigative journalism, or indeed a police report. There are hardly any flourishes, and there is a great deal of technical information. The narrative hardly ever enters anyone's mind, and this gives the novel a strange, chilling tone: things are described as from a distance, as though someone later managed to piece together what had happened, and this makes the events of the novel very convincing indeed.

At the beginning the OAS decide, after many botched attempts, to hire an outsider to assassinate de Gaulle who has, in their opinion, betrayed Algeria. We learn very little about the Jackal, the man they hire: he has no thoughts and hardly any past, he is English, blond, efficient and ruthless. As his plans – perfect weapon, several new identities, perfect location – are made, the police in Paris slowly realize that the danger this time is real. Once this happens you cannot put the novel down, and there are moments when you almost want the Jackal to succeed. The narrative is fast moving, tense, supremely confident and makes this book a classic of its kind.

Frederick Forsyth was born in Kent and now lives in Hertfordshire. His other books include *The Odessa File* (1972) and *The Dogs of War* (1974).

Age in year of publication: thirty-three.

John Fowles 1926–2005

1966　　The Magus

This novel follows in the great tradition of island stories in which our hero, Nicholas Urfe, innocent, raw and English, arrives in a strange and foreign place full of strange and foreign people. He is rational, intelligent and civilized and suddenly now is forced to grapple with dark and hidden forces.

The Magus is set in the years after the Second World War; Nicholas, an Oxford graduate, finds work as a teacher in a school on a remote Greek island. Fowles is brilliant at establishing the island's topography, its bareness and its isolation. He also allows history and myth to hover over the book, so that at times Nicholas seems to be acting out an older story as he comes, like a moth to flame, to the house of Maurice Conchis on the island. Conchis is a conjuror, a story-teller, an art collector. His house is filled with ghosts, strange noises, odd music. And Nicholas is both frightened by what he finds there, and deeply drawn to and intrigued by it.

Fowles is fascinated by the darker aspects of male desire, and by the compulsive and the irrational. He manages to make his island both a real place, rugged and beautiful, and an imaginary place, as though Prospero and Caliban had recently walked these shores. Just as the protagonist is dragged deeper and deeper into the enigma of his host, so too the reader is constantly jolted and surprised by the drama in the novel between the rational and the mysterious.

John Fowles was born in Essex and lived in Lyme Regis. His other novels included *The Collector* (1963) and *The French Lieutenant's Woman* (1969). *The Magus* was reissued with a revised ending in 1977.

Age in year of publication: forty.

Janet Frame 1924–2004

1957   *Owls Do Cry*

Janet Frame's gift is to use a lucid, often comic view of her own experiences as the touchstone for her distinctive work. *Owls Do Cry* fictionalizes her childhood in New Zealand as one of the siblings of the impoverished Withers family. The father is Bob, a shiftworker; the mother the gentle Amy, always wearing a damp pinny; Francie is the eldest, destined for the woollen mills and worse; then comes Toby who is 'a shingle short'; and Daphne, Frame's alter ego, who like Frame herself is given a leucotomy for little reason except as a curb on an excess of imagination. Finally there is Chicks, the youngest, who plunges into the best – or worst – that New Zealand has to offer.

Childhood for the Withers children revolves around scarcity; they are dirty, they are poor. For pleasure they loiter around the town rubbish dump, long to go to the cinema and know the words of every Forties and Fifties popular song. These childhood memories echo with tragic clarity through the adult lives each chooses.

Janet Frame has a relish for words, and for the small details that identify an incident or an event. In *Owls Do Cry* the language shimmers with her poetic sensibility, but there's a toughness too, fortified by her gentle fierceness and her angry calm.

Janet Frame was born in Oamuru, near Dunedin, and lived in that city. She is also famous for her autobiographical trilogy *To the Is-Land* (1982), *An Angel at My Table* (1984) and *The Envoy From Mirror City* (1984) which was filmed by Jane Campion in 1991, under the title of its second volume: *An Angel at my Table*.

Age in year of publication: thirty-three.

Charles Frazier 1950–

1997 *Cold Mountain*

This is an epic historical romance set against the backdrop of the American Civil War. Inman is a wounded Confederate soldier. As his recovery is near completion, his despair at the futility of the fighting and his desire to be reunited with his love Ada lead him to abandon his fellow soldiers in a makeshift hospital and journey home to Cold Mountain in the hills of North Carolina.

Ada's tale of her own heroism in managing a small farm and of the stubborn friendship she cements with her new helper, Ruby, is interspersed with Inman's Odyssean voyage in which he saves the lives of two women, buries a child, is left for dead and is rescued by a slave, and fights off the Home Guard who are looking for deserters.

Frazier has captured the cadences and quotidian miseries of the time and his descriptions of the landscape fully echo the heroic nature of the tale. As the dual narratives converge, the suspense and tension increase along with Ada's and Inman's yearning for each other. They know they have both been changed by their circumstances and wonder if their love can still blossom. The climax is superbly handled and turns a potential saga into a genuine work of literature.

Charles Frazier was born in North Carolina. *Cold Mountain*, his first novel, won the National Book Award in 1998. His second novel *Thirteen Moons* appeared in 2006.
Age in year of publication: forty-seven.

William Gaddis 1922–1998

1955   *The Recognitions*

Readers wishing to enter the strange, dark, rich and difficult world of William Gaddis should probably start with the shortest of his four novels, *Carpenter's Gothic* (1985), but *The Recognitions* is the real masterpiece and repays much rereading and close attention.

The central motif concerns the conflict between the genuine and the fake: one of the main characters is a forger, another character has written a play which may or may not be a forgery. Many of the conversations held at New York gatherings in the novel are also deeply false; religion and consumerism, too, are rendered in-authentic in the novel's vast thousand-page panorama. But it is the texture of the writing which holds the novel together and makes it genuinely exciting: the sheer panache of the parody and satire, the sudden beginnings and endings, the quality of the jokes, the density of the narrative, the weirdness of the characters. Only in Scotland (Kelman, Gray, Welsh) and in the United States (Gaddis, Pynchon, DeLillo) has the true torch of modernism in fiction been carried. *The Recognitions* is one of the great novels of the century.

William Gaddis was born and lived in New York. His other novels include *JR* (1975) and *A Frolic of His Own* (1994).

Age in year of publication: thirty-three.

Mavis Gallant 1922–

1979 *From the Fifteenth District*

Mavis Gallant's range is astonishing. It is hard to make any generalizations about her work because her stories – she has written altogether more than one hundred – are so different in tone and content. In her world people are distant from each other, and the closer they come – in families, in love – the more remote and fraught and strange their behaviour and the more exciting and funny and interesting her story. Her writing is impeccable. Sentences are often startling. In 'The Remission', one of her masterpieces of this collection, a family has moved to the Mediterranean so that Alec can die. His wife is puzzled by the locals: 'Barbara expected them to be cunning and droll, which they were, and to steal from her, which they did, and to love her, which they seemed to.' Alec, of course, doesn't die, at least not for a long time, which gives Barbara the chance to find a new companion. In almost all of the stories, people live in exile. The Anglo-Saxons are bossy and half-impoverished, some of them are truly dreadful people. There is a marvellous story about a German boy who comes home late from the war; there is an extraordinary account of a Polish exile in Paris, and another of a Hungarian mother whose son lives in Scotland. And the last story, 'Irina', has a deeply unsettling version of an old woman ('In loving and unloving families alike, the same problem arises after a death: What to do about the widow?'). In this volume, Gallant writes with wit and intelligence and a unique sort of sharpness.

Mavis Gallant was born in Montreal and has lived in Paris since 1950. Her *Collected Stories* came out in 1996.

Age in year of publication: fifty-seven.

Helen Garner 1942–

1984   *The Children's Bach*

The late twentieth century is Helen Garner's stamping ground. Her novels, short stories and brilliant journalism are marked by an incisive intelligence and an exact command of language. Her writing is spare and sharp, like a sequence of photographs of sour city streets, her characters snatched in celluloid for just one second. In a line or two she captures intimately the habits of the young in the city, and the disorders of adult love. She is at her best in this mordant tale of urban family life in which her wit and singular dialogue are imbedded in an elegant threnody of Bach, Mozart, and a tangy mix of rock and soul.

Athena is married to Dexter, a man who wants to 'live gloriously' and who wears shirts that look like pyjama tops. They have two children, Arthur, and Billy, who is not quite right in the head and about whom Athena, at least, nurses no delusions. Elizabeth erupts from Dexter's past, bringing with her Philip, the cool rock musician, and her younger sister Vicki. Matters and persons rearrange themselves, to the accompaniment of Philip's rock rhythms, Dexter's curly whistling and Vicki's cacophony of vomiting after too much Campari and orange. But really this is the story of Athena's search for her own music, for more than the city sounds, the burble of children and the distant chatter of neighbours. Through it all, Helen Garner's offbeat humour adds wonderfully and contrapuntally to this story of the encounters, adjustments and confrontations of ordinary life.

Helen Garner was born in Geelong and lives in Melbourne. Her award-winning fiction includes *Monkey Grip* (1977), *Honour & Other People's Children* (1980), *Cosmo Cosmolino* (1992), *The Spare Room* (2008) and short stories, *Postcards from Surfers* (1985). Her classic reportage on political correctness in action, *The First Stone*, was published in 1995.

Age in year of publication: forty-two.

William H. Gass 1924–

1968   *In the Heart of the Heart of the Country*

(revised edition 1981)

The five stories in this book have different themes and settings, but there is something distinctive about the tone and the voice; Gass's signature in these stories sets them apart. The style is poetic and at times gnarled. The sentences are worked on and sculpted. Gass is clearly as interested in language as he is in things; he gives the impression that the words he uses were cut out of stone. Yet he manages in the first long story, 'The Pedersen Kid', to give the reader a vivid sense of the fierce cold and the fierce distrust between the characters, to give a sense of danger and mystery to the journey the boy has to take across the freezing landscape with his father and the farm help. In another story, 'Icicles', the tone is more manic, close to William Gaddis perhaps, or even Virginia Woolf. And then the title story is a piece of pure, calm, poetic writing.

It is told in short sections. The narrator is alone in a small town in Indiana: he describes the town and the weather (Gass is brilliant on weather): 'Sometimes I think the land is flat because the winds have levelled it, they blow so constantly.' He writes about houses and neighbours and cats, the mood is meditative and oddly dislocated, as though this was a brilliant translation from the French. And all the time, in stray references, but stitched carefully into the fabric of the story, is an absence, a missing loved one, longed for, loathed (in one section), remembered, brought to mind.

William H. Gass was born in North Dakota and has lived in St Louis since 1969. His novels include *Omensetter's Luck* (1966) and *The Tunnel* (1996). He is also a well-known critic.

Age in year of publication: forty-four.

Maurice Gee 1931–

1978   *Plumb*

'I have never wished for comfort, but for thorns, for battle in the soul's arena. I have had what I wished for.' So speaks George Plumb, a stiff-necked New Zealand clergyman whose story begins in the 1890s and continues through the first half of this century.

Plumb's fanaticism leads him by the nose from Presbyterianism to Unitarianism to pacifism until no religion is good enough for him. But he's a worthy soul and a loving man, one of those men who are always right and like other such paragons considers constant impregnation of his slaving wife Edie '– in her weariness, in her pain, she praised: scouring pans, mopping floors' – to be his Christian duty. And so the novel reaches out to trace the erosive effect of mindless righteousness on their ten children, centring most of all on the homosexual Alf. George's fundamentalism, pinched and sour, placidly overshadows and shrivels all those in his care.

There is a tenderness and charm about Gee's writing, and an understanding in his onslaught on the Puritan tradition – flourishing vigorously in New Zealand – which manages to be compassionate yet deadly. Redolent with the atmosphere of an antipodean world reconstructed with fidelity and warmth, this is a novel thoroughly satisfying in the traditional manner, engraved with the lore of family life.

Maurice Gee was born in Whakatane, North Island, New Zealand. *Plumb* won the New Zealand Fiction Award and the Wattie Book of the Year Award, and was followed by two sequels: *Meg* (1981) and *Sole Survivor* (1983).

Age in year of publication: forty-seven.

Kaye Gibbons 1960–

1987   *Ellen Foster*

There is music in the language of the American South. The sounds come from the words Southerners choose, the dialogue, the laying down of words in a particular order – the nearest to it, when listened to, is Irish.

Kaye Gibbons writes in the cadence of the South, which she puts into the voice of Ellen Foster, whose opening words, 'When I was little I would think of ways to kill my daddy', drop us into the company of a terrified little girl who knows too much about what's going on. Daddy drinks, Mummy is sick to dying; Daddy likes to beat up both of them. Her only place of safety is the coloured house down the road with her friend Starletta, but how can she eat a coloured biscuit or walk down a coloured pathway? She can though, and more, as she is soon to learn.

Ellen has a way of getting through: she must love, and she sets out to find someone to do it with. Her story tells us more about race in the South than any social history, for as we listen to Ellen, we are told Starletta's story too. Kaye Gibbons is a clever writer with an ear for the rhythm and beauty of language, and a way of conveying the fragility of life which is direct and fresh, keen-witted, always original.

Kaye Gibbons was born in North Carolina where she still lives. Amongst her award-winning novels are *A Virtuous Woman* (1989) and *Sights Unseen* (1995).
   Age in year of publication: twenty-seven.

85

William Golding 1911–1993

1954   *Lord of the Flies*

The idea behind this novel should be fatal: it tells us that within us
all, eagerly waiting to be let out, lie savages. But the power of the
narrative and the characterization overcomes the crudity of the idea
and forces the reader to become deeply involved in the story and
the fate of the small English boys who have survived an air crash
on a desert island. At first they are bewildered and find it easy to
pick on a boy called Piggy. They talk in a mixture of school talk
and attempted adult talk, but this changes as the novel goes on. The
older boys take control. 'Apart from food and sleep, [the smaller
boys] found time for play, aimless and trivial, among the white sand
by the bright water. They cried for their mothers much less often
than might have been expected; they were very brown, and filthily
dirty.' They try to keep a fire lit, they eat fruit, attend meetings and
hunt pigs. The pig-hunting scenes are particularly graphic and
bloodthirsty. Leaders emerge, and slowly a war breaks out between
them; two of the older boys get killed and they begin to hunt
another, just as a ship arrives.

Golding has created the unbrave new world of these small boys
so convincingly that when the first adult speaks at the end of the
book, it seems like an odd intrusion.

William Golding was born in Cornwall and was an English teacher in Wiltshire for
many years. He won the Nobel Prize in Literature in 1983. His other books include
Pincher Martin (1956), *The Spire* (1964) and *Rites of Passage*, which won the Booker
Prize in 1980.

Age in year of publication: forty-three.

Nadine Gordimer 1923–

1979   *Burger's Daughter*

Nadine Gordimer is known for her implacable opposition to the enduring apartheid regime in South Africa rather than her extraordinary talent as a stylist or as a novelist who writes better than any of her contemporaries about states of sexual longing and desire. *Burger's Daughter* is the work in which her talent at dramatizing the conflict between public and private life, the individual and the family, history and destiny, escape and entrapment, is best displayed.

Rosa Burger is the daughter of Marxist parents who have been martyred for the cause of a new South Africa. The novel tells the story of her desire to be true to her parents' legacy and her efforts to escape it. It is written in her own voice and the dry voice of a reporter; it takes us through her childhood and her parents' lives, through the years after their deaths, followed by a wonderfully described sensuous sojourn in France, and then the inevitable return. Even though much of the novel deals with cool surfaces, scenes viewed from afar, moments snatched from memory, Rosa Burger, like many of Gordimer's characters, seems desperately real and exact, alive and memorable.

Nadine Gordimer was born in Transvaal, South Africa, and has always lived in South Africa. All her short story collections are wonderful and her strongest novels include *The Late Bourgeois World* (1966), *The Conservationist*, which won the Booker Prize in 1974, and *A Sport of Nature* (1987). She received the Nobel Prize in Literature in 1991.

Age in year of publication: fifty-six.

Alasdair Gray 1934–

1981 *Lanark: A Life of Four Books*

No great Scottish novel emerged from the First World War, nor from the Second. It seems to have taken the unlikely figure of Margaret Thatcher to fire, and perhaps infuriate, the Scottish novelists' imaginations.

Lanark seethes with political rage and is jammed with surrealist invention. It tells the interconnected stories of Duncan Thaw, a young Glasgow artist who draws, and is drawn, in the realist tradition, and the figure Lanark, his science fiction doppelgänger, who comes to the page in full Borgesian dress. Thaw's Glasgow is a place of tenements, canals, middens, Catholics and Protestants, and the man himself is common and depressed, a Fifties lad filled with civic wonder. Lanark's vision of Glasgow is called Unthank, a fiery, darkened, collapsing industrial nightmare, like an illustration from William Blake. Lanark is given to odd skin complaints and strange encounters, and his travels through the underworld give vent to some of the best thinking about citizenship ever to appear in a novel.

Gray is a master of shade and counterpoint. Thaw's world and Lanark's world open on to each other in the most dazzling ways in this novel. At the end of the book, as Lanark contemplates the destruction of the city from his vantage point on the old merchant Necropolis, we are left with nothing less eccentric than a boisterous lament for Gray's native Glasgow and all its past glories. *Lanark* is a circus, and a milestone in contemporary Scottish writing.

Alasdair Gray was born in Glasgow. His other novels include *1982 Janine* (1984), *Poor Things* (1992), which won the Guardian Fiction Prize and the Whitbread Novel Award, and *Young Men in Love* (2007).

Age in year of publication: forty-seven.

Henry Green 1905–1973

1950   *Nothing*

If there is a ball in literary heaven, Henry Green will be waltzing with Ivy Compton-Burnett; masters of dialogue both, it is difficult to imagine which of the two would lead the dance.

In *Nothing* Henry Green gazes upon the English moneyed classes, deprived of wealth by the Second World War and the taxes of the Labour government which followed it. For the first time in their lives, after doing nothing much, they must work. John Pomfret is such a man and Jane Weatherby, his former *amour*, a woman of just that class. Their offspring are quite other: children of the welfare state, they go to work while their parents lunch weekly at the Ritz, making much moan.

In this world no one wishes another well; it is parents first, children second; the rest of the world is there to dance attendance. When John's daughter falls in love with Jane's son, only the accumulated vinegar of many years enables Jane to put her towering self-esteem to good use, and, manipulating malice like a sten gun, lay waste those who stand in her way.

This is a model comedy of manners, lyrical and graphic, rising and falling in perfect tempo to the accompaniment of dialogue at once vivacious and viciously funny. Henry Green had access to wells of wit and caustic perception denied other writers.

Henry Green was born in Gloucestershire and lived in Birmingham and London. *Living* (1929), *Loving* (1945) and *Doting* (1952) are some of the best of his elliptical, enigmatic novels.

Age in year of publication: forty-five.

Graham Greene 1904–1991

1978   *The Human Factor*

It is difficult to decide which of the six wonderful novels that Graham Greene wrote between 1950 and his death is the best: *The End of the Affair* (1951); *The Quiet American* (1955); *Our Man in Havana* (1958); *The Comedians* (1966); *The Honorary Consul* (1973) or *The Human Factor*. There are moments in each of the books which are superb; and there are characters in each book who, in their isolation and shambling struggle with themselves, are among the most memorable in contemporary writing. Greene is certainly the finest English writer of the second half of the century.

The *Human Factor*, the most perfect and poignant of Greene's post-1950s novels, deals with the Secret Service; Maurice Castle, in his sixties, is back in London at the Africa desk. He is a mild man who lives quietly, good with files, as one of his superiors says; he is deeply in love with Sarah, his wife, who is a black South African. He has rescued her once and now he seeks to protect her and her son Sam. The novel, as one would expect from Greene, has some marvellous minor shady characters, and deals brilliantly with the chilling, ruthless nature of Castle's superiors. (It also has the best dog of any novel mentioned in this book; see Iris Murdoch's *The Nice and the Good* for the best cat.) But it is Castle himself who emerges most painfully in the novel: obsessive, driven, haunted, uneasy.

Graham Greene was born in Hertfordshire and lived for many years in the south of France. He published his first novel in 1929 and his last in 1988. Among his most famous works are *Brighton Rock* (1938), *The Power and the Glory* (1940), *The End of the Affair* (1951) and the film script of *The Third Man* (1950).

Age in year of publication: seventy-four.

Patrick Hamilton 1904–1962

1951   *The West Pier*

The West Pier is a study in pure, unmitigated perversity. The novel is set along the seafront and pier in Brighton in the early 1920s; there are only five characters who matter in the plot: three young men who were in school together, and two young women whom they meet on the pier. There are no murders and no violence, and yet there is an atmosphere in the book of constant menace and malevolence.

This book, the first in the Gorse trilogy, explores the mind of one Ernest Ralph Gorse as he takes advantage of one of the young women and makes a fool of her. With all its macabre plots and evil intentions, it has the tone of a very dark psychological thriller. The writing, which is elegant and slightly arch, is also at times world-weary and oddly wise, as though the book were written by the retired headmaster of an old, posh public school. It is full of petty snobberies and dramatic versions of the English class system. Slowly Hamilton allows Gorse to take over the book, and the twisted workings of his agile mind become fascinating; the idea that he wants to cause grief and humiliation and pain for their own sake gives the book a sort of horror that you can only find in other books by Hamilton and certain films by Hitchcock.

Patrick Hamilton was born in Hassocks, Sussex, and lived in London. He is best known for thrillers such as *Rope* (1929), on which Hitchcock based his film, and *Gaslight* (1938). He also wrote *Hangover Square* (1941). The other two books in the Gorse trilogy are *Mr Stimpson and Mr Gorse* (1953) and *Unknown Assailants* (1955).
Age in year of publication: forty-seven.

Elizabeth Hardwick 1916–2007

1979   *Sleepless Nights*

Elizabeth Hardwick sits at her New York table one June 'listening to the birdsong of rough, grinding trucks in the street' and decides to transform memory into fiction. Her 'clever, critical, bookish' heroine – herself – remembers episodes from her childhood in West Virginia in the company of her large family whose destinies 'are linked by a likeness of forehead and nose'. Then there are the bohemian years in New York living at the Hotel Schulyer 'within walking distance of all those places one never walked to', playing games of love with a cherished homosexual friend.

This period includes a portrait of Billie Holiday as Hardwick knew her, drenched in music and drugs; and then come years in America and Europe with the shadowy figure of her real husband, the poet Robert Lowell. All this and more is wrapped around the true heroines of her memories, the 'store clerks and waitresses, those ladies cast off with children to raise', the Idas and Josettes and Angelas whose small women's lives allow Hardwick to conjure up large truths. These splinters of memory, confessions of an insomniac, are recalled in words lovingly and precisely chosen. Hardwick has almost created her own literary form to write this novel; its other originalities lie in its zest for life, for epigram – and in the siren voice of its narrator.

Elizabeth Hardwick was born in Kentucky and lived in New York. A founder and advisory editor of the *New York Review of Books*, she has written other novels and critical works, in particular *Seduction and Betrayal* (1974).

Age in year of publication: sixty-three.

Frank Hardy 1917–1994

1950 *Power Without Glory*

Frank Hardy, an Australian Communist and gambler, wanted to write a fictional exposé of John Wren, the corrupt business magnate who controlled Melbourne – its sporting, gambling and political life, its police force and its Catholic Church – in the decades before 1950. Hardy spent years collecting material and secretly writing the novel, always one step ahead of Wren's machine. With no money, no printer, no publisher and a libellous seven-hundred-page manuscript, bit by bit the book became famous by word of mouth, a triumph of self-publishing.

The result was uproar: Hardy was arrested for criminal libel, and so began the most notorious case in Australian history – which Hardy won.

But above all, this is a passionate work of fiction, with a Balzacian vigour fuelled by Hardy's intense dedication to his epic cause. John Wren – renamed John West – stands before us, rising from his poor Irish immigrant beginnings, discarding family, friends, wife and children – if need be – in his ruthless quest for control of his city. This is not a one-dimensional novel nor is it a political tract. We feel for West: we know what made him what he is, and it is in Hardy's understanding of the evil grandeur of the man and the tangled forces that explain him and bring him down that the value of this novel lies.

Frank Hardy was born in Bacchus Marsh, Victoria, and spent most of his life in Australia. *Power Without Glory* also became a successful Australian TV series in 1976.

Age in year of publication: thirty-three.

Thomas Harris 1941–

1981   *Red Dragon*

Hannibal Lecter, who dominated Harris's bigger bestseller *Silence of the Lambs*, began his career in this thriller of masterly horror that quietly refrigerates the blood.

Thomas Harris does not bother with secrets; we know the infamy we face on the first page. Special agent Will Graham is cooling things off in Miami with his wife and stepson, after being sliced up by Lecter with a linoleum knife. Lecter, in prison, still manages to emit a miasma of iniquity and malignity by letter and phone – almost by osmosis. When Graham comes out of retirement to track down a serial killer who loves to kill families – husband, wife, children and family pet with attendant disagreeable rituals – he encounters a new psychopath, Frank Dolarhyde. Lethally similar, Lecter and Dolarhyde literally savour human flesh. Harris uses meticulous knowledge of forensic science, and domestic detail conveyed with precision and affection. His psychological insight – best illustrated by an account of Dolarhyde's childhood with his glacial grandmother, which is utterly believable, yet beyond belief – brings this intricate thriller to a brilliant climax.

Harris is a master craftsman with a particular talent for inserting horror into the ordinariness of the everyday, as the starting point for incidents of gigantic terror; he is one of a tiny band of popular novelists whose works are in a class and genre of their own.

Thomas Harris was born in Jackson, Tennessee, and lives in New York. This novel was filmed (as *Manhunter*) in 1986 as was, famously, *Silence of the Lambs* (1988), in 1990. A third novel featuring Hannibal Lecter, *Hannibal*, was published in 1999 and made into a film in 2002. A fourth, *Hannibal Rising*, came out in 2006 and was filmed in 2007.

Age in year of publication: forty.

Wilson Harris 1921–

1964   *Heartland*

This is a strange, haunting novel; it reads as though Conrad and Kafka had come together and studied the style of the late Henry James. It is set in a thick jungle close to a waterfall along Guyana's border with Venezuela and Brazil. Zachariah Stevenson is alone in this place: he has time to go over his father's financial ruin and death and then his lover and her husband's disappearance, the husband having embezzled money. He meets several figures in this remote outpost and has strange, portentous conversations with them. The sense of the jungle in the novel is overwhelming; the sense of rot and danger, heat and darkness takes over; the dank, menacing atmosphere is unforgettable; and the closeness of the waterfall lends power to the aura of claustrophobia. The prose is sinewy and dense, with strange twists and turns. In this heartland, habitation and pathways are tentative, so Stevenson's journey from one hut to another is full of uncertainties and odd possibilities. It is therefore not surprising that he should see a half-decomposed dead man and watch a baby being born.

It is impossible to place this novel, or indeed most of Harris's other work, in any tradition. *Heartland*, which is less than a hundred pages, is the sort of book you want to pick up and start again when you have finished it; it is infinitely mysterious and memorable.

Wilson Harris was born in New Amsterdam, British Guiana. He was a land surveyor before moving to London in 1959 where he still lives. His other novels include *Palace of the Peacock* (1960), *Carnival* (1985) and *The Ghost of Memory* (2006).
Age in year of publication: forty-three.

L. P. Hartley 1895–1972

1953   *The Go-Between*

This is one of the great English novels of the post-war period, with, also, one of the most famous opening lines: 'The past is a foreign country: they do things differently there.'

Leo Colston recalls the hot summer of 1900. A schoolboy then, an only child of a widowed mother of modest means, he shyly joins his friend Marcus Maudsley at Brandham Hall in Norfolk, where he confronts the cold conventions of the late Victorian upper classes. Struggling to please the family, he carries messages for Marcus's older sister Marian to the local farmer, Ted Burgess. On the periphery is the charming Hugh, Viscount Trimingham, face scarred by war, attendant on Marian. In the heat of summer Brandham Hall shimmers with deceptions as Leo grapples with crippling loyalties and secrets which, when revealed, are to maim him for life.

The perfection of *The Go-Between* lies in its subtlety, its atmosphere and in its elegiac style. It is one of those books which reveal layer upon layer of meaning with each rereading, so that the anxiety for love and the agony of betrayal as experienced by young Leo open windows to England's larger tragedies: the deathly embrace of the class system, the imminence of the First World War.

L. P. Hartley was born in Cambridgeshire. In later life he divided his time between London and a house near Bristol. His reputation also rests on the Eustace and Hilda trilogy: *The Shrimp and the Anemone* (1944), *The Sixth Heaven* (1946) and *Eustace and Hilda* (1947). *The Go-Between* was filmed by Joseph Losey in 1970.

Age in year of publication: fifty-eight.

Shirley Hazzard 1931–

1980   *The Transit of Venus*

Novels about obsessive love are always absorbing; this one adds intriguing analyses of serious moral issues. Two sisters, Caro and Grace, come to England from Australia in the 1950s. Cook's discovery of Australia is said to be a by-product of travelling to Tahiti in 1769, to watch the transit of Venus. Caro's trajectory across the old world encompasses a cast of interlocking characters and a galaxy of moral predicaments. In this ambitious narrative, science, politics, international affairs and corrupt American governments contend with a particularly felicitous selection of venal bureaucrats and tedious academics.

Caro loves and is loved by three very different men, and so her transit becomes a study first of obsessive love, and then of passion in all its forms. Overarching these human concerns Hazzard places the unwilled determinations of an ironic fate and the importance of truth in private love and in public life. Although this rich mix can sometimes teeter on the edge of excess, the classic structure of the novel, and Hazzard's piercing eye, fixed on the treacheries of people behaving badly, always give her moral puzzles charm. Most characteristic is her way with words, ranging from the constant staccato of witty epigrams to the lambent notes of those professing love, an accompaniment to a romantic melodrama on the grandest scale.

Shirley Hazzard was born in Sydney, Australia, and lives mainly in New York. Other novels include *The Evening of the Holiday* (1966). *The Transit of Venus* won the US National Book Critics Circle Award in 1980. *The Great Fire* (2003) won the American National Book Award and the Miles Franklin Award.

Age in year of publication: forty-nine.

Roy A. K. Heath 1926–2008

1978   *The Murderer*

The Murderer is a powerful novel in which murder and mental breakdown are dealt with coldly and dispassionately. It tells the story of two brothers, Galton and Selwyn Flood, in contemporary Guyana. It is told through the eyes of Galton, who seeks independence and is uneasy with friends and family and crowds. Selwyn has no difficulty settling down with his wife, whom Galton slowly grows to hate. Galton is always watchful and uncertain; it is only after much hesitation that he marries Gemma, whose father owns the boarding house where he stays when he leaves home. He takes her to live first with a friend, with whom he falls out, and then in a tiny, dark room in a crumbling building.

The novel is closer to certain French classic novels such as Camus' *The Outsider* or Sartre's trilogy The Age of Reason than any English or American novels. Part of the novel's power comes from its spare existentialism, but the other part comes from the prose style, which is graceful, old-fashioned, almost Latinate. The dialogue, on the other hand, is pure Guyanese vernacular, and the gap between the two, between the sense of distance in the prose and intimacy in the dialogue, makes the novel chilling and tense and deeply original.

Roy A. K. Heath was born in British Guiana, where most of his novels are set. He lived in London. *The Murderer* won the Guardian Fiction Prize in 1979.

Age in year of publication: fifty-two.

Joseph Heller 1923–1999

1961   *Catch-22*

'It was a vile and muddy war, and Yossarian could have, lived without it, lived forever, perhaps. Only a fraction of his countrymen would give up their lives to win it, and it was not his intention to be among them.'

This novel is set among the American forces in Italy in 1944. Most of the troops are completely insane as well as lazy, greedy, bureaucratic, thieving, bossy, venal and mad for power. All of the generals and colonels are utterly incompetent. The enemy is barely contemplated, nor the effects of the bombing missions. The enemy is sleeping beside you in the tent. Heller explains the meaning of Catch-22: Catch-22 means that if you ask to be let off the bombing missions because you are crazy, so you must be sane, and therefore you can't be let off the bombing missions. The writing is seriously funny, the jokes often intricate and absurd. Everyone has a story to tell – for instance, a Native American whose family, no matter where they go, manage to camp on a valuable oilfield, so that the oil companies begin to follow them around. The novel combines a comedy that is often slapstick and throwaway and at times silly, with images of soldiers who go on bombing missions screaming through the night, and images of a moral universe which has been turned on its head. *Catch-22* is a dark and disturbing anti-war book as well as a great comic novel.

Joseph Heller was born in Brooklyn and was still living in New York when he died. His other novels include *Something Happened* (1974), *Good as Gold* (1979), and the sequel to *Catch-22, Closing Time* (1994).

Age in year of publication: thirty-eight.

Ernest Hemingway 1899–1961

1952   *The Old Man and the Sea*

The style is taut, laconic and yet infinitely expressive. There is an emotional depth somewhere in between the words. Within Hemingway's simple sentence construction and his diction, which can seem innocent and naive, like an early Miro painting, there are odd, disturbing silences.

The story of *The Old Man and the Sea* is simple: an old fisherman in Cuba has had a run of bad luck. One day he goes out alone and catches a giant marlin; he holds it for two days and nights, letting it pull him out into the open sea and then slowly reining it in, letting it circle, and then killing it and tying it to the boat. On the way back to dry land, the marlin is attacked by sharks who eat its flesh, so that the old man arrives on shore exhausted with nothing except the fish's skeleton attached to the boat. There is a great deal of very convincing and not too technical information about the process of fishing; the famous terse style is ever terser as the story proceeds, so that the narrative grips you, every turn the fish makes holds your attention, it feels as though it is happening right in front of you.

The ideas of endurance and futility behind the story are so elemental and stark that the novel has a simplicity and a power which overcome any lingering sentimentality. It remains one of Hemingway's masterpieces.

Ernest Hemingway was born in Chicago and in later years lived largely in Cuba. His other novels include *The Sun Also Rises* (1926) (UK: *Fiesta* 1927), *A Farewell to Arms* (1929) and *For Whom the Bell Tolls* (1940). He won the Nobel Prize in Literature in 1954.

Age in year of publication: fifty-three.

Georgette Heyer 1902–1974

1950   *The Grand Sophy*

Georgette Heyer was a stern realist. She wrote romantic comedies, entertainments set in the Regency period in England, when women concentrated entirely on the essential business of getting married, hopefully for love, preferably with rank or money attached. Immersed in the world of Jane Austen – for whom similar considerations ruled the day, influenced too by Charlotte Brontë's *Jane Eyre*, Georgette Heyer was also a fine Regency scholar. Her novels are a meticulous recreation of that world of manners down to the smallest detail of social code, dress, food, conveyance and language.

In Heyer's milieu lack of looks is always a disadvantage, but Wit and Style make up for it. Requiring an eligible husband, Sophy arrives in London in a chaise drawn by four steaming horses, accompanied by two outriders, a groom, a splendid black horse, a monkey, a parrot and an Italian greyhound. This arrival is impressive, but how can Sophy find a husband when she lacks beauty and has a mind of her own, a wretched thing in a woman?

The resolution of such predicaments was always Heyer's subject matter; her originality lay in the precision and charm of her writing style and in her taste for the wit and frivolities of the period. She was a phenomenon. Widely imitated, within the genre of romantic comedy she was unequalled, and one of the best entertainers of her time.

Georgette Heyer was born and lived in London. Amongst the best of her fifty-seven novels are *These Old Shades* (1926), *Cotillion* (1953) and *Venetia* (1958).
Age in year of publication: forty-eight.

Carl Hiaasen 1953–

1987   *Double Whammy*

Florida produces a variety of miscreants that surpasses anything else in the United States. Carl Hiaasen is the chronicler of this Miami world, the Damon Runyon of its language, circumstances and astounding way of life.

In *Double Whammy* we enter – deeply – the world of competitive bass fishing, a territory of strange clothes, much swearing, companies such as the Happy Gland Fish Scent Company and the flotsam and jetsam of men at fishy sport, which in this case means cheating and murder. An episode with a dog, its head, a wrist, and a man named Thomas Curl begins on page 224 and continues, an inspired running sore of a gag, to the end of this marvellous thriller. Hiaasen is a highly moral writer. His heroes, private eye R. J. Decker and the raw-squirrel eating giant, Skink, are twentieth-century Crusader knights who take on American capitalism in all its glory – the lust for the last dollar, the pollution of the towns, the pollution of the waters, the corruption of politicians and TV shows, particularly those featuring fundamentalist religious crooks such as the repetitive fornicator the Reverend Charlie Weeb, of the Outdoor Christian Network.

Carl Hiaasen is an acerbic thriller writer, inventive and bizarre. His chilling black comedies, with their split-second timing, off-beat dialogue, raging laughter and death, are knowing and provocative records of the way we live now.

Carl Hiaasen was born in and lives in Florida. An award-winning investigative journalist, his other celebrated thrillers include *Native Tongue* (1991), *Strip Tease* (1993), *Lucky You* (1997), *Basket Case* (2002), *Skinny Dip* (2004) and *Nature Girl* (2005).

Age in year of publication: thirty-four.

Patricia Highsmith 1921–1995

1955 *The Talented Mr Ripley*

The art of Patricia Highsmith is cool and detached; this adds power to her depiction of quiet violence and of murderers who could almost be ourselves. This strange identification of reader with murderer – a kind of inverted murder mystery – gives her thrillers an hypnotic attraction.

This novel was the first she wrote about the more than talented Mr Ripley, a neglected and loveless child who grows up to ensure that he compensates for such deficiencies by letting nothing and no one stand in his way. His distinguishing characteristics are his charm, his anxiety to please, and luck, which in this instance whisks him to Italy to coerce the wealthy young Dickie Greenleaf into returning to the USA to take up his responsibilities. The relationship between Tom Ripley and Dickie is one of those troubled tugs-of-war between men in which Patricia Highsmith so eerily excels: fretful, duplicitous, overwrought.

The tension is electric, and Tom's murder of Dickie – in which every ounce of water and blood, every slow motion of struggle is felt almost physically by the reader – is only the beginning of a chase which twists and turns as Tom veers towards his unexpected fate. This is a classic psychological thriller, sinister yet cajoling, swathed in Highsmith's macabre wit.

Patricia Highsmith was born in Fort Worth, Texas, and lived mostly in Europe. Many of her novels were filmed; her first, *Strangers on a Train* (1950), by Alfred Hitchcock. She wrote five novels about Tom Ripley. This novel was awarded the Edgar Allan Poe Scroll.

Age in year of publication: thirty-four.

Oscar Hijuelos 1951–

1989　*The Mambo Kings Play Songs of Love*

This is a novel, written in effortless prose, about Cuban musicians and their families in New York in the 1950s. It throbs with sex, with the pain of desire, with the allure of bodies, with the pure, unadulterated, exotic pleasure of coupling. It is the only novel in this list which makes mention of 'that muscle up at the high end of a woman's thigh, that muscle which intersected the clitoris and got all twisted, quivering ever so slightly when he'd kiss a woman there'; for this alone, the novel is mandatory reading.

It tells the story of two struggling musicians, Cesar and Nestor Castillo, authors of a song called 'Beautiful Maria of My Soul', and their lives in the new country and their memories of the old. It is full of pure style and gorgeous flourishes, like the dance music our two heroes play – tangos, boleros, melancholy tunes. It reads as though it was written in one single hot afternoon. Hijuelos places an aura of huge sadness around his characters' lives, especially that of Nestor, the younger brother, who is eaten up with ennui, despite his enormous sex drive. It is one of the few great books about immigrants to the United States, grappling with the new language and the old ties of affection, the women steady and ambitious, the men hard drinking, locked in the old world and all the more attractive and interesting for their displacement.

Oscar Hijuelos was born in New York, the son of Cuban immigrants. His other novels include *Our House in the Last World* (1983), *The Fourteen Sisters of Emilio Monez O'Brien* (1993), *Empress of the Splendid Season* (1999) and *A Simple Habana Melody* (2002). *The Mambo Kings* won the 1990 Pulitzer Prize and was adapted for film in 1992 and as a broadway musical in 2005.

Age in year of publication: thirty-eight.

Russell Hoban 1925–

1980 *Riddley Walker*

Written in the bastardized fragments of a 'worn-out' English, *Riddley Walker* is set in a brutal tribal world, thousands of years after a nuclear apocalypse. The twelve-year-old Riddley is led by a pack of wild dogs to help an imprisoned mutant, the Ardship of Cambry. Releasing him involves Riddley in a struggle to regain, by shamanistic and alchemical means, the secret of the bomb. On one side are the politicians, the Pry Mincer and the Wes Mincer, travelling showmen, who retell and decode the fragments of ancient stories. On the other are the mutants, whose damaged genes retain some shadows of the bomb that made them. Unknown to both is a simpler secret, the formula for gunpowder. The key is a yellow powder, 'Salt 4'. In the battle for its possession, the Ardship is killed and the Pry Mincer deposed and blinded. Nevertheless, a bomb is made and exploded. Riddley, rejecting all power, except the power of story, becomes a travelling showman, with a new tale to tell.

This is a strenuously, fiercely imagined book. Hoban uses scraps of legend – Punch and Judy, the Green Man, St Eustace – to construct a mythology of original power. Riddley's humanity provokes in the reader a kind of despairing sweetness. The language, which requires concentration, is both brutal and visionary: the effort to understand it becomes an effort to understand something much larger. *Riddley Walker*, which is often compared to *A Clockwork Orange*, releases a strange, raw, spiritual sense that cannot be found in smoother fictions.

Russell Hoban was born in Pennsylvania, but settled in London in 1969. He has written many children's books including *The Mouse and the Child*, and his adult books include *The Lion of Boaz-Jachin and Jachin-Boaz* (1973), *Turtle Diary* (1975), *Angelica's Grotto* (1999), *Her Name Was Lola* (2003), *Linger Awhile* (2006) and *My Tango with Barbara Strozzi* (2007).

Age in year of publication: fifty-five.

Alan Hollinghurst 1954–

1994   *The Folding Star*

Edward Manners, an Englishman in his thirties, goes to teach in a Flemish city – Bruges perhaps? – and like Lucy Snowe in Charlotte Brontë's *Villette* falls obsessively in love. Luc Altidore, one of his pupils, is his adored object, a shadowy, unknowable, golden young man, longed for, lusted after, whilst Edward's other worlds continue imperviously. There are the men he meets at gay bars; another pupil, Marcel, and his father Paul Echevin, curator of the museum devoted to the great Symbolist painter Orst; an entirely different, pastoral, domestic life appears when Edward returns to England for the funeral of his first lover.

Edward's hunger for anonymous sex – for sex whatever – confronts in both a comical and affecting way the idealism of obsessive love. Edward possesses Luc but only for a moment; Luc seems to drift away, eternally elusive, a face glimpsed in a misty glass, unobtainable. Love is trailed by loss, with betrayal waiting in the wings. And shame – or worse, a Nazi past, menacing and tragic – turns romantic love to stone.

There is a mellow beauty to the form and structure of this novel, echoed in its melancholic, elegiac atmosphere. At the same time it is candid, comic, utterly contemporary, with a sly sense of the absurd. This is a luscious and continually fascinating novel; reading it is like contemplating one of the great paintings of the Flemish Old Masters.

Alan Hollinghurst was born in Stroud, Gloucestershire, and lives in London. His other celebrated novels are *The Swimming Pool Library* (1988), *The Spell* (1998) and *The Line of Beauty* (2004) which won the Man Booker Prize.

Age in year of publication: forty.

Kazuo Ishiguro 1954–

1986   *An Artist of the Floating World*

Kazuo Ishiguro's considerable skills as a novelist are especially evident in *An Artist of the Floating World* and *The Remains of the Day* (1989). The novels stand as a fascinating diptych about the atmosphere which created the Second World War, about the small sets of collaborations which make up a society. The former deals with Japan, the latter with England.

An Artist of the Floating World is Ishiguro's best and most subtle novel. It is narrated by an elderly painter in post-war Japan, it plays with ideas of custom and ceremony, tradition and nostalgia, vanity and modesty, as ways for the narrator to disguise himself; information about him and indeed his society come to us in small, carefully modulated, almost perfect moments, when something tiny is disclosed and allowed to stand for a great deal more. This makes the central moment of disclosure in the book immensely powerful. The narration has a withdrawn, distant, stilted tone, and yet it remains readable and engrossing; the tension is kept going by the constant possibility that something more will be said, that all the decorum will break down; by the readers' satisfaction at knowing or guessing rather more than the unreliable narrator wishes to tell them.

Kazuo Ishiguro was born in Nagasaki, Japan. At the age of six, he came to England with his family. His other novels are *A Pale View of Hills* (1982), *The Remains of the Day*, which won the Booker Prize in 1989 and was filmed in 1995, *The Unconsoled* (1995), *When We Were Orphans* (2000) and *Never Let Me Go* (2005), which has recently been adapted to film. His latest work is *Nocturnes* (2009). *An Artist of the Floating World* won the Whitbread Prize.

Age in year of publication: thirty-two.

P. D. James 1920–

1994   *Original Sin*

The classic English detective story has inveigled readers all over the world into the mysteries of English life: class distinctions, eating habits and private passions. While there have been many brilliant male exponents of the genre, it is generally accepted that women such as Margery Allingham, Ngaio Marsh, Dorothy Sayers and Agatha Christie were the Queens of Crime. Today writers of fresh sophistication have taken on their mantle.

P. D. James has the workings of the English establishment at her fingertips – the civil service, medicine, the law, the judiciary, the police, the Church of England: all the bulwarks of the state are grist to her mill. She sets *Original Sin* in the world of book publishing, in Innocent House, on the River Thames in the East End of London, the elegant, marbled, ill-named home of the Peverill Press. James's poetic detective, Commander Adam Dalgleish, is sent to investigate the death of its managing director, found half-naked with a snake draught-excluder stuffed in his mouth.

Uncommon intelligence and an authentic sense of sin mark P. D. James's studies of vengeance and retribution. Most rewarding is her acute sense of place, in this case her atmospheric evocation of the River Thames which dominates this classic detective story as it unravels its secrets past and present to the sounds and scurryings of the great river.

P. D. James was born in Oxford and lives in London. Amongst her best crime novels are *An Unsuitable Job for a Woman* (1972), *A Taste for Death* (1986), *Original Sin* (1994) and *Death in Holy Orders* (2001). In 1987 she was awarded the Crime Writers Association Diamond Dagger.

Age in year of publication: seventy-four.

Elizabeth Jenkins 1905–2010

1954   *The Tortoise and the Hare*

Sometimes a very good writer produces an exceptional work which garners a word-of-mouth reputation as a treasure to be read again and again, increasing in fascination each time. *The Tortoise and the Hare* is one such novel. This is the story of Imogen, quiet, self-effacing, loving and beautiful; of her husband Evelyn, successful barrister; and their country neighbour, the riding, shooting and fishing Blanche Silcox. These are the gentlefolk who have had the whip hand in England for hundreds of years: county people, living in beautiful homes, with servants and smooth cars, capable of sex in strange and desultory ways.

Imogen is the perfect wife and mother, the very model of how we were told women – married women – should be. Observing every gesture, every image, every note – 'the sharp, tinkling sound' of a phone being put down secretly – in her cool, graceful prose, Jenkins negotiates Imogen to a startling and satisfactory finale, producing at the same time a devastating portrait of *mariage à la mode* and of female masochism and timidity. There is an echo of Graham Greene in Elizabeth Jenkins's perception of the bleak, arid wastes of a certain English upper-middle class, reared to mask self-interest with cant, bullying and hypocrisy. All this is revealed in simple but devastating ways, giving this surprising story of domestic betrayal larger, more subtle reverberations.

Elizabeth Jenkins was born in Hertfordshire and lived in London. She was a distinguished historian and biographer; other novels include *Harriet* (1934), winner of the Femina Vie Heureuse, and *Honey* (1968). At the age of 100 she was asked 'Did she read?' to which she replied 'Good gracious, what else would I do?'
Age in year of publication: forty-nine.

Ruth Prawer Jhabvala 1927–

1975   *Heat and Dust*

The love story between England and India has never been better told than in this discerning novel. In 1923 Olivia, married to an English official, Douglas Rivers, stifles amid the staid social habits of the British in India. Fleeing these gatherings of stultifying boredom, Olivia meets the dissolute but charming Nawab and drops the company of her fellow memsahibs for exotic occasions at the palace, which eventually lead to love, and worse. She abandons her husband – abandons England – for the Nawab, and, fifty years later, her ex-husband's granddaughter follows her to India to investigate this family scandal. It is the granddaughter who tells the story, and whilst her experiences imitate and are a counterpoint to the earlier love story, they are entirely different too. Jhabvala conveys the daily realities and teeming profusions of modern India, so that Olivia's story and the days of the Raj and the Nawab seem to settle into the heat and dust of the present as part of a pattern that had to be.

Nothing is stated in this novel which can be implied or imagined; gracefully written, finely constructed, it fascinates both as a love story, and as a sensuous evocation of what the English lost most in India – the soul and feeling those sent out to rule her longed for, yet feared the most.

Ruth Prawer Jhabvala was born in Germany and has lived in England and India; she now lives in New York. She is an acclaimed and prolific novelist and scriptwriter, and won the Booker Prize for this novel. Her screenplays include *Howards End*, *A Room with a View*, *The Golden Bowl* and *Le Divorce*.

Age in year of publication: forty-eight.

B. S. Johnson 1933–1973

1969   *The Unfortunates*

This novel was published in a box. Inside were twenty-seven sections, of which the first and last sections only were to be read in that position. The others could be read in any order, a daunting proposition, but in fact this random method of following the story is perfectly suited to the tale that unfolds.

The narrator is a football reporter, sent to a Midlands city to cover a match. Because we read the workings of his mind, thinking and remembering with him, it becomes clear that the book could be presented in no other way. For when he gets to the city he realizes that this is where his friend Tony had lived, with his wife, and that he had often visited them in the years before Tony's tragic death from cancer.

And so the random form of the novel matches the random insecurities of life and death, all the more so because the voice and experience of recollection are both Bryan Johnson's, and he was so soon to take his own life. There is hunger in this novel, a sense of waste and yearning – for time not to pass and for death not to come. The rugged strength of his writing and the warmth and sensitivity of his vision give B. S. Johnson's unconventional experiments with the form of the novel real meaning and worth.

B. S. Johnson was born and lived in London. He was a poet, dramatist, journalist and film-maker; his other books include *Albert Angelo* (1964) and *Christy Malry's Own Double-Entry* (1973).

Age in year of publication: thirty-six.

Elizabeth Jolley 1923–2007

1988   *The Sugar Mother*

Elizabeth Jolley is always a surprise. She belongs to that flourishing tradition of English tragicomediennes which begins with Jane Austen and wanders on through Emily Eden, Elizabeth Taylor, Ivy Compton-Burnett, Penelope Fitzgerald and Beryl Bainbridge. Like them, her value lies in the absolute originality of her own distinctive voice.

The Sugar Mother is quintessential Jolley. Edwin Page, a hypochondriacal academic of considerable pomposity, is married to Cecilia, a self-satisfied gynaecologist. Cecilia absconds for a year's study leave abroad with a cackling sort of woman called Vorwickl (one of Jolley's great successes is her calm engagement with sexual predilections of a complex kind). Edwin and Cecilia keep in touch: 'Vorwickl she told him ate a cocoon in the muesli. No he said, Yes she said. She said it was delicious even when she knew it was a cocoon.' To fill the gap in the useless Page's life, enter young Leila, and Leila's insinuating mother, who proceeds to take over his life, his house, his bathroom and his sperm count, producing resolutions which are darkly funny, and unpredictably moving.

Jolley's lightness of tone and her wry, sidelong style enable her to deceive us into serious considerations. She is the most disconcerting of novelists, flourishing words and witticisms like an extremely benevolent sorceress enticing us to laugh at, and understand, loneliness and the longing to love.

Elizabeth Jolley, born in Birmingham, England, lived in Western Australia. Her novels have been awarded many prizes and include *The Well* (1986), which won the Miles Franklin Award, *Miss Peabody's Inheritance* (1983) and *Lovesong* (1997).

Age in year of publication: sixty-five.

James Kelman 1946–

1994 *How Late it Was, How Late*

James Kelman is at his best when he has a single male character under pressure and in pain: his novels and his short stories, like much of Beckett's fiction, deal with the workings of the mind, the slow mechanics of thought and memory. He can write brilliant passages of invective and complaint, but these are often underwritten by passages about longing and seeking comfort – anything, a cigarette, a drink, some company, love. The tone of his work moves constantly from hardness and brutality to a kind of tenderness.

In his novel *How Late it Was, How Late*, Sammy, our Glaswegian hero, wakes up in a cell after two days' solid drinking. He has a police record. He has been beaten up and he is in pain. He is also blind. The novel is written in what the American edition calls 'the utterly uncensored language of the Scottish lower classes'. It catches his consciousness at work as he tries to reconstruct what happened, as he tries to walk and move around, deal with the bureaucracy and the police and the fact that his girlfriend has disappeared. The novel is lighter in tone than most of Kelman's work, almost funny at times; it is full of his unique genius for exploring a carefully modulated poetic language of the mind.

James Kelman was born in Glasgow and lives there still. *How Late it Was, How Late* won the Booker Prize in 1994. His books include *Not Not While the Giro* (1983), *A Chancer* (1985), *A Disaffection* (1989), *The Good Times* (1998) and the award-winning *Kieron Smith, boy* (2008).

Age in year of publication: forty-eight.

Thomas Keneally 1935–

1982   *Schindler's Ark*
(US: *Schindler's List*)

This book is based on interviews conducted by the author with survivors of the Holocaust who were protected by the German industrialist Oskar Schindler. None of the book is invented, but it uses the form and tone of a novel. It is a harrowing book which centres in its early chapters on the Jewish ghetto in Cracow, on the beatings and casual murders of Jews, and then on the slow realization that nothing is casual, that all of this is planned.

Schindler, who set about employing and protecting as many Jews as possible while remaining on good terms with the authorities, emerges from the book as enormously sensual, oddly generous, very complex. His urge to save his workers is dramatized sometimes as pure heroism, but also as a strange innocence in his nature. Keneally's version of Amon Goeth, who runs the camp nearby to which many Jews are taken, is dark and disturbing, but equally convincing. He writes with great skill about how systems were put into place and how they were circumvented and then how they prevailed once more. Although *Schindler's Ark* is a story about heroism and ultimate survival, about a good man in a dark time, the atmosphere of the book is deeply depressing and savage, and this is, perhaps, as it should be: a small testament to those who perished as much as to those who survived.

Thomas Keneally was born and lives in Sydney, Australia. His many novels include *The Chant of Jimmie Blacksmith* (1972) and *Confederates* (1979). *Schindler's Ark* won the Man Booker Prize in 1982. It was made into a film, *Schindler's List*, by Steven Spielberg in 1994. A memoir, *Searching for Schindler*, appeared in 2007.

Age in year of publication: forty-seven.

Jack Kerouac 1922–1969

1957   *On the Road*

This book is written with such calm, lazy ease it reads at times like an exercise in pure style, a way of showing that American prose could continue to shine and glitter and perform tricks just as much as it could when Hemingway and Fitzgerald were at their best. It is a book full of carelessness and youth and the search for sensation. It is a deeply American book, full of hope, open to the infinite possibilities which lie ahead; no European has ever written a book like this.

It is based on a number of trips across America which Kerouac made with Neal Cassady between 1947 and 1950 in which they had a lot of fun with drugs and sex and being broke and making friends; Kerouac is Sal and Cassady is Dean. The narrative is written in a straight line; the material seems not to be shaped or structured, the shape of the book remains true, we are led to believe, to what things were like: unplanned, spontaneous, free and easy, beautifully aimless; characters appear and disappear, events happen without meaning, the abiding presence is Walt Whitman rather than Henry James. The spirit of the book took over the lives of young people in half the world in less than ten years. *On the Road* has all the importance of a classic rock album or road movie.

Jack Kerouac was born in Massachusetts and educated at Columbia University. His other semi-autobiographical novels include *The Subterraneans* (1958), *Big Sur* (1962) and *Desolation Angels* (1965).

Age in year of publication: thirty-five.

Balraj Khanna 1940–

1984   *Nation of Fools: Or Scenes from Indian Life*

'God in India doesn't work. Only fools do,' says one of Khanna's post-Partition Hindus. Beginning in one of the camp slums which housed such refugees, this novel is like an Indian movie, rumbustious, vivid, seductive. The wayward Omi is the son of a sweet vendor. In the camp a person who makes buckets in the back garden and sells them in the front is considered an industrialist, but Omi's father is a modern Indian bent on dragging his family up into life in the capital city by his busybody bootstraps, carting along the recalcitrant Omi.

The chaos of Omi's adventurous youth is familiar: what is particular about Khanna's account of Omi's progress is the hilarity and verve of the demotic Indian English in which Omi's family and friends communicate. They address the world lavishly in an idiom of curses, salutations and cries to heaven which brings each of the inhabitants of this Punjabi world pugnaciously to life. All of 1950s India is here, with its love for the movies, its marriages, houses of learning, wife-beaters, families at peace and war. Khanna laughs with his chorus of fools, while his sharp eye makes subtler mincemeat of religious differences and useless taboos. But it is in the character of the resilient Omi, and in his relish for language, that the excellence of this novel lies.

Balraj Khanna was born in the Punjab, India, and lives in England and France. He is one of India's leading contemporary painters, and this was his first novel.

Age in year of publication: forty-four.

Stephen King 1948–

1987   *Misery*

Stephen King has produced a splendid cavalcade of popular horror novels; this one is almost like a subterranean autobiography.

Paul Sheldon, a bestselling writer, has driven himself to drink and boredom by creating a series of relentlessly popular romantic novels featuring Misery Chastain, a heroine of mindbending inanity. Killing her in childbirth in his last novel, Sheldon drives off, liberated, determined to write real fiction, and then crashes his car. Unfortunately he is rescued by a number-one fan of Misery, the lumpen Annie Wilkes, who has even named her pig after his heroine. What follows is a masterpiece of horror and black humour. Paul's legs are smashed: Annie gets him hooked on painkillers, locks him up, torments him and eventually starts slicing off bits of his body, waving a succession of sharp instruments threateningly whenever he shows the slightest sign of not doing what she is forcing him to do: bring back from the dead her heroine Misery Chastain in yet another noxious romantic novel. This Sheldon does, and descriptions of intense physical pain alternate with sections from Sheldon's new Misery novel – a splendid piece of romantic nonsense – and the Samurai prancings of the psychopath Annie.

Stephen King has phenomenal storytelling skills, command of popular culture and everyday things, and a brisk sense of humour. He straps his readers to the page, makes their hair stand on end and in imaginative, contemporary prose provides laughter, intelligence and tremendous entertainment.

Stephen King was born in Maine where he still lives. *Carrie* (1973), *The Shining* (1977), *It* (1986) and *The Stand* (1978) are some of his bestsellers, most of which have been filmed.

Age in year of publication: thirty-nine.

Margaret Laurence 1926–1987

1966   *A Jest of God*

A Jest of God is a monologue written in the present tense by a teacher in her mid-thirties who lives with her mother in a fictional town in Canada. Within one or two pages Margaret Laurence creates a complete emotional landscape and a voice which is perfectly pitched, so that the material, which may seem unpromising to certain readers, becomes intensely interesting and memorable.

The progress of Rachel Cameron, her constant fear of her colleagues and her boss, her extraordinary sensitivity to what is going on around her, to each nuance of right and wrong, are described in a way which is exact and real. Her own ability to see all sides, to understand and resist each person she comes in touch with, gives the reader an extraordinary grasp of the world she inhabits. It is a mark of Laurence's skill as a novelist that she can place Rachel and her mother in a flat above a funeral parlour with regular references to the life and death down below without the reader feeling that this has been added on to the narrative as a way of adding significance to it. Rachel's summer love affair with an old school friend, which is the dramatic core of the book, is riveting; at times you have to put the book aside for a while, so tense is the emotional atmosphere, so full of challenges and possibilities. *A Jest of God* is a small masterpiece.

Margaret Laurence was born in Manitoba, Canada, and lived there, in Africa and in England. Her other novels include *The Stone Angel* (1964) and *The Diviners* (1974). *A Jest of God* won the Governor General's Literary Award and was made into the film *Rachel, Rachel*.

Age in year of publication: forty.

Mary Lavin 1912–1996

1969   *Happiness*

In 'Happiness', the title story of this volume, the tone is rambling, almost anecdotal, like someone chatting. And slowly then, without you noticing, a picture is built up of a whole personality, a voice, a family, a set of relationships and a past. Mother talks about 'happiness', what it is, and how it might be found; she is a widow with daughters living in the Irish countryside. She is visited regularly by a priest; she works in a library and possesses an extraordinary strength which kept her going after her husband died, leaving her a young widow. That experience, the realization that he was going to die, has coloured her life, so that when she too comes to die – by this time the reader is in tears – this is what haunts her. The story is a masterpiece. In another story, 'The Lost Child', Mary Lavin manages as much as most novelists manage: a conversion to Catholicism, Renee's realization that her sister is gay and then the extraordinary graphic account of a miscarriage. There are also moments of pure comedy in some of these stories, as when the priest says to Renee's gay (and Protestant) sister: 'You are a man after my own heart, Iris,' or Annie's brother in 'A Pure Accident' who 'where he used to think sex was the only difference between a man and a woman, it seemed, now, that maybe it was the only thing they had in common'. Mary Lavin's work is full of strange wisdom and insight; she writes brilliantly about marriage and children, but also about celibates and outsiders.

Mary Lavin was born in Massachusetts and moved to Ireland when she was nine, where she lived in County Meath. She is also the author of two novels, *The House in Clewe Street* (1945) and *Mary O'Grady* (1950), and her stories are collected in several volumes. She received many awards, including the Gregory Medal.

Age in year of publication: fifty-seven.

John le Carré 1931–

1963   *The Spy Who Came in from the Cold*

Few writers have used the word 'cold' as well as John le Carré. He gives it a hundred meanings, all of them intimating the absence of good, and the presence of evil, which erupts when squalid men play games that are unnecessary and vicious, in pursuit of aims corrupt in themselves, useless if achieved. Such autocrats flourished in the chilling moral vacuum the Cold War created from the 1950s to the fall of the Berlin Wall in 1989. Modern espionage became our post-war method of warfare, a bitter stamping ground in which spies were instructed that loyalty often meant betrayal.

Such a one is Leamas, about fifty, head of British Command in Berlin, still divided by the Wall. Not a university man, though his spymasters in London – Control – are just that class of English person: right university, right tie, right clubs. Leamas is a tired man, frozen of heart, a failure. Amid an unnerving atmosphere of conspiracy, Control finds a way to send Leamas back for one last attempt to defend the indefensible. Le Carré is a gripping storyteller – spare, ironic, sinewy. He is a master of atmosphere and those dark places of the heart where treachery and tangled moral ambiguities loiter. In this classic novel, full of icy implications and ambiguous truths, he summed up the social and political conditions of an era.

John le Carré was born in Dorset and lives in Cornwall. Other famous novels include his trilogy *Tinker, Tailor, Soldier, Spy* (1974), *The Honourable Schoolboy* (1977), *Smiley's People* (1980), *The Tailor of Panama* (1996) and *The Constant Gardener* (2001), which was made into an award-winning film in 2005. *The Spy Who Came in from the Cold* was also a notable film (1965).

Age in year of publication: thirty-two.

Harper Lee 1926–

1960   *To Kill a Mockingbird*

The voice in this novel belongs to Scout, an immensely intelligent, precocious six-year-old girl. Maycomb, her small town in Alabama in the 1930s, is a stable, conservative place which looks as though it will never change – the blacks live at the edge of town. Scout's mother is dead; she and her older brother Jem are being brought up by their lawyer father, Atticus, who, along with Calpurnia, the black cook, slowly becomes the moral centre of the book. Both adults are portrayed with great, detailed affection, as pillars of society who do not share society's prejudices, as figures of authority who often seem wilful and hard to understand for the six-year-old narrator, but yet are still never cruel or distant.

At first the novel focuses on the childish games of Scout and Jem and their friend Dill, but slowly the real theme of the novel, which is racial prejudice in the Southern states, emerges. A white woman has accused a black man of rape; it is clear that he is innocent. Atticus becomes his defence lawyer. In the scenes which deal with the accusation and the trial, and the bitterness in Maycomb, and the plight of the accused, the child's voice becomes morally powerful, and the narrative, especially in the second half of the book, has a compulsive, thrilling force.

Harper Lee was born in Alabama. *To Kill a Mockingbird*, which won the Pulitzer Prize, is her only novel. The book was made into a film in 1962.

Age in year of publication: thirty-four.

Rosamond Lehmann 1901–1990

1953   *The Echoing Grove*

There is a triangular love affair at the centre of Rosamond Lehmann's elegaic novel – but this entanglement conceals much else. Two sisters are in love with the same man. Madeleine is married to Rickie and is the mother of his children. Her sister Dinah is Rickie's mistress. The place and time are London and southern England in the 1930s and 1940s. Against a backdrop of the Spanish Civil War and the Second World War, Rosamond Lehmann evokes every nuance of the obsession which devours men and women when they love passionately and when loyalties are divided. Time, and outside events, provide the solutions they cannot find for themselves. Lehmann's narrative art is at its most interesting when contemplating the predicaments of women – comic, painful or embarrassing. But she is also an adventurous writer in style and content, technically innovative, using memory and perspective to expose the many meanings human beings can extract from the past. In this novel she mingles the intricacies of social life with the influence of class, politics and much else, in ways that are both deft and imaginative. Rosamond Lehmann's subject was the human heart and the inadequacy of men and women pursuing different goals in the name of love. This haunting novel is a classic exploration of that territory in which self, and love, are always lost, always rediscovered.

Rosamond Lehmann was born in Buckinghamshire and lived in London. Her most famous novels include *Dusty Answer* (1927), *An Invitation to the Waltz* (1932) and its sequel *The Weather in the Streets* (1936).

Age in year of publication: fifty-two.

Elmore Leonard 1925–

1990   *Get Shorty*

Leonard views his country as doused in greed, peopled with fools pursuing the endless dollar: what can we do but laugh? His speciality is America's racial mix, mostly drawn from the bottom of the barrel. In *Get Shorty*, a collection of such persons sashays into Los Angeles, to dabble in the two great American dreams, Hollywood and the Mafia.

There is Chili, hot tempered as a child, coolest of the cool now, debt collector for the Mafia. He encounters the visually challenged film producer Harry Zimm, maker of mutation movies so bad you see 'better film on teeth'. Then there is Karen the Screamer, Leo the Drycleaner, the Bear, Yayo the Colombian mule, Armani-obsessed Bo Catlett and many others equally lyrically named. Will they achieve their life's ambition – to get their hands on money (without being killed) by making a movie? This cast of schemeballs entwine the reader in their scams, heists and smart lines.

Though there is a nostalgia here for a time in America when villainy had a sort of innocence, Leonard avoids sentimentality. His genius lies in his idiosyncratic hipster's prose, amused and inquisitive intelligence and consummate storytelling. This combination makes Leonard an addictive peddler of dreams, a writer whose use of dialogue is unsurpassed, who makes you shake with laughter and suspense, and beg for more.

Elmore Leonard was born in New Orleans and lives in Detroit. Among his best novels are *Glitz* (1985) and *Freaky Deaky* (1988). *Get Shorty* was made into a popular movie in 1995 and *Rum Punch* (1992) became the film *Jackie Brown* (1997).

Age in year of publication: sixty-five.

Doris Lessing 1919–

1962 *The Golden Notebook*

This is one of the most powerful and influential novels of the late twentieth century. Through the experiences of a writer, Anna Wulf, Doris Lessing investigates the moral, intellectual and sexual crises of our age. Anna Wulf is a heroine as vividly imagined as Raymond Chandler's Philip Marlowe or Tolstoy's Anna Karenina. Anna keeps four notebooks: a black notebook for her writing; a red notebook for politics; a yellow notebook which tells stories; and a blue notebook, her diary and a record of breakdown and psychoanalysis. The golden notebook connects each and brings the story full circle. Set in London in the 1950s, the novel is a testament to that decade, with its political tensions and disillusionments, but its centre is Anna's search for truths which are not simple, which match life itself.

The four notebooks describe the scattered quality of women's experience: that time of life when a woman is absolutely wrapped up in lovers, husbands, men's bodies, sex, with a mind always partially elsewhere – with children in particular, and with women friends, ideas, beliefs. And then there is work, usually killed by all the rest of it.

Lessing's distinctive and original mind, tough and prickly, marches in step with her vigorous way of telling a story. *The Golden Notebook*, airing all our dilemmas, holds a mirror to our times.

Doris Lessing was born in Kermanshah, Persia (now Iran), and moved to Southern Rhodesia (now Zimbabwe) at the age of six. She left for England in 1949 where she has lived ever since. She has written thirty novels and ten works of non-fiction, including two volumes of her autobiography. She lives in London. She was awarded the Nobel Prize in Literature in 2007.

Age in year of publication: forty-three.

David Lodge 1935–

1975   *Changing Places: A Tale of Two Campuses*

This is one of three very funny novels, all carefully crafted and plotted, which David Lodge has written about university life in England and the United States. The other two are *Small World* (1984) and *Nice Work* (1989), but there is a sort of symmetry coupled with a rage for disorder in *Changing Places* that makes it his best book.

Two professors change places: Philip Swallow from the University of Rummidge in darkest England does an exchange with Morris Zapp of Euphoric State in the land of opportunity. (Rummidge is a version of Birmingham, Euphoric State a version of San Francisco.) Swallow is 'unconfident, eager to please, infinitely suggestible'; Zapp has 'an apocalyptic imagination'. They leave their wives behind, but take with them their cultural differences. America, to Swallow, is open and glamorous – it is after all 1969 and anything can happen. England, to Zapp, is dank and cold. One of Swallow's former students, a failure at Rummidge, has become a phone-in show host in Euphoric State, and he plays an important part in one of the funniest scenes of the novel. Both men take a serious interest in each other's wives. The moral of the novel is that Americans, at least in the short term, awaken the sleeping sexuality of the English and are therefore a good thing. Another moral may be that people should stay in their own countries unless they want to be deeply unsettled and much misunderstood.

David Lodge was born in London. He has worked for many years as an academic. His comic gifts are apparent in early novels such as *The British Museum is Falling Down* (1965), and his later work includes *How Far Can You Go?* (1980), *Therapy* (1995), *Home Truths* (1999), *Thinks* (2001), *Author, Author* (2004) and *Deaf Sentence* (2008).

Age in year of publication: forty.

Bernard MacLaverty 1942–

1980 *Lamb*

Bernard MacLaverty's three novels, *Lamb*, *Cal* (1983) and *Grace Notes* (1997), and his four volumes of short stories, deal with the dramatic possibilities of the conflict within the human character between the areas of darkness and brutality and the capacity for love and tenderness. His prose is clean and spare, combining a clear and easy tone with moments of pure poetry. He offers his characters a level of understanding and sympathy which is rare among contemporary male novelists; he is not afraid to create scenes of pure unadulterated emotion.

In *Lamb*, Brother Sebastian works in a Borstal in the west of Ireland. Using a legacy from his dead father, he escapes to England with a twelve-year-old boy, Owen Kane. The novel is the story of their misadventures; the boy's vulnerability and his epilepsy make his minder more and more anxious to protect him and love him, and make the outside world of authority – brothers, lawyers, hotel keepers – seem harsh and cruel, and make the ending of this story of the failure of a dream of love inevitable and very moving. The novel is short – just over a hundred and fifty pages – and as tense as a thriller; the set scenes are perfect; the reader knows that this sojourn will be doomed and short-lived, and reads on in terror hoping that the two main characters will survive.

Bernard MacLaverty was born in Belfast but has lived in Scotland for many years. *Lamb* and *Cal* have been made into films. *Grace Notes* was shortlisted for the Booker Prize. His later work includes *The Anatomy School* (2001) and a collection of stories *Matters of Life and Death* (2006).

Age in year of publication: thirty-eight.

Alistair MacLeod 1936–

1976   *The Lost Salt Gift of Blood*

The name Alistair MacLeod does not appear in many surveys of contemporary writing. He has written only two books, *The Lost Salt Gift of Blood* and *As Birds Bring Forth the Sun* (1986), and these contain seven stories each. His tone is old-fashioned, close to certain classic Irish writers, the James Joyce of *Dubliners*, the fiction of John McGahern or Mary Lavin; close also to the tone and timbre of certain Scottish and Irish ballads.

His stories are set in Cape Breton or Newfoundland, his characters are involved in fishing or mining, or, in some of the best work, come from fishing or mining communities but have abandoned them for cities, and are caught now between the two places. MacLeod is, like almost nobody else, able to deal with pure rawness of emotion in the relationship between parents and children, in the drama enacted around ties of blood. His landscapes can be savage and alien, but for those who inhabit them they are real and true, and haunting for those who try to abandon them. He writes simply and clearly; his openings often dry and factual, he uses the present tense with particular skill, some of his accounts of the rituals and sorrows of leavetaking almost unbearably poignant. In Canada his two books are considered classics; he deserves to be better known in the rest of the world.

Alistair MacLeod was born in Saskatchewan. When he was ten his parents moved back to the family farm on Cape Breton. He now lives in Windsor, Ontario. His novel *No Great Mischief* (1999) won the International Impac Dublin Literary Award.
Age in year of publication: forty.

Eugene McCabe 1930–

1992 *Death and Nightingales*

This is a remarkable novel; it is written in prose of bleak, unadorned beauty, closely matching the world in which the narrative takes place, with the sort of hair-raising plot which keeps you up all night wondering how it will end.

It is set on the Monaghan-Fermanagh border in the north of Ireland in 1883. It is full of the bitterness of contemporary politics and family feuds. Beth, a Catholic, is the stepdaughter of Billy Winters, a Protestant landowner. She comes straight out of nineteenth-century fiction: beautiful, intelligent, well read, passionate, just as her stepfather is bigoted, drunken, duplicitous and oddly charming. All around them are the forces that will shape twentieth-century Ireland – ambitious Catholic clergy, ruthless revolutionaries, a sense of Protestant privilege. Neighbours watch each other and bear dark grudges; the landscape itself becomes a significant force in the book, lakeland, bogland, soft hills. The sense of menace, of impending doom, of terrible darkness and hatred is all-pervasive. It would make a superb film. This neglected masterpiece deserves to be much better known.

Eugene McCabe was born in Glasgow, but has lived most of his life on a farm close to the border between Northern Ireland and the Republic of Ireland. His play *King of the Castle* (1964) is a classic of the contemporary Irish theatre. His shorter fiction is collected in *Christ in the Fields* (1993). He also published a fiction *The Love of Sisters* (2009).

Age in year of publication: sixty-two.

Patrick McCabe 1955–

1992   *The Butcher Boy*

This is a relentless and flawless version of grief and madness. It is told in the first person by one Francie Brady, whose mind moves at enormous speed and with considerable logic. He watches the small Irish town he inhabits, the coming and going of a chorus of disapproving housewives, his father, his mother, the doctor, the priest, his friend Joe, a local dog and, most of all, Mrs Nugent and her son Philip. He makes a number of escapes – to Dublin, to a seaside resort, to a Borstal, to a mental hospital. He finds work in the local slaughterhouse. He deals with his mother's madness and death and his father's drinking as though they are normal parts of his experience.

There is an extraordinary amount of pain at the core of the book, and this is made most clear when Francie glosses over it, laughs when he should be crying. He is obsessed with comic books and chocolate bars and pigs and the activities of young Philip Nugent as ways of avoiding what is happening in his own life. He is abandoned by his friend Joe. The account of his abuse by a priest in Borstal is superbly done. McCabe's version of Francie's psychology, and his observation of town life, are comic; using the clarity of Francie's voice and dramatizing with great skill the inevitable consequences of his manic condition, the novel invents its own world and its own set of rules, and remains deeply convincing.

Patrick McCabe was born in County Monaghan in Ireland and lives in Sligo. His other novels include *Carn* (1989), *The Dead School* (1995), *Breakfast on Pluto* (1998), *Winterwood* (2006) and *The Holy City* (2009). Both *The Butcher Boy* and *Breakfast on Pluto* were made into films by Neil Jordan.

Age in year of publication: thirty-seven.

Cormac McCarthy 1935–

1985   *Blood Meridian: Or The Evening Redness in the West*

Cormac McCarthy's vision is dark, apocalyptic and violent. His language takes its bearings from the Old Testament, the Joyce of *Ulysses* and William Faulkner; his syntax is nervous, clotted, he uses short sentences, and then immense, long, curling sentences, like an old preacher. He moves from the vernacular to a high literary style. He mainly writes about men.

Blood Meridian is the book where all his obsessions and his genius as a stylist are most apparent. It tells the story of a group of men in possession of guns and horses on the Texas–Mexico border in the 1840s. McCarthy's Wild West is a barren, hostile landscape; killing is both whim and passion, the book is full of scalpings and hangings, whole villages destroyed, uneasy alliances, further scalpings, dead babies hanging upside down from trees. His group of misfits roam like wild, bloodthirsty animals. His version of the American past as a sort of hell has almost no precedent in American narrative; his refusal to offer meaning and moral shape to his story makes this novel, and his other work, original and disturbing.

Cormac McCarthy was born in Rhode Island but was brought up in Knoxville, Tennessee. He lives in El Paso, Texas. *Child of God* (1973), an account of a necrophiliac on the rampage, is his most savage and disturbing book. *All the Pretty Horses* (1992), *The Crossing* (1994) and *Cities of the Plain* (1998) are labelled 'The Border Trilogy'. He followed these with *No Country For Old Men* (2005) filmed in 2007 and *The Road* (2006) which won a Pulitzer Prize and was filmed in 2009.

Age in year of publication: fifty.

Mary McCarthy 1912–1989

1963 *The Group*

This novel caused a sensation when first published because of its frank descriptions, not so much of sex itself, but of all the contraceptive devices, unguents and general embarrassments that go with it – the bad breath, strange noises, teeth jarring and fiddly birth control methods that coupling requires. Read over thirty years later, the novel is still a diverting tribute to such fumblings.

The group consists of seven upper-middle-class women, Vassar educated, products of everything freedom and money can buy – and even in 1933, when the novel begins, this was considerable. These young women were among the first to benefit from advances in medicine, contraception, education and equality of opportunity. With pitiless wit and a caustic eye, Mary McCarthy shows how the progress of science elevated its voice to entrap them again. The seven friends, Polly, Pokey, Libby, Kay, Dottie, Priss and Helena, founder on the rock of bad judgement, sadistic men and useless doctors and pundits, always shakily clinging to a longing for work, love and marriage.

Mary McCarthy provides an unusual and immensely readable account of the early adult lives of certain young women engaged in life and the practicalities of sex. *The Group* does a prescient and satirical demolition job on those theoretical bullies who are always telling women what to do, and think – and who met their match in Mary McCarthy.

Mary McCarthy was born in Seattle and lived in Paris and the USA. Other notable novels are *The Company She Keeps* (1942) and *The Groves of Academe* (1952).
   Age in year of publication: fifty-one.

Carson McCullers 1917–1967

1951   *The Ballad of the Sad Café*

This short novel tells a story of love. And so it is a ballad, but also an American Gothic opera – a tragi-comic *Carmen*, a poor white *Porgy and Bess*. McCullers's small Southern town is the kind where there is absolutely nothing to do except eat mashed rutabagas, collard greens and the occasional pig, and keep a watchful eye on your neighbour. Here lives Amelia, a six-foot-two, hairy sort of woman, clever at making money, doctoring, and distilling the best liquor in town. When her Cousin Lymon turns up – a malicious four-foot hunchback – she takes a great passion for him, which is incomprehensible but eternally fascinating to the folk who gather every night in the café Cousin Lymon opens in a store. When Cousin Lymon falls in love with the one man most likely to cause Amelia pain, the resolution of these passionate difficulties sees the lights in the café dim and the stage fall empty, Amelia's lament lingering in the air.

Carson McCullers writes in polished Southern tones, and this novel is written in language of singular beauty with not a word out of place. Her explorations of the frustrations of love are never bleak but seem to celebrate human love at its oddest and best, turning humdrum lives into heroic ones, and making a sad love story endearing and droll.

Carson McCullers was born in Georgia, and wrote the equally famous novels *The Heart is a Lonely Hunter* (1940), *Reflections in a Golden Eye* (1941) and *The Member of the Wedding* (1946).

Age in year of publication: thirty-four.

1978   *The Cement Garden*

This novel was published in the year before Margaret Thatcher took power in Britain, and its tone and content seem to imply that there was a very great need for her. The house where the four children – Julie, Jack, Sue and Tomare – are being brought up by their parents is in sight of new tower blocks, and the proposed motorway which caused the houses around them to be knocked down, has never been built. Neither parent has any siblings so there are no relatives. The father dies first, and then the mother after a long illness. The children, three of whom are in their teens, decide to bury her in the cellar and tell no one. This is presented as perfectly normal by Jack, who narrates the story. They loved their mother, but they want the giddy freedom which running the household will offer them.

There is not a false note in the whole book; McEwan makes you feel that this is, perhaps, what you would do too under similar circumstances. In any case, the siblings are locked into their own dramas. Tom, the youngest, wants to dress like a girl and is allowed to do so, then he wants to be a baby and this too is arranged. Jack is obsessed with his own adolescent body. Sue keeps a diary. Julie gets a boyfriend. They settle down into an uneasy and fragile harmony, broken only by Derek the boyfriend and the gradual rise of the smell from the cellar. Their world has been so perfectly created that you feel miserable at the prospect of its being broken up.

Ian McEwan was born in Aldershot, Hampshire. He published his first volume of stories, *First Love, Last Rites*, in 1975. His other novels include *The Child in Time* (1987), *Enduring Love* (1997), *Amsterdam*, which won the Booker Prize in 1998, *Atonement* (2001), which was made into an Oscar-winning film in 2007, *Saturday* (2005), *On Chesil Beach* (2007) and *Solar* (2010).

Age in year of publication: thirty.

John McGahern 1934–2006

1990   *Amongst Women*

In all of John McGahern's fiction – he wrote five novels and three volumes of stories – there is an air of perfection. He works on a small canvas; the same figures and the same landscape and indeed the same hard-won bleakness appear in much of his work. There is a timeless beauty about his fiction which means that it is unlikely to date or seem out of fashion. The opening pages of his first novel, *The Barracks* (1963), contain some of the best prose written in English in the second half of the century.

Twenty-seven years later McGahern's fifth novel *Amongst Women* tells the story of the War of Independence veteran Moran, his three daughters, his two sons and Rose, his second wife. Besides having one of the best first sentences in recent fiction ('As he weakened, Moran became afraid of his daughters.'), the book is remarkable for the plainness of its prose, its seamless structure and its careful delineation of the dark forces which gather around family relationships. Moran is both a violent bully and a man with an enormous capacity to charm; his daughters fear him and love him at the same time. McGahern's genius lies in the relentless accuracy of his prose, and the graceful portrayal of his characters.

John McGahern was born in Dublin and lived in County Leitrim. His novel *The Dark* was banned by the Irish Censorship Board in 1965. *The Leavetaking* (1974) and *The Pornographer* (1979) were followed by his magnificent *Collected Stories* (1992), *That they May Face The Rising Sun* (2001) and *Memoir* (2005). *Amongst Women* won the Irish Times Literature Prize.

Age in year of publication: fifty-six.

Patrick McGrath 1950–

1996   *Asylum*

This novel is written in a language which has been created to preserve order, to describe precisely, to win the reader's trust. This is the first sentence: 'The catastrophic love affair characterized by sexual obsession has been a professional interest of mine for many years now.'

The narrator is the psychiatrist Peter Cleave, who works in a top-security mental hospital in England in the 1950s. He tells the story of how his colleague Max Rafael's wife Stella ran away with the brutal murderer and sculptor Edgar Stark, an inmate of the hospital. As with all of McGrath's work, every word and phrase is carefully weighed and placed; from early on, you cease to trust Dr Cleave's narrative, but despite this, the figure of Stella, obsessed with Stark, becomes more and more clear and engrossing. Her introduction to Stark, his efforts to escape, her flight to London, her life with him there, and all the inevitable consequences are narrated with an almost prurient zeal by Dr Cleave. Her state of mind and the desires which impell her are utterly convincing, and the way in which Stark deals with her and Cleave watches over her make the book dark, disturbing, Gothic. The scenes in a Welsh farmhouse are particularly bleak. This is the sort of book that when you finish, you immediately want to hand to someone else to read.

Patrick McGrath was born in London and grew up near Broadmoor Hospital where his father was Medical Superintendent. His other books include *Spider* (1992), *Dr Haggard's Disease* (1993), *Port Mungo* (2004) and *Trauma* (2008).

Age in year of publication: forty-six.

Larry McMurtry 1936–

1985   *Lonesome Dove*

It is extraordinary and unexpected that two of the best American novels of the past decade have centred on the Wild West. Larry McMurtry's *Lonesome Dove* lacks the poetry and intensity and fierce power of Cormac McCarthy's *All the Pretty Horses*, but it makes up for that in the quality of its characterization and its plain, careful, perfectly pitched style. It is almost a thousand pages in length, the sort of book that you would stay up all night to finish; it has many old-fashioned virtues: a gripping story, action, sex, death, strong silent types (McMurtry is very good on these), human weakness, strong-willed women, harsh landscape.

It tells the story of a journey of a group of men, one woman and a herd of cattle from Texas to Montana at a time when the Native Americans have been all but wiped out and America has been tamed for the white man. It reads like a book of the Old Testament, a battle against nature at a time when old virtues are being replaced, with constant setbacks caused by the weather, cruel Indians (the few remaining), the crossing of rivers and the vagaries of the human heart. The fact that the tone of this book has been unaffected by the advances made in prose fiction by Joyce and Beckett, Faulkner and Pynchon does not lessen its impact, which is immense, or its status as a modern American masterpiece.

Larry McMurtry was born in Texas, where he now lives. His many novels include *Horseman, Pass By* (1961), filmed as *Hud* in 1963 and *The Last Picture Show* (1966) which was made into a film in 1971. *Lonesome Dove* won the Pulitzer Prize in 1985.
Age in year of publication: forty-nine.

Norman Mailer 1923–2007

1979   *The Executioner's Song*

The Executioner's Song is a brilliant work of imagination, based on numerous interviews given by the murderer Gary Gilmore and those around him. Gilmore was executed by firing squad in Utah having demanded the death penalty for himself; he had spent twenty-two of his thirty-five years in jail.

The novel moves like a camera, describing each scene coldly and dispassionately in short paragraphs, never judging, never summing up, never overwriting, allowing each character great latitude and sympathy. It is a triumph of control; the author and his famous ego are totally absent. No one is good or bad; people are motivated by strange, complex passions, longings, compulsions and loyalties. The novel is full of sex and sexual desire in a climate controlled by Mormons. Gilmore's girlfriend Nicole is one of the great creations in contemporary American writing; she is protean and wild and impulsive, deeply loyal and, at the same time, easily distracted. Gilmore emerges as damaged and trapped, his willingness to destroy and be destroyed giving the book a grim tragic power and a sort of grandeur.

Norman Mailer was born in New Jersey and grew up in Brooklyn. His talent as a novelist was often disguised by the extent and uneven quality of his publications. His best books included *The Naked and the Dead* (1948), *Armies of the Night* (1968), *The Fight* (1975) and *Miami and the Siege of Chicago* (1969). *The Executioner's Song* won the Pulitzer Prize in 1980.

Age in year of publication: fifty-six.

Bernard Malamud 1914–1986

1952   *The Natural*

This is one of the best books about sport, which means that it is about much more than the game of baseball which it describes. It is written in a spare clear style, and in a tone in which light and darkness do battle against each other for the body and soul of our hero.

It opens with the nineteen-year-old Roy Hobbs going to Chicago on a train with his scout. He is an orphan who has been discovered as a baseball wizard and he is destined for the big time. When the train has to stop, he pitches his skills against a famous baseball player who is also on the train, and wins. He is watched by a journalist who will follow the rest of his career, and a woman called Harriet, his nemesis, who is crazy and manages to shoot him in the stomach.

The rest of the novel takes place fifteen years later when Roy makes one last effort to succeed. He is too old, and he is still capable of being bewitched by women (all the women in this novel bewitch); he is moody and hungry for sex and love and hero status, but he is still a brilliant player. The games – the crowd, the tension, the next shot – are described in the novel with great verve and excitement. Roy Hobbs's uneasy but ravenous desire, his desperation to avoid the past, give the narrative a stark power and depth. It is the raw simplicity of *The Natural*, his first novel, which makes it so gripping.

Bernard Malamud was born in Brooklyn. His other masterpieces are *The Fixer* (1967) and *Dubin's Lives* (1979), and his *Collected Stories* were published in 1997. *The Natural* was made into a film in 1984.

Age in year of publication: thirty-eight.

David Malouf 1934–

1990   *The Great World*

The Great World is a portrait of Australian life during and after the Second World War. It is hard to make generalizations about Malouf's work. He never repeats himself. His characters are portrayed and handled with great feeling and depth; he is capable of creating moments of pure beauty in his books; he insists always on the complexity of things, the various levels on which things happen.

In his three novels of the 1990s, *Remembering Babylon* (1993), set in a remote part of Queensland in the middle of the nineteenth century, and *The Conversations at Curlew Creek* (1996), a dark, intense novel set in early nineteenth-century Australia and Ireland, he has been constructing a sort of history of Australia, an old and new testament for his own country. *The Great World* deals superbly with the drama of a Japanese prisoner-of-war camp; indeed, the novel could have dealt solely with that experience. But this is a more ambitious book, which follows a number of characters back to Australia and makes what happens to them during subsequent decades, emotionally and domestically, in their work and their families, hugely interesting, so that you feel you know them. *The Great World is* memorable for the range of the characters' emotional response, for the depth and detail and sheer integrity of the writing.

David Malouf was born in Brisbane and lives in Sydney. He is also a poet and librettist. *The Great World* won the Commonwealth Writers Prize. His other books include the magnificent *An Imaginary Life* (1978), a brilliant account of Ovid in exile and after exile, and *The Complete Stories* (2007).

Age in year of publication: fifty-six.

Olivia Manning 1908–1980

1960–1965   The Balkan Trilogy

The Great Fortune (1960), The Spoilt City (1962), Friends and Heroes (1965)

The Balkan Trilogy recounts in fictional form Olivia Manning's Second World War experiences as the young bride of a British Council lecturer, first in Romania, then in Greece and finally in Egypt, moving always away from the advancing German army. Harriet Pringle, Manning's alter ego, lives in cities where revolution, imprisonment and persecution of the Jews are omnipresent, while expatriates and a motley crew of other riffraff pursue the last remaining restaurant in which horse is not served, or finagle money or favours to enable them to survive one more day.

Harriet, a young woman never loved in childhood and about to repeat the experience with her infuriating husband Guy, is a discerning recorder of the cruelties and fragilities of men in pursuit of power, of whatever kind. A parade of eccentrics, led by the seedy emigre Yakomov, the preposterous Lord Pinkrose, the potty Misses Twocurry, alternate with personal lives from which the plangent notes of private love and grief are never absent. Reading The Balkan Trilogy, one of the finest accounts of the impact of war on Europe and on its people, is like reading Jane Austen on a broader canvas, in another time, another place.

Olivia Manning was born in Portsmouth, grew up in Ireland, and except for the Second World War, spent most of her life in London. The Levant Trilogy – *The Danger Tree* (1977), *The Battle Lost and Won* (1978) and *The Sum of Things* (1980) – continues The Balkan Trilogy, the entire sequence entitled The Fortunes of War.

Age in years these books were published: fifty-two – fifty-seven.

William Maxwell 1908–2000

1980   *So Long, See you Tomorrow*

The ghost of *David Copperfield* hovers over this beautiful novel, its evocation of childhood loss – of a father, of a mother, of a friend – is one of the classic accounts of being a motherless boy: 'Other children could have borne it. My older brother did. I couldn't.'

Set in a small farming community in Illinois, the narrator, now an elderly man, recalls his childhood and the influenza which suddenly removed his mother when he was ten. With her death, trust disappears – the world becomes a void through which he tiptoes with caution and he moves his muted gaze to tell the story of another gentle boy, Cletus Smith, his only friend. Cletus' mother is unfaithful; Cletus' father commits murder.

This is the story of two boys who live undefended in an adult world where nothing is said, but everything happens. The passions of insignificant and modest people, precisely placed amongst the animals, milking sheds and flat landscape of the plains, reach Shakespearean heights in Maxwell's exquisite prose. As Maxwell languorously recalls the 'strange and unlikely things washed up on the shore of time' he gives us an elegy to memory which calls forth the vast legacy of seemingly insignificant human suffering.

William Maxwell was born in Illinois and lived in New York, where as fiction editor of the *New Yorker* for forty years, he was a formative influence on a generation of writers. The author of six novels and three short story collections, this novel won the American Book Award in 1980.

Age in year of publication: seventy-two.

Gita Mehta 1942–

1993   *A River Sutra*

'There is a woman at the gate who wants to see you, Sahib.' In *A River Sutra*, she is sure to tell a story. A sutra is a thread or string, but also a literary form; in Gita Mehta's hands a bright necklace which flashes with the religions, philosophies and fables of India.

There are many threads in this necklace. The connecting one is the experiences of a retired bureaucrat, who late in life comes to manage a government resthouse along the banks of the River Narmada, holiest of Indian rivers. This river is a place of pilgrimage, to which come ascetics, minstrels, archaeologists, bandits, musicians, refugees. The tales they tell the bureaucrat are sometimes ecstatic, sometimes, like Mehta's finest achievement here, 'The Teacher's Story', heartbreaking. Piercing each narrative, always, is the question: where does wisdom lie? In the thousand answers, one message is clear: it can only come through experience, and through some experience of love.

Gita Mehta uses the images and mysticism of India to dazzling effect, harmonizing sounds of landscape, animals and music, river and earth. But though these stories draw much from the history and mythology of India, they resonate with the flamboyant presence of modern India too. Mehta has used traditional Indian narratives in an entirely new and muscular way in this exquisite novel.

Gita Mehta was born in Delhi and lives in London, New York and India. Her other books are: *Karma Cola: Marketing the Mystic East* (1976), a novel, *Raj* (1989) and *Snakes and Ladders: Glimpses of India* (1997).

Age in year of publication: fifty-one.

Rohinton Mistry 1952–

1995   *A Fine Balance*

Dickens – Tolstoy – Balzac – Zola: Rohinton Mistry writes in this tradition. The vastness of India and the condition of its people are his subjects, but his genius lies in his exact observation, which brings to life every atom of his characters' experiences, so that we live and breathe with them, laugh when they laugh, suffer as they do.

It is the 1970s, and four people, two Hindu, two Parsi, come together in a dingy Bombay flat. Ishvar and Omprakash are tailors, Untouchables; Dina, their employer, is a widow struggling for financial independence as a seamstress. Her lodger Maneck is a student of 'refrigeration and air-conditioning'. Mistry retraces the background of each, placing the incidents of their insignificant lives against the majestic sweep of Indian history. This is Mrs Gandhi's India, with its vicious Emergency laws bringing forced sterilization, labour camps, thuggery and persecution. Mistry's energetic realism and command of comic nuance capture the long-suffering citizens of India in all their variety and stoic endurance. They burst off the page, making you laugh, weep and rail against the fates.

A Fine Balance is a magnificent novel, beautifully crafted, a political novel which is also the work of an inspiring imagination. Despite its lyrical despair it is full of an exuberance and humanity that fix in the mind and heart a sense of wonder and excitement.

Rohinton Mistry was born in Bombay, India, and has lived in Canada since 1975. His first, equally acclaimed novel was *Such a Long Journey* (1991), which won the Governor General's Award and the Commonwealth Writers Prize.

Age in year of publication: forty-three.

Timothy Mo 1950–

1991   *The Redundancy of Courage*

In 1975 Indonesia invaded the Portuguese colony of East Timor, half an inch above Australia on the map. The USA wanted East Timor's deep-water channels for their nuclear submarines, so allowed Indonesia to annex East Timor: one in three East Timorese died in the slaughter that followed.

Timothy Mo changed names, places, nationalities in this stirring fictional testament to the East Timor resistance fighters, but the connection between fact and fiction has become even stronger with time.

Adolph Ng, an outsider on the island, is a homosexual Chinese hotelier, and his is the knowing voice we hear. Ng's account of the invasion and the years with the freedom fighters in the hills vibrates with crazed brutality, starvation, disease and the gruesome sights which were their daily fare. But resistance is only the backdrop to the humour and humanity that dominate this novel; Adolph is a wry fellow, and as he records the shifting allegiances of the islanders he produces that rarity – a vivid, funny novel about people who fight without hope: not heroes, 'just ordinary people asked extraordinary things in terrible circumstances'.

Mo is a detached yet incisive chronicler of the worst aspects of Empire; in this furiously unsentimental novel about a forgotten war he reveals, with sympathy and political acumen, the real meaning of nobility: courage, exercised when it can achieve nothing.

Timothy Mo was born in Hong Kong and lives elusively around the Pacific Rim and in London. Among his prize-winning novels are *The Monkey King* (1978), *Sour Sweet* (1982) and *An Insular Possession* (1986).

Age in year of publication: forty-one.

144

Brian Moore 1921–1999

1985 *Black Robe*

Brian Moore had three phases. In his first incarnation, he was an Irish novelist. *Judith Hearne*, 1955 (USA: *The Lonely Passion of Judith Hearne*, 1956), is probably his best from this period. In his second coming, he wrote intense novels about faith and morals, obsessions (*The Doctor's Wife*, 1976, is particularly brilliant) and history. In his third phase, he wrote terse novels about contemporary political crises. Always, he was preoccupied by the conflicts surrounding loyalty and belief, and increasingly, he strove for a style which is almost neutral, without flourishes.

Black Robe is set in seventeenth-century Canada. Father Laforgue, a Jesuit, has come to the remote and hostile territory to convert the heathens. The novel dramatizes the conflict between his certainties and the beliefs of the natives, which are presented with immense conviction. The narrative is powerful and emotional, and the violence in the book is shocking, more graphic than anything in Cormac McCarthy. The landscape, the dark forest, the constant menace, the untamed world, are wonderfully evoked. This is Moore's darkest book and most haunting; his account of the Jesuits' colonial enterprise, which echoes other moments in the history of the building of empires, is gripping and deeply disturbing.

Brian Moore was born in Belfast. In 1948 he emigrated to Canada. He lived in California for many years. He wrote numerous novels including *The Emperor of Ice Cream* (1966), *Catholics* (1972), a W. H. Smith Award winner, *The Great Victorian Collection* (1975) and *The Colour of Blood* (1988).

Age in year of publication: sixty-four.

Frank Moorhouse 1938–

1988   *Forty-Seventeen*

The hero of this novel calls himself variously Sean or Ian, seeming unable to make up his mind between the Irish and Scots version of his name, a fitting bafflement for a modern Australian male, floating in beer and fornication yet emitting muffled longings to be otherwise.

About to become forty, a drinking, writing man addicted to women, he is partial to sluts. His grandmother made a fortune being a whore in the caves of Katoomba, and the seventeen-year-old girl he truly loves has departed to London to find herself by becoming a call-girl. His ex-wife Robyn is about to die of cancer. Among the high points of the novel are Robyn's first letters to him; everything that is lost in middle age is plaintively rendered in the naive voice of this young girl. Then there is Belle, one of those sluts who get the blues, and the invaluable seventy-year-old Edith with whom he travels to conferences in Vienna and Israel.

This is a finely crafted work, cleverly moving back and forth through time, written in rueful, mocking prose. Moorhouse's artistic achievement is to give his hero a life that seems casual, but this man on the loose is in fact ligatured to women, and the novel beats with a particular pulse of desperation which is both touching and exhilarating.

Frank Moorhouse was born in Nowra in New South Wales and lives in Sydney. Among his prize-winning novels are *The Americans, Baby* (1972) and *Grand Days* (1993).

Age in year of publication: fifty.

Toni Morrison 1931–

1987   *Beloved*

'For a used-to-be slave woman to love anything that much was dangerous, especially if it was her children she had settled on to love. The best thing, he knew, was to love just a little bit; everything just a little bit, so when they broke its back, or shoved it in a croker sack, well, maybe you'd have a little love left over for the next one.' This is Paul D., whom Sethe, our heroine, has known in slavery. He has not seen her for eighteen years, and now he has come to visit her when her husband has disappeared, her mother-in-law is dead and her two sons have left, her house is haunted by her dead baby daughter, and she is living alone with her daughter Denver. It is 1873 in Ohio. Sethe is torn with memories of the dreadful past, the petty cruelties of being a slave, and then the particular viciousness of certain events which she finds almost impossible to contemplate, and yet cannot forget.

The novel's strength comes from its obsession with the power and the problems of love between people who are enslaved and savagely exploited; there is an extraordinary skill in the way the narrative goes back over events of the past while focusing also on the domestic minutiae, small moments of tension, the play of light, the interior of the house, the constant efforts to survive the catastrophe which haunts the novel and indeed haunts the reader. The figure of the mother-in-law Baby Suggs, who has been bought out of slavery by her son, is especially memorable and sad; the idea of the house being haunted by the dead child is presented calmly and with authority and becomes immensely credible.

Toni Morrison was born in Ohio and lives in New York. Her other novels include *Song of Solomon* (1977), *Jazz* (1992) and *Paradise* (1998). She was awarded the Nobel Prize in Literature in 1993.

Age in year of publication: fifty-six.

Alice Munro 1931–

1990   *Friend of My Youth*

Alice Munro territory is the Ottawa Valley, in the small harsh Munro towns of Logan or Whalley. These are the towns people leave and come back to, but the place and time hardly matter with Alice Munro because she writes about apparently ordinary folk and therefore all of us, wherever. Alice Munro's people are careful souls, you *think*. But here she skewers those moments when change comes about because of one incident which, taken at the flood, leads on to divorce, another husband, another wife, a different town, a different life.

Simply told, these gossipy, wise stories are full of recognitions: 'One evening Raymond had said to Ben and Georgia that it looked as if Maya wasn't going to be able to have any children. "We try our best," he said. "We use pillows and everything. But no luck."' 'I used to sneak longing looks at men in those days. I admired their necks and any bits of their chest a loose button let show.' A wife leaves her husband: 'He said he was giving her a week to decide. No more drinking. No more smoking . . . Karen said don't bother with the week.'

Each story is as rich as a novel. Her characters stand next to you, about to engage you in conversation, their lives laid bare with slashing accuracy so that reading about them, the heart is stopped as something familiar, hopefully hidden, surfaces in a sudden, illuminating way.

Alice Munro is one of the greatest short story writers; only Chekhov comes to mind when contemplating her work. Alice Munro was born and lives in Canada. Some of her award-winning collections are *The Progress of Love* (1987), *Open Secrets* (1994), which won the W. H. Smith Award in 1995, *The Love of A Good Woman* (1998) and *Runaway* (2004). She was awarded the Man International Booker Prize in 2009.

Age in year of publication: fifty-nine.

Iris Murdoch 1919–1999

1968   *The Nice and the Good*

Iris Murdoch had an extraordinarily rich if uneven career as a novelist. She published more than twenty-five novels, and of these the one that we would most recommend readers to begin with is *The Nice and the Good*.

Most of the novel takes place in a large old house beside the sea in Dorset where Octavian Grey, a civil servant, his wife Kate, their daughter Barbara, and an infinite number of friends, servants, house guests and hangers-on spend the summer. The novel has Montrose, the best cat in any of the novels listed in this book (Graham Greene's *The Human Factor* has the best dog): 'a large cocoa-coloured tabby animal with golden eyes, a square body, rectangular legs and an obstinate self-absorbed disposition'. The writing is elegant; Murdoch handles the large cast of characters with great clarity and skill – the children are especially good. She carefully surrounds some events in the novel with echoes of myth and magic, while leaving others as undisturbed pieces of social realism. Her characters are both vividly drawn and credible, but they also operate on other levels, as forces in a field of energy.

Iris Murdoch was born in Dublin and lived in Oxford most of her life. In our opinion her best five novels are *Under the Net* (1954), *The Red and the Green* (1965), *The Nice and the Good, Henry and Cato* (1976) and *The Black Prince* (1973). *The Sea, the Sea* won the Booker Prize in 1978.

Age in year of publication: forty-nine.

Vladimir Nabokov 1899–1977

1955   *Lolita*

Nymphet: a young girl just past puberty; beautiful, semi-divine. Humbert Humbert, born in Paris, comes to the New England countryside in 1947 and encounters Lolita, twelve years old, 'with an impact of passionate recognition'. To take possession of his beloved, he marries her mother. Sex with his dream-child, urgently longed for by Humbert, knowingly accepted by Lolita, becomes more than child abuse – as Lolita pertly points out, it's incest.

Humbert sweeps up his Lolita and for two years lives in heaven and hell, travelling with her through America. Humbert's festering soul chronicles every moment of lust and play, always creating more trouble, inventing dangers. Lolita grows up, the outside world encroaches. There is separation and death – both the same for Humbert.

In *Lolita* Nabokov's imagination is that of a magician puppeteer. Humbert Humbert is a monster, yet we do not always feel so; Lolita the abused girl-child alternately startles and beguiles us. Their story is not sordid but full of yearning, wordplay and jokes – ironic and biting, often erotic. Lolita is one of the immortal love stories. For its fabulous language, its wit, its revolutionary portrait of a different kind of moral monster (not a political one), and because it brilliantly cocks a snook at all known taboos, Lolita is one of the most influential novels of our time.

Vladimir Nabokov was born in St Petersburg, and lived in Europe, the USA and then Switzerland. He was a master prose stylist in both Russian and English. *Lolita* was rejected by many publishers on the grounds of obscenity. Like Joyce's *Ulysses* it was published first in France, in English, and did not appear in the United States until 1958. The first British edition was published a year later.

Age in year of publication: fifty-six.

(1) V. S. Naipaul 1932–

1961   *A House for Mr Biswas*

The expectations of Mohun Biswas are not great. Assured at birth of a miserable life by the village pundit, the curse of his life proves to be the community into which he is born: the Hindus of Trinidad. Overpowering in their vociferous insistence on conformity and control, this swarm of venal, fighting tragicomedians is vividly and preposterously alive. Most ebullient is Mr Biswas, a template of indignation and ambition, albeit modest: all he wants is a house of his own, some dignity, some privacy, where the irritations of his in-laws can be viewed from afar.

Out of this simple wish Naipaul created this masterpiece, and in Mr Biswas, with his stomach powders and fluent Trinidadian English, one of those characters who becomes a part of life. We follow him through a plethora of jobs, from sign painter and sugar-cane overseer – Mr Biswas miserable – to hilariously inventive journalist – Mr Biswas happy. We are with him as son, husband, father and testy family man until his final triumph: a peculiar house of his own.

A House for Mr Biswas is also a history of, and a farewell to, Naipaul's own people, written as the old ways were disappearing. Its greatness lies in its laughing testimony to the frustrations and humiliations of the poor, expressed with magnificent humour and invention, without the bleak despair which marks much of his later work.

V. S. Naipaul was born in Trinidad, but came to England in 1950 and now lives in Wiltshire. His travel books include *An Area of Darkness* (1964), about India and *The Return of Eva Péron* (1980). His other novels include *The Enigma of Arrival* (1987), *Half A Life* (2001) and *Magic Seeds* (2004). His many awards include the Booker Prize for *In a Free State*, the David Cohen Prize for lifetime achievement and in 2001 the Nobel Prize in Literature.

Age in year of publication: twenty-nine.

(2) V. S. Naipaul 1932–

1979   *A Bend in the River*

V. S. Naipaul's most brilliant novels are *In a Free State* (1971), *A Bend in the River* and *The Enigma of Arrival* (1987), with their sombre tone and grave, melancholy wisdom. Of the three, *A Bend in the River* is the best.

The novel takes place in a country very like Zaire, where the narrator, Salim, a Muslim whose family is of Indian trader origin, moves during a time of conflict and sets up shop. The novel deals with history not as a rich legacy full of ancestral voices, but as a set of erasures, and this makes the tone very dark indeed. Against this vision of the past as a void is the deep richness of the present; the minor characters who impinge on Salim's life, such as the servant Metty, the sorceress Zabeth and her son Ferdinand, are wonderfully and vividly drawn, as are the dramatic changes which take place in our narrator's life in the village, and the slow eruption – this is after all Conrad's territory – of civil strife. There is a scene where the President – clearly a version of Mobutu – speaks on the radio, which is utterly electrifying, as are the later scenes of catastrophe in the book.

Age in year of publication: forty-seven.

R. K. Narayan 1906–2001

1952 *The Financial Expert*

Narayan's great novels are set in his fictional town of Malgudi, in southern India. There is something particularly engaging about the stumblings of Margayya, the hero of this one, who luxuriates in an anxious love of money. He begins his financial endeavours sitting under a banyan tree with a tin box, extorting rupees out of any simple soul who comes his way. Fate, in the shape of a sex manual at first called *Philosophy and Practice of Kissing* and later more timidly entitled *Domestic Harmony*, makes him an entrepreneur. An enslaved wife, a house symbolically partitioned from his brother with whom he is forever scratchily at war, and a son, Balu, so loved and so unworthy that he proves to be Margayya's worst investment, complete Margayya's world.

Narayan has been attacked for presenting the miseries of India – poverty, the caste system, etc. – too benevolently. This politically correct position fails to see that Narayan's lightness of touch and unruffled irony reveal a thousand trenchant truths. The bombastic Margayya, with his vanity, his large ambitions and small meannesses and his manoeuvrings around the gods and Mammon, lives the harsh life of those at the bottom of the heap. This is all the more apparent for the vigour, laughter and buoyancy Margayya uses to combat the weaknesses of his pinched soul. That is the real genius of Narayan.

R. K. Narayan was born in Madras and lived in Mysore. Considered one of India's greatest writers, among his best-known novels are *The Painter of Signs* (1977) and *A Tiger for Malgudi* (1983).

Age in year of publication: forty-six.

Patrick O'Brian 1914–2000

1970   *Master and Commander*

This is the first of Patrick O'Brian's sequence of novels about life in the Royal Navy during the French Revolutionary and Napoleonic Wars. For those who entertain dismal notions of the sea and all who sail on it, it is important to know that naval paraphernalia and perfect period detail are only two of the splendours of O'Brian's writing, superseded by the vice-like grip of his storytelling and the instant charm of his characterization and dialogue.

Lieutenant Jack Aubrey, RN, meets Stephen Maturin, a penniless physician, during the performance of Locatelli's C major quartet at the Governor's House in Port Mahon, Minorca, on 1 April 1800. They fall out. Thus begins one of the great literary friendships, as these two very different men – Aubrey a cheerful bulldog Englishman and true man of the sea, and Maturin an enigmatic Irish-Catalan – begin a lifetime of adventure together. Though there are battles aplenty, how men live together, the capering, petty and sometimes lonely qualities of a male society, rather than the tedious brutalities we associate with war, is the subject here. There is nothing monastic or uncultivated about their experiences. Music flows through the novels, which, in turn, are like a series of illustrations, each telling a different story, each one illuminating, through a tiny community on a wooden ship, the confusions and glories of the human condition.

Patrick O'Brian was born in Buckinghamshire, and lived in south-west France and Dublin. A distinguished translator, biographer and novelist, he published twenty Aubrey/Maturin novels.

Age in year of publication: fifty-six.

Edna O'Brien 1932–

1962   *The Lonely Girl*

(renamed *Girl with Green Eyes* in 1964)

The idea that the Republic of Ireland moved from the nineteenth century to the late twentieth century in five or ten years has proved very fruitful for Irish novelists. All Edna O'Brien's work is concerned with the drama between freedom and restriction, between old-fashioned values, and possibilities which are new and untested. In later novels such as *Time and Tide* (1992) or *Down by the River* (1996) she presents this conflict as tragedy, but in her early work, especially her first three novels known as 'The Country Girls Trilogy', she uses a lighter tone.

Of these novels, the second one, *Girl with the Green Eyes*, is the most accomplished. Caithleen and Baba have arrived in Dublin where they are staying in digs and searching for adventure; they are desperate to lose their virginity and desperate to hold on to it at the same time. Baba is full of malice and plans for the future; Caithleen, on whom the novel focuses, is more melancholy and uneasy than her friend, more provincial, but she too wants love and wants to get away from her ghastly family. She meets an older man, a foreigner involved in the movies, who is oddly wise and distant and cynical but great in bed. The tone of the novel is perfectly wry and innocent; some scenes – Caithleen's efforts to cook fish, for example, or her father's visit – are desperately funny.

Edna O'Brien was born in the west of Ireland, but has lived in London for many years. Her other books include *August is a Wicked Month* (1965) and *A House of Splendid Isolation* (1994).

Age in year of publication: thirty.

Flannery O'Connor 1925–1964

1952   *Wise Blood*

'Jesus was a liar' is the oft-repeated cry of Hazel Motes, grandson of a preacher, who returns from the war with his mother's spectacles, the Bible, and his faith gone awry. In Taulkinham, Tennessee, he founds the Church Without Christ, an entirely original concept to the inhabitants of that town, imbued as they are with Bible-belt religion of the more conventional kind. Motes's journey through this novel is a test from God. He is accompanied by bizarre villains such as Asa Hawks, the seeing blind preacher, and his determinedly nauseating daughter Sabbath. And there is the fox-faced young Enoch Emery, driven to absurdities by his wise blood, 'inherited from his daddy'. Animals provide a Greek chorus – a gorilla, a moose, some interesting pigs – even Haze's car looks like a rat. Hoover Shoats, whose rival Holy Church Without Christ precipitates vengeance, completes these 'poor white trash' who have no need for the Lord to mete out punishment; they are a dab hand at doing so themselves.

O'Connor's creations are grotesque but familiar, brutish but funny, every stitch of their clothing and oddity of speech presented to us in fine detail like an etching on glass. Unique in O'Connor's startling use of language and in the intense originality of her Gothic imagination, this is a classic of the American South.

Flannery O'Connor was born in Savannah, Georgia. Her novels include *The Violent Bear It Away* (1960), and her *Complete Stories* won the Pulitzer Prize in 1971. John Huston filmed *Wise Blood* in 1979.

Age in year of publication: twenty-seven.

156

John O'Hara 1905–1970

1958 *From the Terrace*

This is a big, brilliant, old-fashioned novel – all eight hundred and ninety-seven pages of it – which offers a panoramic view of American society in the first half of the twentieth century. It moves slowly, showing scenes and characters in great detail. The dialogue, throughout the book, is inspired: it is hard to think of a writer who uses dialogue so well. It is also full of strange, startling insights into the lives and motives of the characters, which are reminiscent of those of George Eliot.

Our hero Alfred Eaton is born into a prosperous family in a small town in Pennsylvania; his mother drinks and has affairs, his father loved his older brother who died, and has no interest in Alfred. Thus he grows up self-sufficient, he makes an effort, people respect him and admire him. There is a wonderful account in this book of what it is like to be young, rich and good-looking in New York in 1919 and 1920. After the war Eaton goes into business, he gets married, he has children, he has a mistress, he moves to Washington and takes part in government. O'Hara writes well about his most private, intimate thoughts and moments, and then superbly about public events such as the Wall Street crash. And slowly, almost imperceptibly, as time moves on and Eaton's personality coarsens, this great American story darkens, this exemplary character, given every opportunity, somehow fails. This is a deeply convincing and disturbing novel, with myriad small touches of pure genius; it is also very funny. It deserves to be widely read and known.

John O'Hara was born in Pennsylvania. His other books include *Appointment in Samarra* (1934), *BUtterfield 8* (1935) and *Pal Joey* (1940).

Age in year of publication: fifty-three.

Michael Ondaatje 1943–

1987   *In the Skin of a Lion*

This is a short novel about layer and texture and language. It is set in Toronto and south-western Ontario in the 1920s and 1930s: it offers still points, short scenes, moments in the lives of a number of immigrants; it dramatizes the construction of Toronto. The novel is haunted by the building of one bridge, how it was designed and planned, the deaths and accidents during the slow progress. The prose here has a strange, slow, poetic and deliberate tone, which is also present in Ondaatje's subsequent novel *The English Patient* (1992). Great risks are taken with narrative, so that the novel comes to resemble a group of photographs or tiny clips from a film. The main character is Patrick Lewis: in a stunningly beautiful piece at the beginning of the book we see him with his father, who works with dynamite to clear logs. Later, we see him arriving in Toronto, falling in love, spending time in prison, and then telling the story. Ondaatje manages to combine a sense of mystery in the spaces between the words with a deeply solid characterization. His genius is in creating one of the best novels of the century about work, which is also one of the best novels about dreams and disappearances and magic.

Michael Ondaatje was born in Ceylon (now Sri Lanka) and educated in England and in Canada, living there since 1962. His other works include *The Collected Works of Billy the Kid* (1970), *Coming Through Slaughter* (1979), *Running in the Family* (1982) and the novels *Anil's Ghost* (2000) and *Divisadero* (2007). He has also published several volumes of poetry. *The English Patient*, joint winner of the Booker Prize in 1992, was made into a film in 1996.

Age in year of publication: forty-four.

Grace Paley 1922–2007

1959   *The Little Disturbances of Man*

Grace Paley's world is a small but happy one, happy in the sense that nothing worse remains to happen to the creatures she invents. Subtitled 'Stories of Men and Women at Love' (though love–hate would be a more accurate description), her women, the Virginias, Faiths and Annas of these stories, are busy bringing up the children; husbands – Richards, Johns, Peters – having departed for the next woman on the agenda, propelled by testosterone, usually darting a backward glance at wife number one and keeping a careful foot in her door. Elsewhere, bodies age, grandparents fret, kids run riot, and, as always, families demonstrate the American dream to be a species of nightmare.

It is the language she uses, a mélange of New York Russian-Polish-Yiddish, that is the hallmark of her work. Jewish mother lamenting sons: 'First grouchy, then gone.' Jewish son, lamenting mother: 'Me. Her prize possession and the best piece of meat in the freezer of her heart.' This language is much more than inconsequential wisecrackery; it beats with a rhythm that banishes sentimentality and enables Paley's understated and colloquial vignettes to suggest broad spaces of emotion and desire – and enjoyment, for Grace Paley adds greatly to the joy of life, each story like sipping a very strong, very dry Martini. Of the little she has written, these stories show her at her wild and original best.

Grace Paley was born and lived in New York. Her only other story collections were *Enormous Changes at the Last Minute* (1974) and *Later the Same Day* (1985) which appeared in *Collected Stories* (1994). *Begin Again: Collected Poems* appeared in 2000.

Age in year of publication: thirty-seven.

Jayne Anne Phillips 1952–

1984 *Machine Dreams*

This is a most unusual novel, gritty, imaginative, skilful, the family story of the Hampsons, who live in a small town in the USA, during those years when confidence in the American dream disappeared in the Depression, in the Pacific during the Second World War, and in Vietnam.

In 1946 Jean marries Mitch Hampson just after his return from the war. Both are already marked by hardship and family loss. Mitch, in New Guinea and the Coral Sea, has returned from a world of machines and death that deadens him for married life. Their two children, the girl Danner and her brother Billy, who like his father is required by his country to fight in the East, this time in Vietnam, complete the story. There is both charm and power in this novel. Phillips uses stream of consciousness, dreams, images of flying horses, aeroplanes, but always appurtenances of war are buried in the appurtenances of life. Cars, dresses, housework, sex, the clicking of pipes in creaking houses mingle with 'smells of tobacco and men, the sound of men's voices' and 'big machines, earth movers and cranes'.

Artistically, Jayne Anne Phillips's fine understanding of the place of public events in private lives gives a timeless quality to this intently told family story. 'You never see the everyday the way you might,' says Jean Hampson. But Jayne Anne Phillips does.

Jayne Anne Phillips was born in West Virginia and lives in California. Other highly praised books include stories *Black Tickets* (1979) a novel, *Shelter* (1995) and *Lark and Termite* (2008).

Age in year of publication: thirty-two.

Sylvia Plath 1932–1963

1963   *The Bell Jar*

This is Sylvia Plath's only novel. It is written in the same precise, tense, sharp style as the last poems, with the same tone of brutal honesty moving closer and closer to exasperation and breakdown. But the book is also very funny and frank about social and sexual ambition in 1950s America, the worry about sex and boys, the tension between a Puritan upbringing and sudden, bright chances presented to our heroine. There is a marvellous description of looking at an erect penis for the first time: 'The only thing I could think of was turkey neck and turkey gizzard and I felt very depressed.'

The world is watched by Esther Greenwood with the amoral, opportunistic and slightly weary tones of *The Catcher in the Rye*, and this means that Esther's breakdown and suicide attempt in *The Bell Jar* are all the more moving and shocking. The book is full of images of death and decay; the first paragraph opens: 'It was a queer, sultry summer, the summer they electrocuted the Rosenbergs' and ends: 'I couldn't help wondering what it would be like, being burned alive all along your nerves.' The fact that the life and times of the heroine mirror what happened in the life of the young Sylvia Plath gives the book an added immediacy and power.

Sylvia Plath was born in Boston. Her first collection of poetry, *The Colossus*, was published in 1960. She committed suicide in London a month after *The Bell Jar* was published under the pseudonym Victoria Lucas. Her best-known collection *Ariel* was published posthumously in 1965.

Age in year of publication: thirty-one.

Katherine Anne Porter 1890–1980

1962 *Ship of Fools*

It is 1931, the eve of Hitler's accession, and the *Vera*, a German freighter, sets off from Vera Cruz bound for Bremerhaven, carrying a motley collection of persons of differing nationalities, religions and political beliefs. The passengers perform with brio – loving and lusting, revealing smallness of mind and heart and largeness of bigotry and snobbery. Lurking behind each cabin door are stories diverse, disturbingly real and perkily human.

This is a novel written ahead of its time, taking the German attitude to the Jews in the decades before the war as an analogy to be extended to the poor, to women – to all the dispossessed. But in no didactic way: Lowental, Jewish, is almost as repellent as the Germans who persecute him, and the women on the ship treat each other like ghoulish *tricoteuses*. This independence of mind marks Porter's work, as does her style: witty, sometimes acerbic, sometimes beautiful, or languid like the roll of a ship.

The ship itself is, of course, an allegory for mankind on its voyage to eternity. Always celebrating as well as indicting the endless folly of Western Man, about to embark on yet another world war, Katherine Anne Porter shows how from the tiny hatreds and foolishnesses of ordinary souls a great body of hate can grow.

Katherine Anne Porter was born in Texas and lived in Europe and America, North and South. She took twenty years to write *Ship of Fools*, which became an instant bestseller and was filmed in 1965. Her *Collected Stories* won the Pulitzer Prize in 1966.

Age in year of publication: seventy-two.

Anthony Powell 1905–2000

1951–1975   *A Dance to the Music of Time*

*A Question of Upbringing (1951), A Buyer's Market (1952),
The Acceptance World (1955), At Lady Molly's (1957),
Casanova's Chinese Restaurant (1960), The Kindly Ones (1962),
The Valley of Bones (1964), The Soldier's Art (1966),
The Military Philosophers (1968), Books Do Furnish a Room (1971),
Temporary Kings (1973), Hearing Secret Harmonies (1975)*

It is unwise to consult any British person about this novel sequence, which, in the manner of Proust, recounts the life and experiences of Nick Jenkins, a denizen of the English uppermiddle, if not aristocratic, class. The English disease of fussing about class has long prevented Powell from receiving the universal acclaim which is his right.

In Powell's world the Establishment meets Bohemia. Nick Jenkins begins his narration before the First World War and ends in reflective old age, his companions a kaleidoscope of eccentrics, musicians, sluts, women ferocious and loving, men in love or in drink, generals, politicians, necrophiliacs – the cast is as large and as real as life itself. These are comic novels, classical in composition, interweaving sexual entanglements with intricate negotiations for power, with world wars and high matters of state, contemplating always the mysterious nature of love, most particularly of friendship experienced, lost, grieved over. Time dances – and it takes a heavy toll.

There are few masters of English prose with Powell's command of irony and elegance of language. These are tender, amusing, pervasive novels; they remain in the memory. It is unnecessary to read the twelve together, but once begun . . .

Anthony Powell was born in London and lived in Somerset. He wrote other novels, and his memoirs, *To Keep the Ball Rolling* (4 vols 1976–82), illuminate *A Dance to the Music of Time*. His awards included the James Tait Black Memorial Prize and the W. H. Smith Award.

Age in year of publication: forty-six – seventy.

V. S. Pritchett 1900–1997

1998 *The Lady from Guatemala*

A Pritchett sentence is unmistakable. 'She was a smart girl with a big friendly chin and a second one coming.' 'What the unconverted could not forgive in us was first that we believed in successful prayer and, secondly, that our revelation came from Toronto.'

Such words chivvy us into the Pritchett world of shopkeepers, barbers, sailors, small businessmen, religious Nonconformists and women who are much more than a match for any men who come their way. Pritchett delights in writing about human bodies, their shape and protuberances, about marriage, love and everything that leads up to, and away from, marital irritation. His women are powerful creatures, bold-nosed, full-breasted, large-eyed and, quite often, on the rampage. These are not enclosed English people. They often skip overseas and greet foreigners with feisty poise.

Pritchett is the great chronicler of those quotidian institutions which actually keep the wheels of England turning: seedy hotels, small houses, trains and a great deal of rain. His ordinary things are full of vim and bounce. Pritchett is the greatest English short story writer of this century, combining love of the English character with an inquisitive wit. This book, a choice of his best stories, shows his exceptional powers of observation and his effortless command of the use, as well as the beauty, of the English language.

V. S. Pritchett was born in Ipswich and lived in Paris, Spain, Ireland and London. Equally distinguished as an essayist and critic, his other best works are *The Complete Short Stories* (1990) and his autobiographies, *The Cab at the Door* (1968) and *Midnight Oil* (1971).

Posthumous publication.

E. Annie Proulx 1935–

1993   *The Shipping News*

The narrative method here is original, quirky, unforgettable, and so too are the characters. The style is brisk and authoritative, as though this was the only way that the story could be told. There is no nonsense; scenes are short. The author has no interest in heroics, or fine descriptions. The novel is full of details: boatbuilding, housebuilding, knot-making, bad weather, good weather, journalism. No one is perfect.

The place is Newfoundland, where our protagonist – it would be hard to call him a hero – Quoyle, a journalist down on his luck, comes with his aunt, a very tough old bird, and his two daughters. The atmosphere is awash with salt water and conversation and work half done. The sea and the wind and the vagaries of the human heart in equal proportions fuel the narrative. Slowly, Quoyle and his aunt, whose ancestors have come from this place, start to fit in with life in Newfoundland, becoming immensely lovable and credible characters. Proulx has the ability to make the most ordinary moments in their lives shine with a luminous grace, at times a mild incandescence. She keeps the novel moving in scenes which are constantly unexpected and original.

E. Annie Proulx was born in Connecticut. Her other novels include, *Postcards* (1991), *The Shipping News* and *Accordion Crimes* (1996), and *That Old Ace in the Hole* (2002) and the volumes of stories, *Heartsongs* (1988) and three volumes of Wyoming Stories, *Close Range* (1999), *Bad Dirt* (2004) and *Fine Just the Way It Is* (2008). *The Shipping News* won the National Book Award, a Pulitzer Prize and the Irish Times International Fiction Prize.

Age in year of publication: fifty-eight.

Mario Puzo 1920–1999

1969   *The Godfather*

In writing about the Sicilian Mafia at home in the playing fields of
the USA, Mario Puzo created a universal fairy tale in which, crossing
Greek gods with Robin Hood, he produced a new race of heroes,
criminals of honour, murderers with a sense of justice.

Such are the Corleones, ruled by Don Vito, the Godfather, a man
who protects all who belong to him. Within his kingdom he is
omnipotent, capable of arranging for the decapitation of a horse
and its insertion into a recalcitrant's bed whilst tending tomatoes in
his back garden. When we meet him, just after the Second World
War, the Mafia are on the point of change; drugs have entered the
scene, and ritual warfare breaks out between the Mafia families.
Corleone's sons, the rumbustious Sonny and the deceptive Michael,
move to centre stage, encircled by a gallery of Mafiosi men and
women, following the descent into open warfare like the chorus in
an opera. And indeed, in its viciously orchestrated finale, this is
what *The Godfather* is seen to be – a grand opera, in words and
action, its voice reaching the heavens.

One of the reasons *The Godfather*, the movie, is one of the best
ever made is that this novel bursts with Puzo's romantic characterization and unfailing verve for storytelling; it is one of the most
popular ever written.

Mario Puzo was born in Manhattan, New York, and lived in Bay Shore, Long Island.
He won an Oscar for his screenplay for the 1972 Francis Ford Coppola movie of his
book.

Age in year of publication: forty-nine.

Thomas Pynchon 1937–

1973   *Gravity's Rainbow*

The novel opens in London towards the close of the Second World War. A shadowy intelligence department discerns a statistical correlation between American GI Tyrone Slothrop's sexual encounters and V2 rocket hits. The implicit pun – cockup or conspiracy? – is typical and encapsulates one central unresolved theme of this complex novel. The wider canvas of the book is a phantasmagoric vision of Europe at melting point, a teeming zone where national borders and fixed identities of every kind have dissolved into a shimmering chaos of aggressively competing interests. Everyone is a displaced person. But out of the chaos the future is embodied in multinational corporations which transcend old boundaries and variously exploit, encourage, depend on and serve the demands of emerging technologies. As the secrets of the rocket are gathered and assembled, the autonomous human subject is disassembled: Slothrop literally disintegrates as a character. There are vast numbers of other characters and emblematic presences and set pieces idiomatically based on literary and film genres and cultural forms. Mysticism, drug culture, political history, pornography, cabaret, slapstick, comic books and gangster movies all provide frames of reference. Pynchon's sympathies are clearly with the underground, the alternative and the unofficial.

Linguistically, *Gravity's Rainbow* is extremely inventive, its densely textured, hallucinogenic prose keeping us off-balance and engaged, as well as entertained and astonished.

Thomas Pynchon was born on Long Island, New York. His other novels include *V* (1963) *Mason & Dixon* (1997), *Against the Day* (2006) and *Inherent Vice* (2009).
   Age in year of publication: thirty-six.

Jean Rhys 1894–1979

1966 *Wide Sargasso Sea*

Antoinette Cosway, the first Mrs Rochester, is the madwoman in the attic at Thornfield Hall who haunts Charlotte Brontë's *Jane Eyre*. *Wide Sargasso Sea* is set in Jamaica in the 1830s. Antoinette tells us of her childhood on the lush island, with its superstition and troubled colonial inheritance and, hovering over her family, an expression of the decadence of the white community, madness. Antoinette is an heiress and is married off to Rochester on his arrival in Jamaica. Fragile and unloved, she has little to seduce him with except the spells and magic of the island. The cadenced words Rhys uses, breathing the winds and smells of the islands, have a seductive, languid force which cruelly exposes Antoinette's failure.

But the first Mrs Rochester is no more than an imaginative starting point for Jean Rhys to imply larger meanings. In all her novels she is the great chronicler of the unprotected. Here, in dreamlike, exquisite prose, she recreates an experience of madness which is one of the most affecting in literature. Antoinette's fate resonates, it is symbolic. For Rochester can never discover the secrets of the islands; Rhys reveals them to be the forces that lie dormant in the weak, fluttering, disregarded beneath the political, racial and sexual tyrannies of the strong.

Jean Rhys was born in Dominica, and lived in Europe and in England. *Wide Sargasso Sea* appeared twenty-seven years after her earlier four novels and won the W. H. Smith Award and the Royal Society of Literature Award in 1967.

Age in year of publication: seventy-two.

Anne Rice 1941–

1976 *Interview with the Vampire*

There are very few popular novels as strange as this one, in which
Anne Rice began her journey into the world of vampires, beings of
beauty and horror whom she uses to tell us about how and what
we are.

Interview with the Vampire famously begins with a boy in a room
in San Francisco, listening, with a tape recorder, to the life story of
Louis, since 1791 a reluctant vampire consumed with anguish for
his lost mortal world. For two centuries he has endured the life of
a vampire, awake only at night, nauseated that he must kill human
beings to survive. New Orleans is the setting, and in that ravishing
city Louis's longing for redemption conflicts with the outrageous
enthusiasm for evil of his companion, the vampire Lestat. Vampires
live – and love – and drink blood for ever, so the story Louis tells
moves out to encompass other vampires' extravagant experiences.

Anne Rice imagines her erotic and mysterious tale in prose which
is luscious, decadent, rueful. The reader is transfixed by writing of
intense sexuality, conveying desire and desperation with vehement
force. With Mary Shelley's *Frankenstein* and Bram Stoker's
Dracula, this is one of the great tales of the supernatural, a mythic
exposition of the meaning of good and evil.

Anne Rice was born in and lives in New Orleans. This is the first of her bestselling
'Vampire Chronicles', and *The Witching Hour* (1990) is the first of her sequence of
novels about the Mayfair dynasty of witches. *Interview with the Vampire* was
adapted for film in 1994.

Age in year of publication: thirty-five.

Mordecai Richler 1931–2001

1971   *St Urbain's Horseman*

It is the 1960s. Jake Hersh and his large Jewish family have moved from Montreal to London, where he sets about making his career as a film director and raising his children. This novel is about the fate of being Jewish, male, ambitious and Canadian during those years. Jake's wallet and his penis, not to speak of his conscience, also play important roles in the novel. He is constantly under siege from producers; from his father; from his shadowy cousin who flits about the world as gambler, singer, horseman, rake and freedom fighter; as well as from the taxman; from an old friend who is slowly becoming rich and famous; and from his own mortality. He has broken his father's heart by marrying the beautiful Nancy, who is a gentile, and now he has also broken his mother's heart by being accused in an obscenity trial. This does not prevent her arriving in London to be by his side: she is nosy, racist and aggressive, and she drives Jake and Nancy out of their minds.

Jake is in constant flight from all that raw emotion. In England, he finds it hard to make much sense of the natives – there is a marvellous description of a ghastly English dinner party. While Jake's background renders him powerless in the public world of the Swinging Sixties – with actors, producers and TV people everywhere – he is tender and human in his own house with his wife and his three children. Jake Hersh is one of the great Jewish creations of the North American novel.

Mordecai Richler was born in Montreal and lived in England between 1959 and 1972, before he returned to Montreal. His other novels include *Cocksure* (1968), *Solomon Gursky Was Here* (1989) and *Barney's Version* (1997), which was adapted for film in 2010.

Age in year of publication: forty.

Marilynne Robinson 1943–

1980   *Housekeeping*

This is a most unusual novel, steeped in imagery of water and light, lakes and trains, and the mountains and snows of the north-eastern USA, where the town of Fingerbone seems to float.

Here live three generations of women. Sylvia, the grandmother, has three daughters: Molly, who becomes a missionary in China; Helen, who is mother to Lucille and Ruthie, but follows her father into the bottom of the lake; and Sylvie, a drifter. Ruthie is the teller of the tale and through her eyes we witness the quiet desperation of children at loose in the world. Grandmother dead, mother dead, they end up with Sylvie, who like all her sisters has eschewed for ever the accepted ways of being a woman. No housekeeping, cake-making or doily-crocheting for her, but magic in the mountains and love when required. As the disapproving townsfolk of Fingerbone move in, Sylvie and Ruth and Lucille variously set off on pilgrimage, the past travelling with them.

Marilynne Robinson has a rare eye for nature. Every insect, gnat on the wing, the shifting colours of snow, water, ice 'the colour of paraffin', 'plaited light' is closely observed. Smells too – woods with the odour of 'the parlor of an old house', cleanliness that smells like a sun-warmed cat. This is a wistful, laconic novel, illuminated by a haunting sense of the spirit of nature, and the spirit of place.

Marilynne Robinson was born in Idaho and lives in New England. Her other novels are *Gilead* (2004) which won the American National Book Critics Circle Award and a Pulitzer Prize and *Home* (2008) which won the Orange Prize. *Housekeeping* was filmed by Bill Forsyth in 1987.

Age in year of publication: thirty-seven.

171

Philip Roth 1933–

1997   *American Pastoral*

Swede Levov has everything: he is good-looking, a superb athlete, rich, a good father, a good son, a good citizen and a good employer; he is married to a former Miss New Jersey, with whom he has a pretty good sexual relationship; he is even-tempered, at ease with himself, mild-mannered, and much admired. Philip Roth establishes him convincingly and in great detail as one of the most contented men in America, post-Jewish, but deeply alert to his family's recent history as immigrants. Why then, does his daughter, Merry, become such a difficult presence in the house, refusing first to eat her food and then slowly becoming obsessed with the Vietnam War until she puts a bomb in the local store-cum-post office and disappears? Why do the riots in Newark, where the main Levov factory is sited, occur?

Roth dramatizes the significant events of the second half of the century in the United States in the life of one family, in one all-American consciousness. The result is a novel which is intensely absorbing and readable with some magnificent set scenes such as a forty-fifth anniversary high school reunion at which the narrator meets the Swede's brother among many others, and a dreadful dinner party at the end of the book which must be the best worst dinner party in all fiction. Swede Levov is alive in this book not as a recognizable type, but as a uniquely vivid personality. His character and his consciousness stay in your mind.

Philip Roth was born in Newark, New Jersey, and now lives in New York State. His other books include *Portnoy's Complaint* (1969), *Sabbath's Theater* (1995), *I Married a Communist* (1998), *The Plot Against America* (2001), *Everyman* (2006), *Exit Ghost* (2007) and *Indignation* (2008). *American Pastoral* won a Pulitzer Prize in 1998.
Age in year of publication: sixty-four.

Norman Rush 1933–

1991 *Mating*

Sometimes a novel appears which seems to have no direct literary antecedents, which is written in a tone which is new and fresh, and takes an approach which is original and startling. Norman Rush's *Mating* is such a book; it deals with Americans in Africa; it is narrated by a female anthropologist on the make in Botswana. She is urbane, intelligent and has read thousands of books, now she is in search of new sensations and a warm climate and useful research material. She is knowing and cynical and pushy, too selfconscious as a narrator to make the reader dislike her too actively, but so adept with sentences and paragraph endings and exciting prose rhythms, not to speak of self-knowledge, that the reader is full of admiration for her and deeply amused by her antics.

The novel, like all good comic writing, has a dark side: our heroine sets out on a lone journey across the desert to find the brave, remote Utopia which a shady and attractive American called Nelson Denoon has set up in a place called Tsau. While some of this is very funny indeed, there is something strange and un-settling about the social control which Nelson insists on, and the world he has invented. The tone of this book is flawless, the voice is utterly convincing.

Norman Rush was born in San Francisco and now lives in New York. He is the author of three works of fiction: a book of stories, *Whites* (1986), *Mating* which won the *Irish Times* Literature Prize and *Mortals* (2007). He lived and worked in Africa between 1978 and 1983.

Age in year of publication: fifty-eight.

Salman Rushdie 1947–

1981 *Midnight's Children*

Salman Rushdie is a born storyteller, whose work has been a turning point in the development and perception of modern Indian fiction. Rushdie vibrates with moral passion, with opinion and political belief. He is a dominating writer who engulfs his readers in fabulous stories. A master of comic invention, his characters, full of snot, ego and physical abnormality, leave you with a sense of having sneezed violently and laughed too long and too loudly. *Midnight's Children* – an allegory for India's recent history – leaves you with a great love for its Indian world.

Saleem Sinai is born on 15 August 1947, one of 1001 children, magically endowed, whose birth coincides with India's severance from Britain. Rushdie takes a savage swipe at Mrs Indira Gandhi and her notorious 1971 Emergency measures, whilst the fantastical plot and flamboyant narrative, centring on the swapping of two babies at birth, give entirely new excitement to the most traditional of British comic literary fancies. Rushdie is the kind of writer whose work is too much surrounded by academic contemplations of his 'magical realism' and 'post-modernism'. Readers need only concentrate on the ebullient Rushdie imagination and the wonder and entertainment of the novel itself.

Salman Rushdie was born in Bombay and educated in England. *Midnight's Children* won the Man Booker Prize. Other novels include *Shame* (1983), *The Moor's Last Sigh* (1995), *The Satanic Verses*, which won the Whitbread Fiction Award (1988), *The Ground Beneath Her Feet* (1999), *Fury* (2001), *Shalimar the Clown* (2005) and *The Enchantress of Florence* (2008). *Midnight's Children* was awarded the Man Booker of Bookers for the best Man Booker winning novel of the first forty years in 2008.

Age in year of publication: thirty-four.

J. D. Salinger 1919–2010

1951 *The Catcher in the Rye*

It is against the odds that this book, which had such a cult following in its day, and during the twenty years after publication, should still be fresh and fascinating. But it is still fresh and fascinating.

It tells the story of a few days in the life of a sixteen-year-old boy, Holden Caulfield who, about to be thrown out of another expensive school, escapes to New York. He books into a hotel, tries to lose his virginity, meets his kid sister – the scene where he sneaks into the apartment is magnificent – and ponders on the nature of things. His thought process is direct and unforgettable, he has odd fascinations and desires, he has great loves and hates, and he has a most peculiar and impressive sort of intelligence. Clearly, he needs psychiatric help, but psychiatric help also needs him (and his version of the encounter would be by far the more interesting). In other words, Salinger created a character who stays in the mind, whose first-person narrative the reader enters completely, whose verbal quirks – and he has many – remain funny and do not irritate, and whose story is likely to survive into the far future.

J. D. Salinger was born in New York. His other books include *Franny and Zooey* (1961) and two collections of stories. At the time of his death he had lived in seclusion in New Hampshire for many years.

Age in year of publication: thirty-two.

Frank Sargeson 1903–1982

1965   *Memoirs of a Peon*

Michael Newhouse, New Zealand Casanova, is the protagonist of this picaresque satire, which takes us from his childhood through his youth to his later years, by way of the procession of vociferous women who catch his eye.

Michael is a puffball of conceit, one of those oblivious men who specialize in making others aware of their own intelligence and emotional requirements. Thus a puzzled sense of indignation wafts through Michael's story, as he perambulates around Hamilton, Auckland, Wellington, Rotorua and the farms and towns of the North Island, extending his favours to mothers and daughters, utterly unconcerned with his country's complacent, puritanical values. Circumstance constantly foils him as he snuffles around for a corner of New Zealand life where a more diverse sexuality and a more willing attitude to copulation can be discovered.

Much of the pleasure of the novel comes from the comic grace of its narrative. Michael, raised by his Edwardian grandparents, has mastered a sedate New Zealand version of their formal prose which fluently decorates his descriptions of the 'raging pit of disappointment' fate always seems to place in his path. Seeming artless, this novel is artful, a radical work using the life and times of an intelligent rake to stick pins into conventional pomposities, in New Zealand in particular, and in the world in general.

Frank Sargeson was born in Hamilton, New Zealand, and lived and wrote in New Zealand. Important works are stories, *Conversations with My Uncle* (1936) and the novel *The Hangover* (1967).

Age in year of publication: sixty-two.

Paul Scott 1920–1978

1966   *The Jewel in the Crown*

India was the jewel in the crown of the British Empire, the possession most loved, most influential, most mourned. This is the first volume of Scott's grand work The Raj Quartet, and is set in 1942, the beginning of tumultuous times, with Europe at war and India in ferment, raging with anti-British riots, on the road to Independence.

Rape is at the centre of events, the political rape of India by the British, the physical rape of Daphne Manners by Indian peasants in the Bibighar Gardens in Mayapore, an outrage which reverberates immediately and for many years to come throughout the British community in India. And throughout the Indian communities too, for Daphne Manners had committed the unforgivable sin of falling in love with a Hindu, Hari Kumar. He, in turn, a Hindu educated at an English public school, is an outcast in both worlds.

Over Scott's vast landscape hovers the magnificence of India itself, almost a spectator, watching as Scott moves through the past, present and future to show that just as there was no mercy in British India for those who transgressed Imperial rules so, subtly, mercilessness became the weapon upon which the British impaled themselves.

Paul Scott was born and lived in London. The books that follow *The Jewel in the Crown* in The Raj Quartet, which became a successful television series in 1983 as *The Jewel in the Crown*, are *The Day of the Scorpion* (1968), *The Towers of Silence* (1971) and *A Division of Spoils* (1975). *Staying On*, a coda to The Raj Quartet, won the Booker Prize in 1977.

Age in year of publication: forty-six.

Hubert Selby Jr. 1928–2004

1964   *Last Exit to Brooklyn*

This is written with a freedom and flow and use of vernacular and voice that make it compelling and hugely readable. It is full of dirty language and dirty longings and dirty activity in general, including the most appalling violence; it is *strictly* for maiden aunts. It is a set of loosely connected stories in which some characters reappear, in which an all-night diner called The Greek regularly features. It includes some of the most unsavoury characters in modern fiction: a crowd who hang around the bar and beat up soldiers; a 'hip queer' called Georgette who is in love with a man called Vinnie and gets her leg cut by a knife by the crowd from the bar; and a woman called Tralala, one of the strongest characters in the book, who does the most appalling things to a soldier, generally hangs around looking for trouble and gets badly beaten in the end. One of the longest scenes is about a strike and a man called Harry, who is lazy and drunken and bloody-minded and unhappily married. Slowly, he realizes he is gay, and there are terrible consequences. The last scene is set in a low-life housing project. The tone of the book is cold and angry; Selby moves among the damned with an urge to tell us – to yell at us, if necessary – that this is what the American dream looks like now, that this is what hell is like, and there is no possibility of redemption. Some people, including the man who owned Blackwell's bookshop and Robert Maxwell, if you don't mind, succeeded in having the book banned for a short while when it was first published in England.

Hubert Selby Jr. was born in Brooklyn and lived in Los Angeles. His other books include *The Room* (1971) and *The Demon* (1976).

Age in year of publication: thirty-six.

Will Self 1961–

1993   *My Idea of Fun*

A Cautionary Tale

The junkies' group therapy session on page 175 of this novel would be its most savagely funny episode were it not for the ending, which provides the best last paragraph in modern fiction since Evelyn Waugh's *The Loved One*.

Will Self is a master of the grotesque and a pricker of conventional bubbles. In his hands the gentility of the English is hung, drawn, quartered and then incinerated for good measure. What could be more genteel than the south-coast town of Saltdean where Ian Wharton, our hero, first makes an appearance? Ian has eidesis, or photographic memory, which is good news for the Fat Controller, who descends upon Saltdean, Ian and anyone who gets in his way. He knows what to do with eidesis and how to turn the repulsive Ian into his significant other, using disgusting notions such as washing the face with semen soap as part of his regime.

This is a familiar England, where emphysemic pigeons land hacking on window sills and keel over dead, and where babies munch razor blades and happily burble blood. In this pungent Swiftian attack, using as many nasty images as possible, Self cuts to the gut and watches his subject bleed, usually to death. His writing is always elegant, his invention lurid and his mind a whirlpool of ideas.

Will Self was born and lives in London. His acclaimed short story collections are *The Quantity Theory of Insanity* (1991), *Grey Area* (1994) and *Tough, Tough Toys for Tough, Tough Boys* (1998). His other novels include *Great Apes* (1997), *How the Dead Live* (2000), *The Book of Dave* (2006) and *The Butt* (2008).

Age in year of publication: thirty-two.

Vikram Seth 1952–

1993   A Suitable Boy

At almost fifteen hundred pages long, *A Suitable Boy* is a sprawling, engaging and supremely confident novel set in the early years of independent India. It is essentially an old-fashioned tale of manners with a political background, as though Anthony Trollope had applied his skills to modern India. Its power and its extraordinary popularity derive from its array of characters and the real aura of warmth and glow and even love which surrounds their creation.

The main story is that of Mrs Rupa Mehra's efforts to find a suitable husband for her daughter Lata. Mrs Mehra is bossy, emotional and ambitious, and Lata is intelligent, wilful and also ambitious, but in a different way. The novel dramatizes the clash between traditional morals and manners and the vagaries of the young. Seth loves playing off the haughty against the humble, the feckless and charming against the conservative and staid. There is an infinite number of minor characters, and long, fascinating digressions about land reforms and other aspects of political life in India. The light tone, the delight in the detail, the eye for pure comedy and drama, and the fearless use of nineteenth-century literary devices make the book easy to read, and justify its astonishing length.

Vikram Seth was born in Calcutta. His other books include *An Equal Music* (1999), *The Golden Gate: A Novel In Verse* (1986), *From Heaven's Lake: Travels Through Sinkiang and Tibet* (1983) and *Two Lives* (2005).

Age in year of publication: forty-one.

Bapsi Sidhwa 1938–

1988   *Ice-Candy-Man*
(US: *Cracking India*)

From the lap of her beautiful Ayah, or clutching her skirts as Ayah is pursued by her suitors through the fountains, cypresses and marble terraces of the Shalimar Gardens, little Lenny observes the clamorous horrors of Partition. It is 1947. Lenny lives in Lahore, in the bosom of her extended Parsee family – Mother, Father, brother Adi, Cousin, Electric-Aunt, Godmother and Slavesister. Working for them, or panting after Ayah, are Butcher, the puny Sikh zoo attendant, the Government House gardener, the favoured Masseur, the restaurant-owning wrestler and the shady Ice-Candy-Man – Muslims, Christians, Sikhs, Hindus, friends and neighbours – until their ribald, everyday world disintegrates before the violence of religious hatred.

No other novel catches as this one does India's centuries-old ways of living with religious difference before Partition. Lenny is inquisitive and notices everything: clothes, smells, colour, the patina of skin, sex everywhere, and eyes – olive oil coloured, sly eyes, fearful eyes. In writing which is often lyrical, always tender and clever, with a nuance here, a touch there, Sidhwa shows us the seedbed of the Partition massacres – an abused Untouchable, the ritual disembowelling of a goat, a priest shuddering over the hand of a menstruating woman. This laughing, gentle tale, told through the eyes of innocence, is a testament to savage loss, and a brilliant evocation of the prowling roots of religious intolerance.

Bapsi Sidhwa was born in Karachi, grew up in Lahore and lives in Pakistan and the USA where she teaches. Other novels are *The Crow Eaters* (1978) and *The Bride* (1983).

Age in year of publication: fifty.

Alan Sillitoe 1928–2010

1958   *Saturday Night and Sunday Morning*

If this novel were written in French, it is possible that its protagonist, Arthur Seaton, would be an existentialist hero and the book an essential modern text; instead, it was written in English and it is known as a story about the antics and highjinks of the northern English working class.

In the first chapter our Arthur gets drunk, falls down the stairs, vomits all over a man and then takes a woman not his wife back to her house to bed while her husband is away. All of this is good fun, clearly written and well paced. But the novel then becomes darker and stranger.

Arthur lives at a considerable distance from his own experience. He prefers other men's wives, and feels only slightly uneasy when he meets the husband. He barely exists during his time in the factory. He has no religion, and the idea of England for him and his family, especially his cousins, is a sour joke. Even the idea of family and community has broken down. Arthur is unusual in modern fiction: he does not use his intelligence, it is not important for him, and yet he is never stupid – his instincts and his appetites dictate his behaviour, and this gives the novel great integrity and originality.

Alan Sillitoe was born in Nottingham and lived in both London and France. He wrote many novels including *The Loneliness of the Long Distance Runner* (1959). His *Collected Stories* were published in 1995.

Age in year of publication: thirty.

Iain Sinclair 1943–

1991 *Downriver (or the Vessels of Wrath): A Narrative in Twelve Tales*

This novel reads like an Old Testament for the east side of London. The tone is sombre and sinister, at times bitter and satirical, at times unsparing in its venom and hatred for England under Margaret Thatcher, who appears here as The Widow, and for ad-men, TV people and property speculators, not to speak of wine bars. The stories are loosely connected: there is a long interview; there are letters; characters appear, disappear, reappear, but Sinclair is at his most content when they disappear mysteriously, leaving strange traces. *Downriver* is a big *Ulysses* of a book which can contain anything and everything including echoes of and references to Conrad, Eliot (there is a newspaper-seller called Tiresias), William Blake, Lewis Carroll, Hawksmoor and many others living and dead, including the 'author' himself. There is an extraordinary rhythmic energy in Sinclair's prose; he loves big, long snaky sentences; huge lists; apocalyptic moments; quotations; arcane references; titles of obscure books; new characters; pubs; the Irish in London; place names. For him, capitalism is a form of terrorism, with money moving across London like napalm. Sinclair is interested in layers of narrative and layers of time and experience: he allows the past to haunt the book, allows whole sections to become quests for something half-lost, half-forgotten and misunderstood. His London is a dark ghostly place whose spirit is available only to the few; his book is one of the several enduring, playful – dare one say Modernist? – monuments to Thatcher produced by British novelists.

Iain Sinclair was born in Cardiff. He has lived in London for many years. His books include poetry, novels and the non-fiction *Lights Out for the Territory* (1995), a celebration of London, *London Orbital* (2002), *Edge of the Orison: In the Traces of John Clare's Journey Out of Essex* (2005) and *Hackney, That Rose-Red Empire: A Confidential Report* (2009).

Age in year of publication: forty-eight.

Khushwant Singh 1915–

1956   *Train to Pakistan*

'The summer of 1947 was not like other summers. Even the weather had a different feel in India that year.' So begins Singh's famous novel about the Partition of Pakistan from India, set in the small Punjabi frontier village of Mano Majra, where Hindu, Muslim and Sikh have lived together for thousands of years. This place of about seventy families is best known for its railway station; as the book opens a Sikh boy and a Muslim girl are making love in the fields.

But in 1947 nothing is really the same; there is quiet unease, then, dreadfully, the first train from Pakistan arrives. At first glance the train seems normal, then its ghostly silence reveals a thousand corpses, emitting the incredible stench of putrefying flesh. Soon, in the rains, comes a second train, with an even more horrific cargo. The effect is devastating; religious warfare breaks out, the Muslims of the village are evicted and put on a train for Pakistan. The massacres of Partition are just beginning.

The strength of this political novel lies in the vivacity and life Singh gives to the people of the Punjabi community. You can feel the presence of Mano Majra and hear the rhythm and laughter of its days. The loss of this, in this fine novel, is a striking testament to the devastating human cost of religious prejudice.

Khushwant Singh was born in Hadali, now in Pakistan, and lives in Delhi. Critic, journalist, historian, short story writer and distinguished editor, this was his first novel.

Age in year of publication: forty-one.

Jane Smiley 1951–

1991   *A Thousand Acres*

Zebulon County, Iowa, is the centre of the universe. Larry Cook owns one thousand acres of land there and farms it well. When the old monster suddenly decides it's time to pass the inheritance on to his daughters, he is infuriated when the youngest, Caroline, refuses the gift, whilst the older two, Rose and Ginny, accept it with reservations. Here we have the plot of *King Lear* transferred to the American Midwest, where it flourishes embedded in a recreation of every particular of farming and family life – the crops, the technology, the strawberry rhubarb pies, the mucking-out of farrowing pens, pizza with pepperoni and extra cheese – a multitude of tiny details evoking a world in which the land and its people seem indivisible.

Listening to the conversational voice of Ginny, we learn to see beyond the horizon. Jane Smiley's skill here is to use the great play but to look at *King Lear* through a different microscope. This transforms it into an epic study of a tyrant and of a family slowly disintegrating as old sins see the light of day. There is an airy clarity about this novel, echoing the rolling landscape of the American Midwest. Jane Smiley's graceful prose gives a similar beauty to the novel's moral twists, its passion for life and its emotional vitality.

Jane Smiley was born in Los Angeles and lives in California. *A Thousand Acres* won a Pulitzer Prize for Fiction and the US National Book Critics Circle Award.
Age in year of publication: forty.

Wole Soyinka 1934–

1965   *The Interpreters*

This is, to some extent, a dark and intricate comedy of manners set in Nigeria in the years after independence. It centres around the lives of a number of young intellectuals who are ambitious and uneasy in the new society, who meet regularly, drink a lot and talk all of the time. Much of the novel is made up of their dialogue. In scene after scene – the setting and tone change in each chapter – they confront their own idealism and sophistication, their own concern (or lack of concern) with manners and morals versus the concern (and lack of concern) of the society all around them. Religion, voodoo, art, government, journalism, sex, negritude, whiteness, etiquette (the wearing of gloves by women at certain parties, for example), Americans and Germans all come in for discussion and examination. (The American and the German in the book are treated with a good deal of contempt.) Soyinka makes none of his characters heroic in any way: they all have their weaknesses, but they also have a sort of innocence which makes them vulnerable. His ability to make dialogue sparkle – especially in the party scenes, where our intellectuals are at their most cynical and observant – is astonishing. At times, the novel demands close attention as Soyinka refuses to deal in easy realism; he makes no judgements or psychological assessments; he wrings a lot of emotion out of surface detail and moments of pure, careful observation, and manages – and this is one aspect of the genius of the book – to suggest that the people he has written about are doomed and will not have the strength to withstand the pressures of the society all around them.

Wole Soyinka was born in Nigeria. He was imprisoned for two years without trial in Nigeria in 1967–69. He has written many plays and has also published volumes of poems, memoirs and diaries. In 1986 he was awarded the Nobel Prize in Literature.

Age in year of publication: thirty-one.

Muriel Spark 1918–2006

1961   *The Prime of Miss Jean Brodie*

Muriel Spark is a novelist whose every line contains at least three insinuations. The oft-used phrase of Miss Jean Brodie, teacher *extraordinaire*, proclaiming that she is 'in her prime', are words now used by millions of women as they leave youth behind them.

It is Edinburgh in the 1930s. Miss Brodie is a mighty woman, forcefully politically incorrect, an individualist. She has her 'set' at Marcia Blanc School, five girls she raises to follow her principles, providing them with high culture, homing in particularly on Love. She involves them in her affairs with Teddy Lloyd the art master and Gordon Lowther the music master, and in her unfortunate penchant for Mussolini and his attractive fascisti. Her colleagues long to see the back of her. Miss Brodie confounds all their attempts until betrayed by one of her girls, raised to bite the hand that fed her.

This is a novel about nonconformity and spiritual pride and the nastiness of mankind, in particular in the shape of growing girls with peg legs and skinny souls. In spare, quirky dialogue, Miss Brodie and her disciples tempt fate with self-composure, accepting retribution with an imperturbable sense of guilt. This is a perfect novel, a classic, not a word out of place, laced with mother's wit and wisdom.

Muriel Spark was born in Edinburgh and lived in Rome. This novel has been adapted for the stage, the screen and for television. Her other novels included *Memento Mori* (1959), *The Girls of Slender Means* (1963) and *The Mandelbaum Gate* (1965).
   Age in year of publication: forty-three.

Christina Stead 1902–1983

1966   *Cotters' England*
(US: *Dark Places of the Heart*)

The rushing force of Christina Stead's novels explodes with words and myriad personalities and images: reading her is like standing under a gigantic waterfall, shouting your head off with glee. Nellie Cook, née Cotter, is a spellbinder and a possessive manipulator, one of those Socialists to the left of everything, living in a tatty house in Islington, working as a journalist on a London newspaper in those harsh years which followed the end of the Second World War. Nellie never draws breath. She lies, she fantasizes, she drinks, she smokes, wandering round the house all night blowing smoke into sleeping faces, talking to the moon. She is a seductress, an emotional gangster. Her brother Tom, to whom she remains locked in adolescent intimacy, uses women's hearts to wreak his havoc, oozing into them then out again, leaving a trail of slime behind. Cotters' England made them what they are: the poor Northern town of Bridgehead where poverty – incest? – has stunted and perverted them, like trees growing underground. Christina Stead writes at full pelt about politics, domestic life and sexual politics. She fizzes with ideas, making no judgements, revealing everything through the monologues and encounters of the people of Cotters' England. This is a great novel, savagely comic, demanding angry understanding for people and a country whose lives are blighted by the past.

Christina Stead was born in Sydney and lived in Europe and the USA from 1928 to 1974; on her return to Australia she was the first winner of the Patrick White Award. The best known of her eleven novels are *The Man Who Loved Children* (1940) and *For Love Alone* (1944).

Age in year of publication: sixty-four.

John Steinbeck 1902–1968

1952   *East of Eden*

Has there ever been a male American novelist who did not want to write a vast, defining history of the American soul? *East of Eden*, John Steinbeck's version, is set in rural California in the years around the turn of the century. It is the story of two families of settlers, the Trasks and the Hamiltons, but it is also the story of settlement itself, of the formation of the modern United States. 'The Church and the whorehouse arrived in the Far West simultaneously . . . the singing, the devotion, the poetry of the churches took a man out of his bleakness for a time, and so did the brothels.'

East of Eden is a rambling, garrulous family saga, with some deeply memorable characters (such as the Irishman Samuel Hamilton, the narrator's grandfather, and the dark, almost innocent Adam Trask), and some wonderful set scenes (such as the birth of the twins Aron and Caleb, whose lives dominate the second half of the book). In the novel there is a constant struggle, epic, almost biblical (sometimes knowingly echoing the Bible), between light and darkness, money and penury, bad land and good land, water and drought, men and women, fathers and sons and, perhaps most starkly and dramatically, brother and brother. Steinbeck has a natural skill as a storyteller, and manages to make this long and powerful saga hugely credible, readable and vivid.

John Steinbeck was born in rural California and spent most of his working life there and in New York. He won the Nobel Prize in Literature in 1962. His other novels include *Tortilla Flat* (1935), *Of Mice and Men* (1937) and *The Grapes of Wrath* (1939). *East of Eden* was made into a film in 1955 starring James Dean.

Age in year of publication: fifty.

Robert Stone 1931–

1981   *A Flag for Sunrise*

This novel is set in a fictional Central American country, its tone and sense of darkness and impending doom a cross between Conrad and Greene. Stone is at his best when he deals with loners and drifters, with drugs, uncertainty, paranoia, hallucinations, violence. There is a very accurate sense of the mixture of strange innocence and pervasive malevolence of the American intelligence services, and the novel is haunted by Vietnam, where Holliwell, one of the protagonists, has served.

A number of characters are moving and being moved towards catastrophe. One of them is a nun who has been told to be prepared to treat the injured in an insurrection, another a gunrunner, another a drug-crazed refugee from the United States, another a CIA man, another our friend Holliwell, an anthropologist, another a local cop. All of them are oddly powerless, only half-motivated; the writing is dense, concentrated and often powerful. Right in the middle of the book, there is a sensational description of Holliwell diving and the world under water: 'On the edge of vision, he saw a school of redfish whirl left, then right, sound, then reverse, a red and white catherine wheel against the deep blue.' At the novel's heart is the drama of covert action versus botched revolution, how easily things are misunderstood and half understood, and how strong the lure of violence.

Robert Stone was born in Brooklyn and now lives in Connecticut. His other novels include *A Hall of Mirrors* (1967), *Dog Soldiers* (1974), *Damascus Gate* (1998) and *Bay of Souls* (2003). *A Flag for Sunrise* won the PEN/Faulkner Award in 1981.
Age in year of publication: fifty.

David Storey 1933–

1976 *Saville*

For the English, the class system has been as fruitful a subject and as devastating to contemplate as serfdom was for the great Russian writers. *Saville* is an epic account of English life in the mid-twentieth century, told through the story of young Colin Saville, son of a miner, living in a worn-out mining community in south Yorkshire. Colin is an observer, strong in his silence, watching the weary lives of his father and mother – subsistence allowed them, but little else – as gradually the education he earns by winning a scholarship removes him from them and from his community. The school sequences are worthy of Dickens, all the more astonishing because they tell of such recent times.

Saville examines the consequences of poverty, class and environment, but there is patience and a sturdy intensity about this novel that makes the absence of so much a rich seam, for Storey elaborates many other themes – the conflict between the spiritual and the physical, the force of sexuality, the exact price paid by the English working class as they left the old ways behind. This is a realistic novel of power and beauty, full of sardonic humour and feeling and desire, using those passions of the soul which D. H. Lawrence and the Brontës drew upon to provide Storey's people with a stoic testament.

David Storey was born in Wakefield and lives in London. A playwright and a novelist, his famous first novel was *This Sporting Life* (1960). *Saville* won the 1976 Booker Prize. His other novels include *Radcliffe* (1963), *Pasmore* (1972) and *Thin-Ice Skater* (2004).

Age in year of publication: forty-three.

Francis Stuart 1902–2000

1971　*Black List, Section H*

This is an awkward book which has become a sort of underground classic. It is told in the third person by H, whose life and opinions mirror those of the author. Real characters such as Iseult Gonne, Stuart's first wife, Maud Gonne, her mother, and writers such as W. B. Yeats and Liam O'Flaherty stalk the pages. H is a damaged individual, estranged from accepted morality. Prison seems his natural habitat: he is incarcerated – as was Stuart – by the pro-Treaty side in the Irish Civil War and later by the Allies in the aftermath of the Second World War.

The story takes place in the literary bohemias of Dublin and London in the 1920s and 1930s and then in Berlin, where our hero goes to spend the war, as did Stuart. He is in search of punishment and redemption; he seeks an ark away from the hypocrisy he detects all around him. He finds solace among the defeated and the damned. He is obsessed by life in all its rich (and often funny) detail, by women, by horse-racing and poultry farming, by Dostoevsky, but he never loses sight of his own distance from things, his deep alienation. *Black List, Section H*, written in the early 1960s, in its mixture of nihilism and visionary anarchism makes William Burroughs look like a pussycat.

Francis Stuart was born in Australia and brought up in Northern Ireland. He lived in Dublin. His other novels include *The Pillar of Cloud* (1948) and *Redemption* (1949), both of which deal with the war and its aftermath.

Age in year of publication: sixty-nine.

William Styron 1925–2006

1967   *The Confessions of Nat Turner*

This book caused considerable controversy when it was first published. It is based on the true story of Nat Turner, who led a slave revolt in Virginia in 1831; it is narrated in the first person. Styron, who is white, took considerable liberties with the historical context; he also – and this caused the greatest offence – invented a black consciousness and an African–American voice and sensibility at a time when black intellectuals no longer thanked white liberals for inventing their voices. Thirty years later, however, read as a novel, *The Confessions of Nat Turner* has great emotional impact; as a psychological portrait, it is credible and complex and unexpected.

Styron's Nat Turner is not a typical slave: he learns to read, he knows the Bible and he is, at one point, offered the possibility of freedom. Thus the drudgery and misery of his later years are rendered all the more sharply painful, and make his coldness and calculating determination to exterminate 'all the people in Southampton County and as far beyond as destiny carried me' understandable. The narrative is beautifully written, with echoes of the Bible; the mind which is dramatized here is educated and sophisticated, capable of subtle analysis and careful discrimination. Styron's triumph is to make this voice convincing and absorbing and to make Nat Turner's actions plausible and dramatic.

William Styron was born in Virginia and lived in Connecticut. His other novels include *Set This House on Fire* (1960) and *Sophie's Choice* (1979).
Age in year of publication: forty-two.

Graham Swift 1949–

1996   *Last Orders*

Vic and Ray, Lenny and Vince set off in a car from Bermondsey in the East End of London to throw into the sea off Margate Pier on the Kent coast the ashes of their friend Jack, the butcher. In their laconic voices – memories expressed in the vernacular of South London – secret histories are revealed so that the journey becomes a Chaucerian pilgrimage with every character placed before us as in a lost medieval fresco in some old English church.

Among Swift's accomplishments as a novelist are his great technical skill and his imaginative intimacy with his characters: we hear the accents in which they speak and think. Jack, Ray, Mandy, Amy – all their separate voices, talking to us, give them living shape. These are ordinary English human beings who live on an island surrounded by sea, battered by wars and plagued by institutions distinguished for their lack of concern for lesser lives and vanishing ways. Their dense little world is crammed with the grief of families, but also with the jokes, popular songs, boozers, betting shops and the sad 'things that do and don't get told'.

Last Orders is an inspired novel about love, patience and redemption, about great events remembered in the tiny bits and pieces of memory and feeling which make up a people's history.

Graham Swift was born in and lives in London. He is the author of several other novels, among which are *Waterland* (1983), *Ever After* (1992), *The Light of Day* (2003) and *Tomorrow* (2007). *Last Orders* won the 1996 Booker Prize.

Age in year of publication: forty-seven.

Amy Tan 1952–

1989   *The Joy Luck Club*

One of the most fascinating aspects of emigration is that moment when the last generation to remember the old country gives way to the next. The Chinese who fled the invading Japanese in the Second World War and escaped to San Francisco are Amy Tan's emigrants. Turn and turn about, four Chinese mothers and their Chinese–American daughters tell us their stories. Their meeting place is the Joy Luck Club, source of all laughter and news from the past and present: here the mothers meet, eat, play mah-jong and boast about their Chinese–American daughters. The women expect every achievement from their American-educated offspring, but illogically continue to demand Chinese obedience and compliance. This conflict, together with their vibrant misuse of the American language, give the battles between mother and daughter an irresistible tang, as, gradually, past catastrophes are revealed that make their anxious bullying entirely understandable. How can mother not always know best when she has survived arranged marriages, concubinage, abandonment and worse?

Amy Tan is a natural entertainer, her Joy Luck ladies emitting a quickness of wit and a particularly attractive and Chinese kind of inquisitiveness and gossipy good sense. She writes simply, with laughter always on the tip of her pen. And she is wise: through her eyes intolerable tragedies become part of life, to be accepted, remembered and honoured.

Amy Tan was born in California and lives there. This first novel was an international bestseller and was followed by *The Kitchen God's Wife* (1991), *The Hundred Secret Senses* (1996), *The Bonesetter's Daughter* (2001) and *Saving Fish from Drowning* (2005).

Age in year of publication: thirty-seven.

Donna Tartt 1964–

1992   *The Secret History*

Richard Papen recalls in solitude his years as an impressionable student amongst a small but gilded group at Hampden College, Vermont, a hermetically sealed place of education in the chilly north-east of the United States. In that longed-for but exclusive world he becomes infatuated with Henry, Bunny, Francis and the twins Charles and Camilla, privileged and self-confident youths studying classical Greek under the effete care of Julian Morrow, Svengali of this elite coterie. The Dionysian murder these five have already committed is as far from ancient truth and beauty as you can get: their second murder, to conceal the first, gradually reveals how flimsy an edifice the life of the intellect can be. This is a bravura performance, a novel of high ambition fully achieved. Tartt elaborates the style and tone of this favoured world with chilling control, making the arrogance and snobbery of her chosen few seem almost innocent. Vermont itself and the habits of college life are so solidly created that whether munching cream cheese and marmalade sandwiches, gobbling alcohol and drugs or declaiming in ancient Greek, the charm and individuality of each member of the group are firmly established. These are only a few of the secrets of this unusual literary thriller. Others lie in Tartt's clever manipulation of suspense and the sardonic note she injects into these confessions, final touches of literary magic.

Donna Tartt was born in Mississippi and lives in New York. This, her first novel, was an international bestseller, as was her second, *The Little Friend* (2002).

Age in year of publication: twenty-eight.

Elizabeth Taylor 1912–1975

1957 *Angel*

Elizabeth Taylor is one of those English novelists who choose small parameters in which to work upon the monumental fragilities of life. Of her eleven novels, models of graceful prose and sharp humour, *Angel* is her magnum opus. This story of the life and times of Angelica Deverill – Angel – is told with ironic elegance. Angel, prickly, vain and deluded, writes popular novels notable for their romantic asininity and for their vast sales. She uses her money to discard her humble beginnings, to buy a beautiful husband – Esme Howe Nevinson, minor painter, major rogue – and to live in Paradise House, ultimately only with her sister-in-law Nora and an assembly of cats. *Angel* is resolutely single-minded but Elizabeth Taylor, always an emotional wizard, so cleverly insinuates the isolation behind her cranky misbehaviour that when Angel dies we are loath to see her go. In the Taylor world, lives that seem uneventful prove quite otherwise. She has an iron-like but delicate way of disinterring maggots of egoism, self-deceit and hypocrisy, for which sins she has much compassion, moving on, an expert observer of the vagaries of desire and love, to reveal the small cruelties we inflict upon those nearest to us, wryly pointing out where real love often lies.

Elizabeth Taylor was born in Berkshire and lived in Buckinghamshire. This novel was chosen by the British Marketing Council in 1983 as one of the best ten novels published since the Second World War. She was equally famous for her short stories.
Age in year of publication: forty-five.

Peter Taylor 1917–1994

1986   *A Summons to Memphis*

This novel is written in a style which is deceptively languid and effortless. The story it tells is tangled and disturbing even though it is set in a world of good manners and considerable comfort in the South of the United States in the years between about 1930 and 1970. The Carver family come from old money; old Mr Carver's rebellion consisted of going to Vanderbilt University instead of Princeton, and marrying slightly above himself. He, however, did not allow his four children to rebel at all; *A Summons to Memphis* tells the story of what they did to him in return. The central event in their childhood was a move from Nashville, where they were happy, to Memphis after their father was half-ruined by a colleague. They never got used to the new city. Their father broke up central love affairs in three of their lives; the fourth was killed in the war. The two girls never married; they run a business now and move around Memphis like teenagers. The narrator Philip is the one who got away. He lives uneasily in Manhattan, but in the months after his mother's death he is constantly summoned to Memphis where his father, aged eighty-one, is also acting like a teenager and is planning to get married. That is, until the two sisters, brilliant creations both, pounce on him and his intended and then move in on top of him and set about making his life a misery. Taylor steers between a Southern Gothic and a deeply civilized, deadpan and almost distant style, all the more to inspire the reader with awe and fascination. This book can be read in one sitting without once looking up.

Peter Taylor was born in Tennessee and lived in Charlottesville, Virginia. He is the author of many collections of short stories. *A Summons to Memphis* won a Pulitzer Prize.

Age in year of publication: sixty-nine.

Ngugi Wa Thiong'o 1938–

1967   *A Grain of Wheat*

This subtle, melancholy novel is set on the eve of Kenyan independence; its characters include a number of British administrators, but the narrative focuses mainly on a group of characters who have been involved in one way or another in the struggle for independence. They are Karanja, who worked for the British and is now in great danger; Gikonyo, who was detained by the British and whose wife had a baby with Karanja while he was away; and Mugo, who was viewed as a hero for his resistance to torture and beatings while in detention, and has been asked to make the main speech on Independence Day in his village. But Mugo was, in fact, the one who betrayed Kihiki, a man who was hanged by the British.

There is a very sharp portrait in this novel of the British as irrational and defeated, misguided idealism mixed with vicious cruelty. But the violence of the Mau Mau years has defeated everybody, has left a legacy of treachery and fear and poison. There is no disillusion, because there was no illusion in the first place. Courage is shown as a form of hatred or a form of passivity. In all the accounts we have of a national liberation, this is the most sober and clear-eyed, and the most angst-ridden, even though it allows the characters, even the British, golden moments which are rendered with great beauty and affection. But, it is clear, nothing has been solved by independence.

Ngugi Wa Thiong'o was born in Kenya and after a brief teaching spell in the USA, now lives in Nairobi. His early novels, including *A Grain of Wheat* and *Petals of Blood* (1977), were written in English, but more recent novels such as *Wizard of the Crow* (2006) have been written in Kikuyu.

Age in year of publication: twenty-nine.

John Kennedy Toole 1937–1969

1980   *A Confederacy of Dunces*

This book, set in New Orleans, is written with an enormous flawless comic flair, an eye for the absurd detail and an ear for the perfectly placed non sequitur. It tells the story of the truly dreadful Ignatius Reilly, vastly overweight, an intellectual bully, constantly burping and deeply unpleasant in every possible way. Other characters include his long-suffering mother and several of her acquaintances and a policeman whose job it is to sit in the public toilets of a bus station seeking out suspicious characters when he is not made to dress up in absurd costumes by his superior. Ignatius's mother wants him to get a job; she has spent a fortune on his education. He is so arrogant and smelly and rude that no one, it seems, will employ him until he approaches Levy Pants, whose employees are even more wildly insane than our hero; later he works selling hot dogs, but eats more than he sells. His views on the question of race do not bear repetition: 'I do admire the terror which Negroes are able to inspire in the hearts of some members of the white proletariat and only wish . . . that I possessed the ability to similarly terrorize.' The writing is always controlled, and brilliant and pointed. This is Southern Gothic at its most complete and perfect.

John Kennedy Toole was born in New Orleans and committed suicide after this book had been turned down for publication by innumerable publishers. The novel was finally published by Louisiana State University Press due to his mother's persistence and the novelist Walker Percy's help. It then won a Pulitzer Prize.

Posthumous publication.

William Trevor 1928–

1991   *Reading Turgenev*

'Only love matters in the bits and pieces of a person's life,' writes William Trevor. A splendid evoker of such bits and pieces, his novels are sometimes set in England, sometimes in Ireland, but always, in ironic, simple prose, he delves into the iniquities and failures and necessary forgiveness which constitute our lives.

Mary Louise Dallon, his heroine, lives outside a small Irish town, a daughter of one of its few Protestant families. Suitable men to marry are thin upon the ground, and when she marries Elmer Quarry, a bachelor twice her age and owner of the town's drapery shop, she confronts his sexual inadequacies and his two sisters' viperous natures with an innocence which is fatal. Things go from worse to worst when Mary Louise meets her cousin Robert again, and childhood love re-emerges, taking up every inch of Mary Louise's heart. He reads her Turgenev; they look for herons. Matters resolve themselves by means of rat poison, fishcakes, toy soldiers and homes for the insane. William Trevor is a writer in the finest tradition; one with particular sensitivity for people who cannot manage as others do. His exquisite style uses laughter and pity in classic contemplations of the tidal dramas human flesh is heir to.

William Trevor was born in County Cork, educated in Ireland and has lived in Devon in later life. He has won many awards for his fiction which includes *The Children of Dynmouth* (1976), *Fools of Fortune* (1983), *Felicia's Journey* (1994) and *Love and Summer* (2009). *Reading Turgenev* was published with another novella, *My House in Umbria*, in a single volume entitled *Two Lives*.

Age in year of publication: sixty-three.

1953   *The Palm-Wine Drinkard and his dead Palm-Wine Tapster in the Deads' Town*

'I was a palm-wine drinkard since I was a boy of ten years of age,' the novel begins. But on the death of his palm-wine tapster, our narrator, who is not satisfied, saying that 'the whole people who had died in this world did not go to heaven directly, but they were living in one place somewhere in the world.' He decides to travel in search of his palm-wine tapster in the world between heaven and earth. The novel is the story of his fantastic adventures. It reads like a folk tale, part of an oral tradition; it is told simply, and the style is artless and increasingly effective. In every paragraph a new monster or threat appears, or a new journey, or a new strange vision; there is constant metamorphosis. He finds a wife along the way; the tone is wide-eyed, innocent, even-handed. Most of his escapades are from a world of nightmare and unconscious dread; both Jung and Freud would have had a field day with this book. What distinguishes it is the quality of its imaginative energy, its refusal to settle for a single story or a single meaning. The sense of the dead and the living and the half-dead sharing this strange world is very powerful and the use of the storyteller's art and the sheer verve of the narrative make this one of the best African novels to appear over the past fifty years.

Amos Tutuola was born in Nigeria and worked in Lagos and Ibadan in Western Nigeria most of his life. His other novels include *My Life in the Bush of Ghosts* (1954) and *Pauper, Brawler and Slanderer* (1987).

Age in year of publication: thirty-three.

Anne Tyler 1941–

1988   *Breathing Lessons*

Maggie Moran, wife to Ira for twenty-eight years, is a 'whiffle-head', one of those women who tell a perfect stranger the entire story of their life, with attendant husband and children standing by, rigid with embarrassment. *Breathing Lessons* tells the story of twenty-four hours in the life of the sublime Maggie, Ira and their two disappointing children, Jesse and Daisy: 'Mom? Was there a certain conscious point in your life when you decided to settle for being ordinary?'

Maggie pursues happiness, indeed insists upon it. As they take a trip to the funeral of the husband of Maggie's best friend Sabrina (where Maggie sings 'Love is a Many Splendoured Thing', one of Anne Tyler's unsurpassed virtuoso performances), dreams end in disaster, but real life taps Maggie buoyantly on the shoulder.

Anne Tyler's novels chronicle with intricate delicacy the scratchy habits of domestic life; her affectionate disembowellings of marital and family arrangements send out simultaneous signals of anguish and humour, always captured in small details, delicately inserted, almost thrown away. Baffled but hopeful, Tyler people are in total command of pathos and humour, and, using the author's greatest gift, they keep the reader teetering on the edge of laughter – the out-loud kind, and the flickering kind – producing a constant humming impatience for the next page.

Anne Tyler was born in Minneapolis and lives in Baltimore. *Dinner at the Homesick Restaurant* (1982) and *The Accidental Tourist* (1985, filmed 1988) are two of the best of her novels. *Breathing Lessons* won a Pulitzer Prize.

Age in year of publication: forty-seven.

John Updike 1932–2009

1960–1990   The Rabbit Quartet

Rabbit, Run (1960), Rabbit Redux (1971), Rabbit is Rich (1981), Rabbit at Rest (1990)

These four novels tell the story of Harry 'Rabbit' Angstrom, American male. We first meet him aged twenty-six, an ex-basketball player married to Janice whom he abandons, pregnant, for Ruth. Rabbit's women – his wife, his mom, his mother-in-law, his sister, his daughter-in-law and his varied mistresses and encounters are alive in every varicose vein, as is Rabbit's organ itself which takes on a life of its own, leading Rabbit to infidelities and betrayals, always rising and falling, jiggling around, no peace to be had at all. Life with Janice under these circumstances always remains complex and reflects the times – the Vietnam War, race relations, a society in turmoil on all fronts. The misdemeanours of Rabbit and Janice's son Nelson echo everything that has gone before, and as their lives progress, sex overapplied and misused becomes a mordant, always explicit, analogy for the disintegration of the United States under a barrage of drugs, wars, junk food and TV; eerily predicting too, Clintonesque adventures to come.

Updike is an irresistibly funny writer with a deceptively easy style. His sense of comedy and his quirky philosophical contemplations flash through this quartet, a contemporary American classic. Each novel can be read separately, but read them all; each one seems even better than the one before.

John Updike was born in Pennsylvania and lived in Massachusetts. Novelist, poet, essayist and short story writer, he was awarded a Pulitzer Prize for both *Rabbit is Rich* and for *Rabbit at Rest*.

Age in years these books were published: twenty-eight–fifty-eight.

Barbara Vine (Ruth Rendell) 1930–

1986   *A Dark-Adapted Eye*

Ruth Rendell writes under two names, her own and that of Barbara Vine. The Rendell novels are, generally, detective novels centring on Chief Inspector Wexford and the fictional southern English town of Kings Markham, whilst those written under the name of Barbara Vine are psychological novels in the manner of Dickens or Wilkie Collins. To start on her detective novels, read *From Doon with Death* (1964), a Rendell classic. And so too is *A Dark-Adapted Eye*, her first Barbara Vine novel. Set in Suffolk, mostly in the 1950s, this story of the Longley women, Vera and Eden, uses the things that English gentlewomen do – embroidery, baking, keeping a spotless house, making do and behaving as women should – as a foil for what they also do in secrecy, in pursuit of power. This story of love and murder between sisters has such impact that the very trees in the Suffolk lanes arch up to warn of the damage wreaked, particularly on their menfolk, by women such as these, tight-laced in snobbery, fighting for life within rigid social rules.

There is more to this wily novel than meets the eye. The Longley clan always speak in 'half-shades and half-truths' and thus Barbara Vine ends this novel . . . the other half of the truth being there for us to find out if we can.

Ruth Rendell was born in London and lives in Suffolk. Many of her novels have won awards and have been televised. *A Dark-Adapted Eye* won the Mystery Writers of America Edgar Allan Poe Award.

Age in year of publication: fifty-six.

Alice Walker 1944–

1982   *The Color Purple*

'Take off they pants, I say, and men look like frogs to me.' This is the voice of Celie, who writes most of the letters in this novel. Her voice is vivid and strong, her intelligence is sharp. Although the novel is set in the American Deep South, whites appear in the book as a sort of afterthought; the book is more concerned with the relationships between black men and women, between Celie and her stepfather (who is the father of her children), between Celie and her wastrel husband, between Celie's stepson Harpo and his wonderful wife Sophie and his second wife Squeak. These relationships are all fraught and difficult, if also various and immensely interesting, in sharp contrast to the relationships between the women, especially that between Celie and the singer Shrug, whom her husband loves and brings home and who eventually rescues Celie, which is tender and complex and sexual (it is clear from very early in the book that Celie is gay).

The other letter-writer in the book is Celie's sister Nettie, the clever one in the family, who has escaped and gone to Africa and whose letters have been withheld by Celie's husband. This relationship, too, is full of tenderness, love and warmth. Alice Walker risks a great deal with Celie's voice – her spelling, for example, is often wildly inaccurate and there is an innocence about her observations which plays against her general shrewdness – but succeeds in creating one of the most memorable characters in contemporary American fiction.

Alice Walker was born in Georgia and now lives in San Francisco. *The Color Purple* won a Pulitzer Prize and was made into a film by Steven Spielberg in 1985.

Age in year of publication: thirty-eight.

Sylvia Townsend Warner 1893–1978

1954   *The Flint Anchor*

There is no one quite like Sylvia Townsend Warner. She has her own way of looking at the world and a breadth of vision as open as the East Anglian sea and sky she writes about here.

In the early nineteenth century, Anchor House in Loseby, Norfolk, is the home of John Barnard, a house made of the dark flint of the area, as is the soul of the man himself. A man of lofty morality, he fears 'nothing but God', an emotion which sours his life and that of his family – wife Julia, sipping rum all day, and wimpish children, the Wilberforces and Euphemias of the time. But then there is his pretty daughter Mary, a serio-comic creation of the first order, who raises the pursuit of self-interest to a high art. Around them bustle those instigators of teas, dinners, walks, visits, attendances at church – not to mention the surprising fishermen of the village: inventive disturbers of all of those who live behind the sharp walls of the House of Flint.

Warner is not a romantic: she has a keen eye for malevolence and other flaws of the soul, yet she absorbs us totally in the personalities and daily concerns of her characters, unheroic though they be. Every novel Sylvia Townsend Warner wrote was entirely different from its predecessor in subject, period and story, but all of them are the work of a great English stylist, and all are diverting, funny and very, very clever. This little-known novel is a lost treasure.

Sylvia Townsend Warner was born in Harrow, Middlesex, and lived mostly in Dorset. She was a poet, novelist, short story writer and biographer. Her other notable novels are *Lolly Willowes* (1926), *Mr Fortune's Maggot* (1927) and *The Corner That Held Them* (1948).

Age in year of publication: sixty-one.

1952–1961   The Sword of Honour Trilogy

Men at Arms (1952), Officers and Gentlemen (1955),
Unconditional Surrender (1961)

This is a beautifully structured and deeply melancholy account of England and the Second World War, which also contains moments and scenes of pure hilarity. It is written in a spirit of great tenderness and tolerance and a sort of humility. Guy Crouchback is the scion of one of the great English recusant families now down on its luck. He lives alone in a castle in Italy. His wife, the irrepressible Virginia – a figure straight out of Waugh's earlier fiction – has left him, marries twice more, and pops up throughout the trilogy to humiliate him. The first novel opens at the outbreak of war when Guy, at the age of thirty-five, returns to England and joins up. The trilogy then deals with his sensations and experiences. He is sensitive, watchful, loyal, good-humoured and a devout Catholic, but he is also distant, awkward, slightly priggish and self-centred. His character works superbly in the books because his loneliness and sadness are absorbed by the war, and his personality undergoes many tests and changes – he sees action in Africa, Egypt, Crete and Italy. The novels move fast in a series of short scenes; Waugh's comic skills are used with great effect, especially in minor characters and the whole business of military operations and regulations. Guy's father, retired now, living in a hotel by the sea, is one of the miraculous creations in the books.

Evelyn Waugh was born in West Hampstead, London. Most of his working life was spent in London and travelling until he finally settled in Somerset. He wrote many novels and travel books. They include *Decline and Fall* (1928), *A Handful of Dust* (1934), *The Loved One* (1948), *Brideshead Revisited* (1945) and *The Ordeal of Gilbert Pinfold* (1957).

Age in years these books were published: forty-nine – fifty-eight.

Fay Weldon 1933–

1980   *Puffball*

Fay Weldon's role in late twentieth-century literature is that of the good witch, her special brew being woman and man, particularly when both are embroiled in marriage. In *Puffball* she adds to the potion by placing the marriage of Liffey and Richard within a larger structure, in which the spite of woman for woman is hilariously and lethally exposed.

Liffey is an excellent Weldon heroine – a good woman, kind and loving. Husband Richard is an ambitious advertising man, pompous in London, a bore when they move to the country, near Glastonbury, to breed. It is hell: the cottage is hell, the neighbours, Mabs and Tucker, are hell. Liffey's womb takes on a life of its own as it battles to survive the general onslaught; and indeed there is no modern novel that so nimbly takes us through that rarely described experience, the biological stages of pregnancy, and the exact surgical instructions necessary to perform a Caesarean. If there is a message here, and all novels with happy endings like *Puffball* offer one, it is that women are biologically discriminated against by God, should he exist, and by Nature, if he doesn't.

Fay Weldon is a perspicacious, compelling storyteller who makes you laugh – and weep – for the malice and ill-will we mortals hurl at each other in the name of love.

Fay Weldon was born in Worcestershire, brought up in New Zealand, and lives in London. She is a novelist, TV, radio and stage dramatist, journalist and commentator. Among her novels are *Praxis* (1979) and *The Life and Loves of A She-Devil* (1986).
  Age in year of publication: forty-seven.

Irvine Welsh 1958–

1993   *Trainspotting*

'Ah don't hate the English. They're just wankers. We are colonized by wankers. We can't even pick a decent, vibrant, healthy culture to be colonized by. No. We are ruled by effete arseholes. What does that make us? The lowest of the fuckin low, the scum of the earth.' Meet Mark Renton – Scottish heroin junkie, fan of Hibs United, hopeless shoplifter, Iggy Pop fiend, and the hero of Irvine Welsh's explosive and hilarious novel.

Set among Edinburgh's troubled housing estates, *Trainspotting* brings a whole new world into the novel, a new kind of person, a low-life humour and demotic energy. These are mostly characters who have never known work, who defy the materialist ethos of 1980s Britain, and who embrace music, drink and drugs as the only truth in a nation of lies.

Though Welsh owes something to Burroughs and Ballard, and to his late compatriot Alexander Trocchi, he draws much more from popular culture, punk rock and the rave scene. The episodic rush of *Trainspotting* is remarkable because of the way it deals with class politics and for the power and range of its voice. It is interesting also because it offers a breathtakingly vivid picture of lives that are never written about. The world of *Trainspotting* is not a charming Scotland of castles and Bravehearts; it is a place of new sicknesses. As Renton says of an old auntie who falls in love with Romantic Edinburgh: 'Instead ay a view ay the castle she'd goat a view ay the gasworks. That's how it fuckin works in real life, if ye urnae a rich cunt wi a big fuckin hoose n plenty poppy.'

Irvine Welsh was born in Edinburgh and now lives in London. His other books include *The Acid House* (1994), *Ecstasy* (1996), *Filth* (1998), *Glue* (2001), *Porno* (2003) and *Crime* (2008). *Trainspotting* was filmed in 1996.

Age in year of publication: thirty-five.

Eudora Welty 1909–2006

1972 *The Optimist's Daughter*

Eudora Welty is a writer who has listened closely all her life. Living in Mississippi, her language merits recording – the singing, teasing English of the South.

She is the alert observer of small communities of people, families, everyday things. There is a Welty miasma, an atmosphere in which wildly comic words and vigorous behaviour scuffle with a sense of loss, failure or grieving. Thus, minor incidents take on major significance, and this is exactly so in this account of Laurel's return home for the illness and death of her father, Judge McKelva. Born optimist, 'fairest, most impartial, sweetest man', after the early death of Laurel's mother Becky – beloved Becky – he has married the young and malign vulgarian Wanda May, a vixen on green high heels. Every neighbour and friend comes to greet Laurel, and each object in the old family home comes alive for her return: the sewing machine, the gooseneck lamp, cupboards 'with the earnest smell of mouse'.

Welty's theme is memory, the confusion of life and the comedy of love, love of all kinds: the friends and neighbours at the funeral are a melodic Mississippian Greek chorus to Laurel's recollections. Eudora Welty is a southern magician, a mistress of words that tell us the meaning and value of the things and people we live among, and of the past.

Eudora Welty was born and lived in Jackson, Mississippi, and wrote five novels and many short stories. This partially autobiographical novel won a Pulitzer Prize in 1973.

Age in year of publication: sixty-three.

211

Rebecca West 1892–1983

1957   *The Fountain Overflows*

Everything Rebecca West did, and wrote, had determination about it. This novel has the intense charm of a classic Edwardian novel recounted in the expressive prose of that time, yet it was written in the 1950s.

Rose Aubrey tells the story of her childhood. She lives with her parents, brother and two sisters in South London, in the sort of poverty associated with wayward and improvident fathers. This adored man, Piers, is given to gambling and speculation, whilst security of some kind is provided by Rose's artistic, serious mother, so that some of what we associate with such childhoods is still there: the hearths, the gaslight, the walks, the teas, and most of all the music – for the love of music and the talent to make it is the only deliverance the girls can hope for.

Much of the novel is autobiographical. Rebecca West was Rose Aubrey, and the power of the novel comes from her resolute belief in the way things were. Into her portrait of Piers Aubrey, her father, she pours dreams of worship: 'Our Papa was far handsomer than anybody else's . . . he stood like a fencer in a picture . . .' These long-remembered cries are like ghosts in the novel giving it the keenness of a lament – for a family life that could have been, for the artistic aspirations that, instead, made life worth living.

Rebecca West was born in London of a Scottish mother and Irish father. She lived in London and was a celebrated journalist, novelist, political commentator and critic. Her classic study of the Balkans, *Black Lamb, Grey Falcon* was published in 1942.

Age in year of publication: sixty-five.

Edmund White 1940–

1982   *A Boy's Own Story*

Edmund White's *A Boy's Own Story* tells the story of an unnamed American white boy growing up gay in the 1950s. It is a careful and close examination of an effort to invent an identity. Nothing is taken for granted. His parents seem distant and strange even before their divorce, and after the divorce they emerge as capricious and irrational, as does the boy's sister. He is alone with his sexuality. He wants, and the sense of his desire in the book is overwhelming, to sleep with a man, an older man, a younger man, any man, just as he wants to escape from home. But he does not want to deal with the implications of any of this and this makes his story complex and fascinating. He does not want to become the narrator of *The Beautiful Room Is Empty* (1988) or *The Farewell Symphony* (1997), White's two novels which deal with our hero as a young gay man on the rampage and an older man in the age of AIDS. The sense of honesty in the book is matched by the writing, which is wonderfully dense and sharp at the same time; White understands, as almost no one before him did, how perfect the novel form is for a dramatization of gay identity, how a gay character's search in a hostile environment for recognition and completion remains, for the moment, intrinsically interesting and tense.

Edmund White was born in Ohio in 1940, and lived in Paris for many years. He has now returned to the United States. His other books include *States of Desire: Travels in Gay America* (1980), *Genet: A Biography* (1993), *The Married Man* (2000), *Fanny: A Fiction* (2003) and *Rimbaud* (2008).

Age in year of publication: forty-two.

Patrick White 1912–1990

1961   *Riders in the Chariot*

A Jewish refugee scholar, Himmelfarb, the half-caste painter Alf Dubbo, a washerwoman from the English Fens, Ruth Godbold, and the spinster and innocent Miss Hare, alone in the abandoned wilderness of the mansion Xanadu, are Patrick White's riders. Their stories become a study of love and hate, of good and evil; evil as epitomized by the Holocaust, but also the persecution everywhere of those who see a vision by those who don't, of the publicly weak by the publicly strong. This is the most compassionate and the most beautiful of all Patrick White's works; colours fly everywhere; his words, comic, ecstatic, are like the brushstrokes on a canvas by Nolan or Blake.

Each rider is a creator and misfit – outcasts all. Circling them, in contest, are the citizens of Sarsaparilla, Patrick White's mythic Australian suburban town. Patrick White's account of the Holocaust is an epic achievement; but Himmelfarb's experiences are balanced by portraits of the female harridans of Sarsaparilla which are acute and farcical – a fierce battalion of Barry Humphries' Edna Everages, taking the Holocaust from European isolation into neighbourhood life. Patrick White tells us in *Riders in the Chariot* 'that all faiths . . . are in fact one' – and so the greatness of the novel also rests on the fact that it remains thunderously relevant.

Patrick White, born in London of Australian parents, divided his time between England and Australia until 1948 when he settled in Sydney. Awarded the 1973 Nobel Prize in Literature, his other major novels include *The Tree of Man* (1955), *Voss* (1957) and *The Twyborn Affair* (1979).

Age in year of publication: forty-nine.

214

Jeanette Winterson 1959–

1985   *Oranges Are Not the Only Fruit*

There is something effortless about this novel; the tone is a mixture of almost innocent wonder at how richly strange things are and shrewd memories and sour observations. The narrator is both knowing and unknowing, and the play between the two makes the novel absorbing and fascinating.

Our heroine has been adopted by a most religious lady, and, it should be said, a most neurotic one, in the North of England. Prayer-meetings, stirring sermons and Bible-readings fill her childhood, as well as strange urges (and a fortune teller) which lead her to believe that she will never marry. Odd fairy tales are spliced into the narrative, which helps give this story of a charmed young girl a mythic quality. Everyone around her intrigues her, puzzles her and amuses her. She goes deaf, and the people in church think that she is full of the spirit. She goes to school, but fails to fit in, and the description of the failure contains some classic comic writing. She works in an undertaker's. She then falls in love with her friend Melanie, much to the horror of the church. She suffers from a mixture of religious fervour and lesbian passion: it is clear that one of them will have to give. She cannot go on preaching by day and doing the other by night, although she sees no reason why not. And it is this seeing no reason, this pure (or impure) determination, that lends great drama to the narrative and makes this book fresh and original, one of the best English novels since the war.

Jeanette Winterson was born in Lancashire and now lives in Gloucestershire. *Oranges Are Not the Only Fruit* won the Whitbread First Novel Prize. Her other novels include *The Passion* (1987), *Lighthousekeeping* (2004) and *The Stone Gods* (2007).

Age in year of publication: twenty-six.

Tim Winton 1960–

1991   *Cloudstreet*

Cloudstreet is an Australian novel remarkable for its sense of the country, for the atmosphere of the streets and houses, the weather, the aboriginal people who are the ghosts in every city, and their companions at the bottom of the heap, the ordinary Australian women and men who live on the cities' fringes.

Two families, the hardworking, God-fearing Lambs and the drinking and gambling Pickles, escape their diverse rural catastrophes and end up in Cloudstreet, making do, but uneasy in the midst of the city. With their children they settle into one of those vast ramshackle houses which have a life of their own, furnished with a pig outside that sings its head off 'like a bacon choir'.

Winton has an excellent ear for the words and phrases Australians use. The Lambs and Pickles argue, fight and pass the time of day in an Australian idiom which is inventive, amusing and pithy, a perfect match for Winton's natural skill at giving voice to the dreams and myths buried in everyday affairs.

Using sentiment with an exhilarating energy Winton carries each Pickle and each Lamb to magical or prosaic conclusions. It is rare to find a novel which so successfully combines family observation with unsugary charm and such easygoing cleverness, stirred into the entertainment and laughter of the people in the street.

Tim Winton was born in Perth, and lives near there, in Western Australia. His novels include *That Eye, The Sky* (1986), *Shallows* (1984), *Cloudstreet* (1990), *The Riders* (1994), *Dirt Music* (2002) and *Breath* (2008). He is also the author of a collection of stories, *The Turning* (2005). *Shallows*, *Cloudstreet* and *Dirt Music* all won the Miles Franklin Award.

Age in year of publication: thirty-one.

P. G. Wodehouse 1881–1975

1960   *Jeeves in the Offing*
(US: *How Right You Are, Jeeves*)

Jeeves is about to go on holiday (to Herne Bay for the shrimping), and Aunt Dahlia has invited our hero Bertie Wooster to her country seat at Brinkley Court, Market Snodsbury, near Droitwich, where Roberta Wickham, 'the red-haired menace', will be in residence, not to speak of Bertie's former headmaster Aubrey Upjohn MA and his daughter Phyllis, and, to thicken the plot, Adela Cream, the mystery writer, and her son Willy. Very soon all is not well: Roberta has announced her engagement to Bertie in *The Times* so that her mother, who hates Bertie, will not object to her attachment to Bertie's friend 'Kipper' Herring. 'Kipper', in turn, has written a vicious review of Upjohn's new book, he also being a former pupil of Upjohn.

Is Willy Cream mad? Should Phyllis become engaged to him? Aunt Dahlia has cleverly lured Sir Roderick Glossop, the brain surgeon, to pretend he is her butler Swordfish and thus observe young Cream. 'Kipper', in the meantime, is invited to distract Phyllis. He is in love with Roberta but enraged by her ad in *The Times*. Ma Cream, the mystery writer, is snooping around. Upjohn is suing the reviewer of his book for libel. 'Kipper' will be ruined. Where is Aunt Dahlia's husband's eighteenth-century silver cow-creamer? Luckily for everybody, Jeeves, who has been reading Spinoza's *Ethics*, returns from his holiday, and the day is saved. The writing, as always, is sharply comic, and the plotting is as elaborate as ever. This is vintage Wodehouse.

P. G. Wodehouse was born in Guildford, Surrey. He lived in Berlin for several years and eventually settled in the USA. He wrote vast numbers of books, including the Blandings series of novels, and the series of books about Bertie Wooster and his valet Jeeves.

Age in year of publication: seventy-nine.

Tom Wolfe 1931–

1988   *The Bonfire of the Vanities*

Tom Wolfe is a brilliant 'reporter novelist', one of those writers who, avoiding literary 'isms', take life as his subject. Tom Wolfe was lucky. For his version of *The Rake's Progress*, he had the comic insanities of 1980s New York for his material and, cool pioneer of the 'New Journalism', a baroque writing style to match.

This is a panoramic, rumbustious cartoon of a novel, encompassing every chicanery and vanity New York has to offer. Sherman McCoy is a Wall Street man with an annual salary of a few bucks less than a million dollars, a wife Judy and a mistress Maria. As with so much else in Sherman's life Maria is a mistake: she involves him in a car accident with two black youths one of whom is mortally wounded and . . . bingo! Enter black ghetto leader Reverend Reggie Bacon, poisonous English hack Peter Fallow, harassed Assistant District Attorney Larry Kramer, and creepily ambitious District Attorney Abe Weiss – living, walking and talking examples of the seven deadly sins. All bring about Sherman's downfall with brio and enthusiasm.

Tom Wolfe comes at the vanities of man like a boxer punching the air, using wit, audacity and ridicule as weapons. As a demolition job on the prancing snobberies, arrogance, greed and ambitions of American man, the novel is unsurpassed, and as a novel of unlimited entertainment and social comment, likewise.

Tom Wolfe was born in Virginia and lives in New York. His renowned non-fiction includes *The Electric Kool-Aid Acid Test* (1968) and *The Right Stuff* (1979). His other novels are *A Man In Full* (1998), and *I am Charlotte Simmons* (2004).

Age in year of publication: fifty-seven.

Tobias Wolff 1945–

1996   *The Night in Question*

The Americans encountered in these short stories could, with a bit of adaptation of surroundings and preoccupations, just as easily be Muscovites or New Zealanders. Wolff's people are loners living together. 'Even together, people were as solitary as cows in fields all facing off in different directions.' But there is no self-pity and little sadness here. Instead, Wolff conjures up certain moments of recognition, moments when the riddles posed by the bewildering behaviour of others rise to the surface for baffled inspection.

Each story is firmly placed within the traumas and trivia of daily life: the jumble of bottles and tubes on a dressing table, the flickering of the television set, 'chemical gizmos' that turn the lavatory water blue. Amid this entirely recognizable world Wolff's men and women, fathers and mothers, suitors, soldiers and schoolteachers negotiate safe passage. Children look after their parents (a favourite Wolff topic), dogs bark, newspapers are read and discarded, people hope for the wrong kind of love and create their own disappointments. Wolff records all this in writing of beauty and simplicity, a lemon twist of irony or wit often present. These are stories flavoured too with Wolff's sense of delight in humankind at its most precarious, but there is always a notion of happiness fluttering in the air, like a delicate kite or a multicoloured balloon.

Tobias Wolff was born in Birmingham, Alabama, and lives in California. His books include the famous memoirs *This Boy's Life* (1989), and *In Pharaoh's Army* (1994). He has also written the acclaimed novel *Old School* (2003) and *Our Story Begins: New and Selected Stories* (2008).

Age in year of publication: fifty-one.

Francis Wyndham 1924–

1987   *The Other Garden*

In Francis Wyndham's novel, which quietly marks the end of a certain kind of English life, the narrator is a young man living in a village near Marlborough before and during the Second World War, an atmosphere recalled here through the songs and movies of that time. In this village live Sybil and Charlie Demarest, the class of English person young men were supposed to be defending, in fact odiously snobbish, boring and preternaturally cruel, most of all to their daughter Kay, whom they detest. She is not like them. Kay is awkward, undistinguished, with simple affections for the sun, for film stars and for friends. Kay has a droll penchant for not quite managing things, but she is not a snob, she loves what crumbs of life come her way, and most of all the dog Havoc whom she passionately adopts, abandoned as she is. Kay is the personification of those people who do not so much wish to be different, as are, and have to be. What happens to Kay and Havoc and the narrator is the stuff of this report from the Other Garden of England, the untended one, and nothing quite like it exists. The Other Garden gives an alternative view of the accepted world, always in subtle ways, not a word too many or out of place. Quizzically wise, irresistibly funny, this is a poignant novel of great intelligence.

Francis Wyndham was born in and lives in London. He is also a distinguished journalist, critic and short-story writer.

Age in year of publication: sixty-three.

Autobiographies and Memoirs

TWENTY OF THE BEST WRITTEN SINCE 1950

J. R. Ackerley
My Father and Myself   1968

Nirad C. Chaudhuri
The Autobiography of an Unknown Indian   1951

Frank Conroy
Stop Time   1968

Jill Ker Conway
The Road to Corain   1989

Harry Crews
A Childhood: The Biography of a Place   1978

Quentin Crisp
The Naked Civil Servant   1968

G. H. Hardy
A Mathematician's Apology   1951

Lillian Hellman
An Unfinished Woman   1969
Pentimento   1973
Scoundrel Time   1976

Michael Herr
Dispatches   1977

Christopher Hope
White Boy Running   1988

Mary Karr
The Liar's Club   1995

Maxine Hong Kingston
The Woman Warrior: Memoirs of a Childhood Among Ghosts
1976
China Men   1980

Robert McAlmon and **Kay Boyle**
Being Geniuses Together 1920–1930   (1984 edition)

Frank McCourt
Angela's Ashes   1997

Rian Malan
My Traitor's Heart   1990

Arthur Miller
Timebends   1987

Jessica Mitford
Hons and Rebels   1977

Frank Moorhouse
Martini: A Memoir   2005

Sally Morgan
My Place   1987

Blake Morrison
When Did You Last See Your Father?   1996

Nuala O'Faolain
Are You Somebody   1997

Literary Biographies

TWENTY OF THE BEST WRITTEN SINCE 1950

Peter Ackroyd
T. S. Eliot: A Life   1984

Walter Jackson Bate
Samuel Johnson   1978

Jane Dunn
Antonia White: A Life   1998

Leon Edel
Henry James 1953–1972
(5 volumes)

Richard Ellmann
James Joyce   1959

Roy Foster
Yeats   1997

Ian Gibson
Federico Garcia Lorca: A Life   1988

Gordon Haight
George Eliot   1968

Ian Hamilton
Robert Lowell   1977

Richard Holmes
Footsteps, Adventures of a Romantic Biographer   1985

Michael Holroyd
Lytton Strachey   1994
(one-volume edition)

Hermione Lee
Virginia Woolf   1996

Fiona MacCarthy
William Morris: A Life for Our Time   1994

Bernard Martin
Tennyson: An Unquiet Mind   1980

George Painter
Marcel Proust: A Biography   1989
(one-volume revised edition)

Graham Robb
Victor Hugo   1997

Richard B. Sewell
Emily Dickinson   1996

Jon Stallworthy
Wilfred Owen   1974

Claire Tomalin
Jane Austen   1997

Jenny Uglow
Elizabeth Gaskell: A Habit of Stories   1993

Poetry

TWENTY OF THE BEST COLLECTIONS PUBLISHED SINCE 1950

John Ashbery
Self-Portrait in a Convex Mirror   1977

W. H. Auden
City Without Walls   1969

Elizabeth Bishop
Complete Poems, 1927–1979   1986

Paul Durcan
A Snail in My Prime: New and Selected Poems   1993

Thom Gunn
My Sad Captains   1961

Seamus Heaney
Field Work   1979

Anthony Hecht
Millions of Strange Shadows   1977

Geoffrey Hill
King Log   1968

Ted Hughes
The Hawk in the Rain   1957

Philip Larkin
The Whitsun Weddings   1964

Robert Lowell
Robert Lowell's Poems: A Selection   1974

Derek Mahon
The Snow Party   1974

Les Murray
The Vernacular Republic   1982

Howard Nemerov
The Western Approaches   1975

Sylvia Plath
Ariel   1965

Adrienne Rich
*The Fact of a Doorframe: Poems Selected and New
1950–1984*   1984

Theodore Roethke
Collected Poems   1966

Anne Sexton
Complete Poems   1981

R. S. Thomas
Song at the Year's Turning   1955

Derek Walcott
The Star-Apple Kingdom   1979

Autobiographies and memoirs by novelists chosen in this book

Chinua Achebe
Home and Exile   2000

Martin Amis
Experience   2000

Kingsley Amis
Memoirs   1991

J. G. Ballard
Miracles of Life: Shanghai to Shepperton   2008

Julian Barnes
Nothing to be Frightened of   2008

Sybille Bedford
Quicksands: A Memoir   2005

Elizabeth Bowen
Seven Winters   1942
Bowen's Court   1942

John Cheever
The Journals of John Cheever   1991

Agatha Christie
Autobiography   1977

Joan Didion
The Year of Magical Thinking   2005

Isak Dinesen
Out of Africa   1937

Anthony Burgess
Little Wilson and Big God   1987
You've Had Your Time   1990

John Fowles
The Journals Volume 1 1949–1965   2003
The Journals Volume 2 1965–1990   2006

Janet Frame
To the Is-Land   1983
An Angel at My Table   1984
The Envoy from Mirror City   1985

Graham Greene
A Sort of Life   1971
Ways of Escape   1980

Shirley Hazzard
Greene on Capri: A Memoir   2000

Roy Heath
Shadows Round the Moon: Caribbean Memoirs   1990

Joseph Heller
Now and Then: From Coney Island to Here   1998

Ernest Hemingway
A Moveable Feast   1964

P. D. James
Time to be in Earnest   2000

Margaret Laurence
Dance on the Earth   1990

Rosamond Lehmann
The Swan in the Evening   1967

Doris Lessing
Under My Skin, Volume 1 of my Autobiography   1994
Walking in the Shade, Volume 2 of my Autobiography   1996

David Lodge
The Year of Henry James   2006

Mary McCarthy
Memoirs of a Catholic Girlhood   1957
How I Grew   1987
Intellectual Memoirs, New York 1936–1938   1992

John McGahern
Memoir   2005

David Malouf
12 Edmonstone Street   1985

Frank Moorhouse
Martini: A Memoir   2005

R. K. Narayan
My Days   1975

Vladimir Nabokov
Speak, Memory   1951
(new edition 1966)

Sylvia Plath
The Journals of Sylvia Plath   1982

Anthony Powell
Infants of the Spring   1978
Messengers of the Day   1978
Faces in My Time   1980
The Strangers All Are Gone   1982
Published as one volume: *To Keep the Ball Rolling*   1983

V. S. Pritchett
The Cab at the Door   1968
Midnight Oil   1971

Philip Roth
The Facts: A Novelist's Autobiography   1989

Frank Sargeson
Once is Enough   1972
More Than Enough   1975
Never Enough   1978
Published as one volume: *Sargeson*   1981

Vikram Seth
Two Lives   2005

Alan Sillitoe
Life Without Armour   1995

Kushwant Singh
Truth, Love and a Little Malice   2002

Wole Soyinka
Ake: The Years of Childhood
Ibadan: The Penkelemes Years: A Memoir   1946–1965

Muriel Spark
Curriculum Vitae – Autobiography   1992

Robert Stone
Prime Green: Remembering the Sixties   2007

William Styron
Darkness Visible: A Memoir of Madness   1991

William Trevor
Excursions in the Real World: Memoirs   1994

John Updike
Self-Consciousness: Memoirs   1989

Evelyn Waugh
A Little Learning   1964

Eudora Welty
One Writer's Beginnings   1984

Tobias Wolff
This Boy's Life   1989
In Pharoah's Army   1995

Literary biographies of novelists chosen in this book

Chinua Achebe
Christophe Tshikala Kamgaji
Chinua Achebe: A Novelist and A Portrait of His Society   2004

Kingsley Amis
Zachary Leader
The Life of Kingsley Amis   2006

James Baldwin
James Campbell
Talking at the Gates: A Life of James Baldwin   1992

Samuel Beckett
Anthony Cronin
Samuel Beckett. The Last Modernist   1996
James Knowlson
Damned to Fame: The Life of Samuel Beckett   1996

Elizabeth Bowen
Victoria Glendinning
Elizabeth Bowen: Portrait of a Writer   1977

William Burroughs
Ted Morgan
Literary Outlaw: The Life and Times of William Burroughs   1988

Raymond Chandler
Tom Hiney
Raymond Chandler: A Biography   1997

Bruce Chatwin
Susannah Clapp
With Chatwin: Portrait of a Writer   1997

Nicholas Shakespeare
Bruce Chatwin   1999

John Cheever
Scott Donaldson
John Cheever: A biography   1988
Blake Bailey
Cheever: A life   2009

Agatha Christie
Laura Thompson
Agatha Christie: The Biography of Agatha Christie   2004

Ivy Compton-Burnett
Hilary Spurting
Ivy When Young: The Early Life of Ivy Compton-Burnett 1884–1919   1974
The Secrets of a Woman's Heart: The Later Life of Ivy Compton-Burnett 1920–1969   1984

Robertson Davies
Judith Skelton Grant
Robertson Davies: Man of Myth   1994

Isak Dinesen
Judith Thurman
Isak Dinesen: The Life of A Story Teller   1986

Daphne du Maurier
Margaret Forster
Daphne du Maurier   1993

Ralph Ellison
Lawrence Jackson
Ralph Ellison: Emergence of Genius   2002

J. G. Farrell
Lavinia Greacen
J. G. Farrell: The Making of A Writer   1999

William Faulkner
Frederick R. Karl
William Faulkner: American Writer   1989

John Fowles
Eileen Warburton
John Fowles: A Life in Two Worlds   2004

William Golding
John Carey
William Golding, A Life   2009

Nadine Gordimer
Ronald Suresh Roberts
No Cold Kitchen: A Biography of Nadine Gordimer   2005

Alasdair Gray
Rodge Glass
Alasdair Gray: A Secretary's Biography   2008

Henry Green
Jeremy Treglown
Romancing: The Life and Times of Henry Green   2001

Graham Greene
Norman Sherry
The Life of Graham Greene Vol 1: 1904–1939   1989
The Life of Graham Greene Vol 2: 1939–1955   1995
The Life of Graham Greene Vol 3: 1956–1991   2004

Patrick Hamilton
Sean French
Patrick Hamilton   1993

Ernest Hemingway
Carlos Baker
Ernest Hemingway: A Life Story   1969

Georgette Heyer
Jane Aiken Hodge
The Private World of Georgette Heyer

B. S. Johnson
Jonathan Coe
Like A Fiery Elephant: A Life of B. S. Johnson   2005

Jack Kerouac
Barry Miles
Jack Kerouac: King of the Beats   1998

Rosamond Lehmann
Selina Hastings
Rosamond Lehmann: A Life   2002

Norman Mailer
Peter Manso
Mailer: His Life and Times   1989

Mary McCarthy
Frances Kiernan
Seeing Mary Plane: A Life of Mary McCarthy

Carson McCullers
Virginia Spencer
Carr The Lonely Hunter: A Biography of Carson McCullers   1975

Olivia Manning
Neville Braybrooke and June Braybrooke
Olivia Manning: A Life   2004

William Maxwell
Barbara A. Burckhardt
William Maxwell: A Literary Life   2005

Brian Moore
Patricia Craig
Brian Moore: A Biography   2003

Vladimir Nabokov
Brian Boyd
Vladimir Nabokov: The Russian Years   1990
Vladimir Nabokov: The American Years   1991

V. S. Naipaul
Patrick French
*The World is What it Is: The Authorised Biography of
V. S. Naipaul*   2008

John O'Hara
Frank Mac Shane
The Life of John O'Hara   1987

Sylvia Plath
Janet Malcolm
The Silent Woman: Sylvia Plath and Ted Hughes   1994
Jacqueline Rose
The Haunting of Sylvia Plath   1991

Katherine Anne Porter
John Givner
Katherine Anne Porter: A Life   1990

Anthony Powell
Hilary Spurling
*Invitation to the Dance: A Handbook to Anthony Powell's Dance to
the Music of Time*   1976

Jean Rhys
  Carol Angier
Jean Rhys: Life and Work   1990
  Lillian Pizzichini
The Blue Hour   2009

Frank Sargeson
  Michael King
Frank Sargeson: A Life   1995

Paul Scott
  Hilary Spurling
Paul Scott: A Life   1990

Christina Stead
  Hazel Rowley
Christina Stead: A Biography   1993

John Steinbeck
  Jay Parini
John Steinbeck: A Biography   1995
  Jackson J. Benson
The True Adventures of John Steinbeck, Writer: A Biography   1989

Peter Taylor
  Hubert Horton McAlexander
Peter Taylor: A Writer's Life   2004

John Kennedy Toole
  George Hardy
Ignatius Rising: The Life of John Kennedy Toole   2001

Sylvia Townsend Warner
  Claire Harman
Sylvia Townsend Warner: A Biography   1989

Evelyn Waugh
   Selina Hastings
Evelyn Waugh: A Biography   1995

Eudora Welty
   Paul Binding
The Still Moment: Eudora Welty, Portrait of a Writer   1994

Patrick White
   David Marr
Patrick White: A Life   1991

P. G. Wodehouse
   Frances Donaldson
P. G. Wodehouse: The Authorised Biography   1992
   Robert McCrum
P. G. Wodehouse: A Life   2004

Literary Prizewinners

BOOKER PRIZE

Author must be a citizen of the Commonwealth, Pakistan, or the Republic of Ireland. No short stories or novellas. No English translation. Formerly named the Booker McConnell Prize.

1969   **Something to Answer For**   P. H. Newby

1970   **The Elected Member Bernice**   Rubens

1971   **In a Free State**   V. S. Naipaul

1972   **G**   John Berger

1973   **The Siege of Krishnapur**   J. G. Farrell

1974   **The Conservationist**   Nadine Gordimer
Holiday   Stanley Middleton

1975   **Heat and Dust**   Ruth Prawer Jhabvala

1976   **Saville**   David Storey

1977   **Staying On**   Paul Scott

1978   **The Sea, the Sea**   Iris Murdoch

1979   **Offshore**   Penelope Fitzgerald

1980   **Rites of Passage**   William Golding

1981   **Midnight's Children**   Salman Rushdie

1982	**Schindler's Ark** Thomas Keneally (US: *Schindler's List*)
1983	**Life and Times of Michael K** J. M. Coetzee
1984	**Hôtel du Lac** Anita Brookner
1985	**The Bone People** Keri Hulme
1986	**The Old Devils** Kingsley Amis
1987	**Moon Tiger** Penelope Lively
1988	**Oscar and Lucinda** Peter Carey
1989	**The Remains of the Day** Kazuo Ishiguro
1990	**Possession** A. S. Byatt
1991	**The Famished Road** Ben Okri
1992	**The English Patient** Michael Ondaatje **Sacred Hunger** Barry Unsworth
1993	**Paddy Clarke Ha Ha Ha** Roddy Doyle
1994	**How Late It Was, How Late** James Kelman
1995	**The Ghost Road** Pat Barker
1996	**Last Orders** Graham Swift
1997	**The God of Small Things** Arundhati Roy
1998	**Amsterdam** Ian McEwan

1999	**Disgrace**	J. M. Coetzee
2000	**The Blind Assassin**	Margaret Atwood
2001	**True History of the Kelly Gang**	Peter Carey
2002	**Life of Pi**	Yann Martel
2003	**Vernon God Little**	D. B. C. Pierre
2004	**The Line of Beauty**	Alan Hollinghurst
2005	**The Sea**	John Banville
2006	**The Inheritance of Loss**	Kiran Desai
2007	**The Gathering**	Anne Enright
2008	**The White Tiger**	Aravind Adiga
2009	**Wolf Hall**	Hilary Mantel
2010	**The Finkler Question**	Howard Jacobson

THE CNA AWARD

Authors must be of South African birth or registered permanent residents of South Africa. Books entered for the award must be published in a South African edition. Any original work written in any of the indigenous or official languages of South Africa is eligible for consideration.

1961   **The Desert Place**   Siegfried Stander

1962   **The Bull from the Sea**   Mary Renault

1963   **The Seed and the Sower**   Laurens van der Post

1964   **Hofmeyr**   Alan Paton

1965   **British Supremacy in South Africa 1899–1907**
G. H. le May

1966   **No Ordinary Woman**   Thelma Gutsche

1967   **The Hunter and the Whale**   Laurens van der Post

1968   **The Horse Thief**   Siegfried Stander

1969   No award

1970   **The Stone Fish**   John McIntosh

1971   **The Rain-Maker**   Jack Cope

1972   **The Castaways**   Sheila Fugard

1973   **Apartheid and the Archbishop**   Alan Paton

243

COMMONWEALTH PRIZE

Any work of prose fiction first published in year prior to the award.
Author must be a member of a Commonwealth country.

1987   **Summer Lightning**   Olive Senior

1988   **Heroes**   Festus Iyayi

1989   **The Carpathians**   Janet Frame
Women of Influence   Bonnie Burnard

1990   **Solomon Gursky**   Mordecai Richler
Visitors   John Cranna

1991   **The Great World**   David Malouf
Shape-Shifter   Pauline Melville

1992   **Such a Long Journey**   Rohinton Mistry
Divina Trace   Robert Antoni

1993   **The Ancestor Game**   Alex Miller
The Thousand Faces of the Night   Githa Hariharan

1994   **A Suitable Boy**   Vikram Seth
The Case of Emily V.   Keith Oatley

1995   **Captain Corelli's Mandolin**   Louis de Bernières
Seasonal Adjustments   Adib Khan

1996   **A Fine Balance**   Rohinton Mistry
Red Earth and Pouring Rain   Vikram Chandra

1997   **Salt**   Earl Lovelace
Fall on Your Knees   Ann-Marie MacDonald

246

GOVERNOR GENERAL'S LITERARY AWARD

Selected by the Canada Council and given for outstanding English- and French-language works.

1950   **The Outlander** (translation)   Germaine Guevremont

1951   **The Loved and the Lost**   Morley Callaghan

1952   **The Pillar**   David Walker

1953   **Digby**   David Walker

1954   **The Fall of a Titan**   Igor Gouzenko

1955   **The Sixth of June**   Lionel Shapiro

1956   **The Sacrifice**   Adele Wiseman

1957   **Street of Riches** (translation)   Gabrielle Roy

1958   **Execution**   Colin McDougall

1959   **The Watch that Ends the Night**   Hugh MacLennan

1960   **The Luck of Ginger Coffey**   Brian Moore

1961   **Hear Us O Lord from Heaven Thy Dwelling Place**   Malcolm Lowry

1962   **Running to Paradise**   Kildare Dobbs

1963   **Hugh Garner's Best Stories**   Hugh Garner

1964   **The Deserter**   Douglas LePan

2001 **Clara Callan**   Richard B. Wright

2002 **A Song for Nettie Johnson**   Gloria Sawai

2003 **Elle**   Douglas Glover

2004 **A Complicated Kindness**   Miriam Toews

2005 **A Perfect Night to Go to China**   David Gilmour

2006 **The Law of Dreams**   Peter Behrens

2007 **Divisadero**   Michael Ondaatje

2008 **The Origin of Species**   Nino Ricci

2009 **The Mistress of Nothing**   Kate Pullinger

2010 **Cool Water**   Dianne Warren

HUGHES & HUGHES IRISH NOVEL OF THE YEAR

The Hughes & Hughes Award is part of the annual Irish Book Awards.

2003   **That They May Face The Rising Sun**   John McGahern

2004   **Dancer**   Colum McCann

2005   **Havoc In Its Third Year**   Ronan Bennett

2006   **The Sea**   John Banville

2007   **Winterwood**   Pat McCabe

2008   **The Gathering**   Anne Enright

2009   **The Secret Scripture**   Sebastian Barry

2010   **Room**   Emma Donoghue

MILES FRANKLIN AWARD

Awarded for a novel or play of the highest literary merit, written by an Australian, presenting aspects of Australian life, and published during the preceding year.

1957   **Voss**   Patrick White

1958   **To the Islands**   Randolph Stow

1959   **The Big Fellow**   Vance Palmer

1960   **The Irishman**   Elizabeth O'Connor

1961   **Riders in the Chariot**   Patrick White

1962   **The Well-Dressed Explorer**   Thea Astley
      The Cupboard Under the Stairs   George Turner

1963   **Careful He Might Hear You Sumner**   Locke Elliott

1964   **My Brother Jack**   George Johnston

1965   **The Slow Natives**   Thea Astley

1966   **Trap**   Peter Mathers

1967   **Bring Larks and Heroes**   Thomas Keneally

1968   **Three Cheers for the Paraclete**   Thomas Keneally

1969   **Clean Straw for Nothing**   George Johnston

1970   **A Horse of Air**   Dal Stivens

1971   **The Unknown Industrial Prisoner**   David Ireland

2009 **Breath** Tim Winton

2010 **Truth** Peter Temple

MONTANA NEW ZEALAND BOOK AWARD

This was the Goodman Fielder Wattie Book Award until 1994. Author must be a New Zealand citizen. From 2010 the prize was renamed the New Zealand Post Book Award.

1968 **The New Zealand Sea Shore**   John Morton/M. Miller

1969 **Augustus Earle in New Zealand**   A. Murray-Oliver

1970 **Fateful Voyage of the St Jean Baptiste**
John Dunmore

1971 **William and Mary Rolleston**   Rosemary Rolleston

1972 **200 Years of New Zealand Painting**   Gil Docking

1973 **Strangers and Journeys**   Maurice Shadbolt

1974 **Tangi**   Witi Ihimaera

1975 **Nothing Venture, Nothing Win**   Sir Edmund Hillary

1976 **The Wind Commands**   Harry Morton

1977 **Charles Brasch**   James Bertram

1978 **Sovereign Chief: A Biography of Baron de Thierry**   J. D. Raeside

1979 **Plumb**   Maurice Gee

1980 **Leaves of the Banyan Tree**   Albert Wendt

1981 **Eruera**   Eruera Stirling/Anne Salmond
Te Rauparaha   Patricia Burns

1982 **Craft New Zealand** Doreen Blumhardt, Brian Brake
Other Halves Sue McCauley

1983 **To the Is-Land** Janet Frame

1984 **Maori: A Photographic and Social History**
Michael King

1985 **The Envoy from Mirror City** Janet Frame

1986 **The Matriarch** Witi Ihimaera

1987 **Season of the Jew** Maurice Shadbolt

1988 **The Treaty of Waitangi** Claudia Orange

1989 **Sylvia** Lynley Hood

1990 **Moriori** Michael King

1991 **The Burning Boy** Maurice Gee

1992 **Portrait of the Artist's Wife** Barbara Anderson

1993 **Going West** Maurice Gee

(Name change to Montana Book Award)

1994 **Let the River Stand** Vincent O'Sullivan

1995 **Bulibasha** Witi Ihimaera

(Name change to Montana New Zealand Book Award)

1996 **Redemption Songs – A Life of To Kooti Arikangii
Te Turuki** Judith Binney

259

NATIONAL BOOK AWARD

Author must be an American citizen. Books cannot be submitted for this but are selected by a panel.

FICTION PRIZEWINNERS

1950 **The Man With the Golden Arm**   Nelson Algren

1951 **Collected Stories**   William Faulkner

1952 **From Here to Eternity**   James Jones

1953 **Invisible Man**   Ralph Ellison

1954 **The Adventures of Augie March**   Saul Bellow

1955 **Ten North Frederick**   John O'Hara

1956 No award

1957 **Field of Vision**   Wright Morris

1958 **The Wapshot Chronicle**   John Cheever

1959 **The Magic Barrel**   Bernard Malamud

1960 **Goodbye, Columbus**   Philip Roth

1961 **The Waters of Kronos**   Conrad Richter

1962 **The Moviegoer**   Walker Percy

1963 **Morte d'Urban**   J. F. Powers

1981	**Plains Song**	Wright Morris
1982	**Rabbit is Rich**	John Updike
1983	**The Color Purple**	Alice Walker
1984	**Victory over Japan**	Ellen Gilchrist
1985	**White Noise**	Don DeLillo
1986	**World's Fair**	E. L. Doctorow
1987	**Paco's Story**	Larry Heinemann
1988	**Paris Trout**	Pete Dexter
1989	**Spartina**	John Casey
1990	**Middle Passage**	Charles Johnson
1991	**Mating**	Norman Rush
1992	**All the Pretty Horses**	Cormac McCarthy
1993	**The Shipping News**	E. Annie Proulx
1994	**A Frolic of His Own**	William Gaddis
1995	**Sabbath's Theater**	Philip Roth
1996	**Ship Fever and Other Stories**	Andrea Barrett
1997	**Cold Mountain**	Charles Frazier
1998	**Charming Billy**	Alice McDermott

NOBEL PRIZE IN LITERATURE

Awarded by the Swedish Academy for a writer's contribution to literature, language and society.

1950 **Bertrand Russell**

1951 **Pär Fabian Lagerkvist**

1952 **François Mauriac**

1953 **Sir Winston Churchill**

1954 **Ernest Hemingway**

1955 **Halldór Laxness**

1956 **Juan Ramon Jimenez**

1957 **Albert Camus**

1958 **Boris Pasternak** (obliged to decline award)

1959 **Salvatore Quasimodo**

1960 **Saint-John Perse**

1961 **Ivo Andrić**

1962 **John Steinbeck**

1963 **George Seferis** (pseudonym of Giorgos Seferiadis)

1964 **Jean-Paul Sartre** (declined award)

1965	Michail Sholokhov
1966	Shmuel Yosef Agnon; Nelly Sachs
1967	Miguel Angel Asturias
1968	Kawabata Yasunari
1969	Samuel Beckett
1970	Aleksandr Solzhenitsyn
1971	Pablo Neruda
1972	Heinrich Boll
1973	Patrick White
1974	Eyvind Johnson; Harry Martinson
1975	Eugenio Montale
1976	Saul Bellow
1977	Vicente Aleixandre
1978	Isaac Bashevis Singer
1979	**Odysseus Elytis** (pseudonym of Odysseus Alepoudhelis)
1980	Czeslaw Milosz
1981	Elias Canetti
1982	Gabriel García Márquez

1983	Sir William Golding
1984	Jaroslav Siefert
1985	Claude Simon
1986	Wole Soyinka
1987	Joseph Brodsky
1988	Naguib Mahfouz
1989	Camilo José Cela
1990	Octavio Paz
1991	Nadine Gordimer
1992	Derek Walcott
1993	Toni Morrison
1994	Kenzaburo Oë
1995	Seamus Heaney
1996	Wislawa Szymborska
1997	Dario Fo
1998	José Saramago
1999	Günter Grass
2000	Gao Xingjian

2001   V. S. Naipaul

2002   Imre Ketersz

2003   J. M. Coetzee

2004   Elfriede Jelinek

2005   Harold Pinter

2006   Orhan Pamuk

2007   Doris Lessing

2008   Jean-Marie Gustavo Le Clezio

2009   Herta Muller

2010   Mario Vargas Llosa

PRIX FEMINA ÉTRANGER

French literary prize awarded by an all-women jury of twelve, to novels written in a foreign language. No restrictions on nationality. Books can be translations from any language.

1985 **Life and Times of Michael K**   J. M. Coetzee

1986 **Bathsheba**   Torgny Lindgren

1987 **Monkeys**   Susan Minot

1988 **The Black Box**   Amos Oz

1989 **The Truth about Lorin Jones**   Alison Lurie

1990 **The Lost Morning**   Vergilio Ferreira

1991 **The Great World**   David Malouf

1992 **Talking it Over**   Julian Barnes

1993 **A Child in Time**   Ian McEwan

1994 **Restoration**   Rose Tremain

1995 **Decanted Red**   Jeroen Brouwers

1996 **Tomorrow in the Battle, Think on Me**   Javier Marias

1997 **The Fallen City**   Jia Pingwa

1998 **Full Moon**   Antonio Munoz Molina

1999 **The White Buddha**   Hitonari Tsuji

PRIX MÉDICIS ÉTRANGER

French literary prize awarded by a jury of twelve to novels written in a foreign language. No restrictions on nationality. Books can be translations from any language.

1970 **Jump of Death**   Luigi Malherba

1971 **Deliverance**   James Dickey

1972 **Cobra**   Severo Sarduy

1973 **Life is Elsewhere**   Milan Kundera

1974 **Manuel's Book**   Julio Cortazar

1975 **The Too Brief Life of Edwin Mulhouse**
Steven Millhauser

1976   No award

1977 **The Treatise of Seasons**   Hector Biancotti

1978 **Radiant Future**   Aleksandr Zinoviev

1979 **The Harp and the Shadow**   Alejo Carpentier

1980 **A Dry White Season**   André Brink

1981 **The Day of the Countess**   David Shahar

1982 **The Name of the Rose**   Umberto Eco

1983 **The Blue Road**   Kenneth White

1984   **Aracoeli**   Elsa Morante

1985   **God Knows**   Joseph Heller

1986   **Adventures of the Fur Trade in Alaska**   John Hawkes

1987   **Indian Nocturne**   Antonio Tabucchi

1988   **Ancient Masters**   Thomas Bernhard

1989   **The Admiral's Snow**   Alvaro Mutis

1990   **The Shadow Lines**   Amitav Ghosh

1991   **The Story that was Happy then Painful then Funereal**   Pietro Citati

1992   **Wartime Lies**   Louis Begley

1993   **Leviathan**   Paul Auster

1994   **Brother Sleep**   Robert Schneider

1995   **The Castles of Anger**   Alessandro Baricco

1996   **Himmelfarb**   Michael Kruger
       Sonietchka   Ludmila Oulitskaia

1997   **The Tortilla Curtain**   T. C. Boyle

1998   **The House of Sleep**   Jonathan Coe

1999   **The Captain of his Dreams**   Bjorn Larsson

2000   **Anil's Ghost**   Michael Ondaatje

PULITZER PRIZE FOR FICTION

Author must be an American citizen. Books cannot be submitted for this, but are selected by a panel.

1950   **The Way West**   A. B. Guthrie Jr.

1951   **The Town**   Conrad Richter

1952   **The Caine Mutiny**   Herman Wouk

1953   **The Old Man and the Sea**   Ernest Hemingway

1954   No award

1955   **A Fable**   William Faulkner

1956   **Andersonville**   Mackinlay Kantor

1957   No award

1958   **A Death in the Family**   James Agee
(posthumous publication/award)

1959   **The Travels of Jamie McPheeters**
Robert Lewis Taylor

1960   **Advise and Consent**   Allen Drury

1961   **To Kill a Mockingbird**   Harper Lee

1962   **The Edge of Sadness**   Edwin O'Connor

1963   **The Reivers**   William Faulkner

1964	No award	
1965	**The Keepers of the House**	Shirley Ann Grau
1966	**Collected Stories**	Katherine Anne Porter
1967	**The Fixer**	Bernard Malamud
1968	**The Confessions of Nat Turner**	William Styron
1969	**House Made of Dawn**	N. Scott Momaday
1970	**Collected Stories**	Jean Stafford
1971	No award	
1972	**Angle of Repose**	Wallace Stegner
1973	**The Optimist's Daughter**	Eudora Welty
1974	No award	
1975	**The Killer Angels**	Michael Shaara
1976	**Humboldt's Gift**	Saul Bellow
1977	No award	
1978	**Elbow Room**	James Alan McPherson
1979	**The Stories of John Cheever**	John Cheever
1980	**The Executioner's Song**	Norman Mailer
1981	**A Confederacy of Dunces**	John Kennedy Toole

1982 **Rabbit is Rich**   John Updike

1983 **The Color Purple**   Alice Walker

1984 **Ironweed**   William Kennedy

1985 **Foreign Affairs**   Alison Lurie

1986 **Lonesome Dove**   Larry McMurtry

1987 **A Summons to Memphis**   Peter Taylor

1988 **Beloved**   Toni Morrison

1989 **Breathing Lessons**   Anne Tyler

1990 **The Mambo Kings Play Songs of Love**
Oscar Hijuelos

1991 **Rabbit at Rest**   John Updike

1992 **A Thousand Acres**   Jane Smiley

1993 **A Good Scent from a Strange Mountain**
Robert Olen Butler

1994 **The Shipping News**   E. Annie Proulx

1995 **The Stone Diaries**   Carol Shields

1996 **Independence Day**   Richard Ford

1997 **Martin Dressler: The Tale of an American
Dreamer**   Steven Millhauser

1998 **American Pastoral**   Philip Roth

1999	**The Hours**	Michael Cunningham
2000	**Interpreter of Maladies**	Jhumpa Lahiri
2001	**The Amazing Adventures of Kavalier and Clay**	Michael Chabon
2002	**Empire Falls**	Rick Russo
2003	**Middlesex**	Jeffrey Eugenides
2004	**The Known World**	Edward P. Jones
2005	**Gilead**	Marilynne Robinson
2006	**March**	Geraldine Brooks
2007	**The Road**	Cormac McCarthy
2008	**The Brief Wondrous Life of Oscar Wao**	Junot Diaz
2009	**Olive Kitteridge**	Elizabeth Strout
2010	**Tinkers**	Paul Harding

STAKIS PRIZE FOR SCOTTISH WRITER OF THE YEAR

Author must have been born in Scotland, have Scottish parents or have been resident in Scotland for a considerable period, or have taken Scotland as his or her inspiration. Entries in Scots, English and Gaelic are all eligible. Until 1997, named the McVities Prize for Scottish Writer of the Year.

1987   **Nairn in Darkness and Light**   David Thomas

1988   **The Great Profundo and Other Stories**
Bernard MacLaverty
Antarctica: Beyond the Frozen Sea
Edwin Mickleburgh

1989   **MacDiarmid**   Alan Bold

1990   **From Wood to Ridge**   Sorley Maclean

1991   **Brazzaville Beach**   William Boyd

1992   **Scotland's Music**   John Purser

1993   **Landscapes and Memories**   John Prebble

1994   **Foreign Parts**   Janice Galloway

1995   **Something Very Like Murder**   Frank Kuppner

1996   **Stone Garden and Other Stories**   Alan Spence

1997   **Oideachadh Ceart agus dáin ede/A Proper Schooling**   Aonghas MacNeacail

1998   **The Good Times**   James Kelman
Virtual and Other Realities   Edwin Morgan

277

SALTIRE SOCIETY SCOTTISH BOOK OF THE YEAR

1996   **The Kiln**   William McIlvanney

1997   **Grace Notes**   Bernard MacLaverty

1998   **The Sopranos**   Alan Warner

1999   **Pursuits**   George Bruce

2000   **The Lantern Bearers: A Novel**   Ronald Frame

2001   **Medea**   Liz Lochhead

2002   **Clara: A Novel**   Janice Galloway

2003   **Joseph Knight**   James Robertson

2004   **In Another Light**   Andrew Greig

2005   **Case Histories**   Kate Atkinson

2006   **A Lie About my Father**   John Burnside

2007   **Day**   A. L. Kennedy

2008   **Kieron Smith, boy**   James Kelman

2009   **The Bard: Robert Burns, A Biography**
Robert Crawford

2010   **And the Land Lay Still**   James Robertson

WHITBREAD NOVEL AWARD

The Whitbread Book Awards are made up of six awards: first novel, novel, biography, poetry and children's. The winners of each adult category then go forward to the Whitbread Book of the Year Award. Author must have been resident in the UK or the Republic of Ireland for three years. Since 2006 this award has been called the Costa Novel Award

1971 **The Destiny Waltz**   Gerda Charles

1972 **The Bird of the Night**   Susan Hill

1973 **The Chip Chip Gatherers**   Shiva Naipaul

1974 **The Sacred and Profane Love Machine**   Iris Murdoch

1975 **Docherty**   William McIlvanney

1976 **The Children of Dynmouth**   William Trevor

1977 **Injury Time**   Beryl Bainbridge

1978 **Picture Palace**   Paul Theroux

1979 **The Old Jest**   Jennifer Johnston

1980 **How Far Can You Go?**
David Lodge (and Book of the Year)

1981 **Silver's City**   Maurice Leitch

1982 **Young Shoulders**   John Wain

1983 **Fools of Fortune**   William Trevor

1984 **Kruger's Alp**   Christopher Hope

1985 **Hawksmoor**   Peter Ackroyd

1986 **An Artist of the Floating World**
Kazuo Ishiguro (and Book of the Year)

1987 **The Child in Time**   Ian McEwan

1988 **The Satanic Verses**   Salman Rushdie

1989 **The Chymical Wedding**   Lindsay Clarke

1990 **Hopeful Monsters**
Nicholas Mosley (and Book of the Year)

1991 **The Queen of the Tambourine**   Jane Gardam

1992 **Poor Things**   Alasdair Gray

1993 **Theory of War**   Joan Brady (and Book of the Year)

1994 **Felicia's Journey**
William Trevor (and Book of the Year)

1995 **The Moor's Last Sigh**   Salman Rushdie

1996 **Every Man for Himself**   Beryl Bainbridge

1997 **Quarantine**   Jim Crace

1998 **Leading the Cheers**   Justin Cartwright

1999 **Music and Silence**   Rose Tremain

2000 **English Passengers**   Matthew Kneale

2001 **Twelve-Bar Blues**   Patrick Neate

2002 **Spies**   Michael Frayn

2003 **The Curious Incident of the Dog in the Night-Time**
Mark Haddon

2004 **Small Island**   Andea Levy

2005 **The Accidental**   Ali Smith

(Here renamed the Costa Novel Award)

2006 **Restless**   William Boyd

2007 **Day**   A. L. Kennedy

2008 **The Secret Scripture**   Sebastian Barry

2009 **Brooklyn**   Colm Tóibín

2010 **The Hand That First Held Mine**   Maggie O'Farrell

WHITBREAD FIRST NOVEL AWARD

Author must have been resident in the UK or the Republic of Ireland for three years. Renamed the Costa First Novel Award in 2006.

1981 **A Good Man in Africa** William Boyd

1982 **On the Black Hill** Bruce Chatwin

1983 **Flying to Nowhere** John Fuller

1984 **A Parish of Rich Women** James Buchan

1985 **Oranges Are Not the Only Fruit** Jeanette Winterson

1986 **Continent** Jim Crace

1987 **The Other Garden** Francis Wyndham

1988 **The Comfort of Madness**
Paul Sayer (and Book of the Year)

1989 **Gerontius** James Hamilton-Paterson

1990 **The Buddha of Suburbia** Hanif Kureishi

1991 **Alma Cogan** (US: *Alma: A Novel*) Gordon Burn

1992 **Swing Hammer Swing!**
Jeff Torrington (and Book of the Year)

1993 **Saving Agnes** Rachel Cusk

1994 **The Longest Memory: A Novel** Fred D'Aguiar

1995	**Behind the Scenes at the Museum** Kate Atkinson (and Book of the Year)
1996	**The Debt to Pleasure** John Lanchester
1997	**The Ventriloquist's Tale** Pauline Melville
1998	**The Last King of Scotland** Giles Foden
1999	**White City Blues** Tim Lott
2000	**White Teeth** Zadie Smith
2001	**Something Like a House** Sid Smith
2002	**The Song of Names** Norman Lebrecht
2003	**Vernon God Little** D. B. C. Pierre
2004	**Eve Green** Susan Fletcher
2005	**The Harmony Silk Factory** Tash Aw
2006	**The Tenderness of Wolves** Stef Penney
2007	**What Was Lost** Catherine O'Flynn
2008	**The Outcast** Sadie Jones
2009	**Beauty** Raphael Selbourne
2010	**Witness the Night** Kishwar Desai

Acknowledgements

COLM TÓIBÍN

Aidan Dunne; Anne Enright; Mary Mount; Andrew O'Hagan; Jon Riley; The London Library; The Library of Trinity College, Dublin.

CARMEN CALLIL

All my friends helped me with this book, and I am grateful to them for their suggestions, advice, conversations and for listening to me. Special thanks to:

Tariq Ali; Hanan Al Shaykh; Christine Bell; Liz Calder; Lorraine Callil; Susannah Clapp; Frances Coady; John Cox; David Davidar, Penguin Books, India; Polly Devlin; Peter Eyre; Bob Gottlieb; Sandy Grant; Kate Griffin; Clare Harman; Philippa Harrison; John Hayes; Michael Healy, The Cornstalk Bookshop, Sydney, Australia; Michael Herr; Michael Holroyd; Helena Ivins; Pat Kavanagh; Helena Kennedy; Hermione Lee; Suzanne Lowry; Roger Mackell, Gleebooks, Sydney, Australia; Mary Mackintosh and all at the Elgin Bookshop, London W11; Anthony McConnell; Hilary McPhee; David Matthews; Sonny Mehta; Di Melly; Tom Melly; Caroline Michel; Ivan Nabokov; The North Kensington Library, London W11; Craig Raine; Gail Rebuck; Jon Riley; Ann Victoria Roberts; Deborah Rogers; John Ryle; Alison Samuel; Harriet Spicer; Jenny Uglow; Caroline Upcher; Marina Warner; Joshua White; Kitty Wishart, University Bookshop, Auckland, New Zealand; to my agent Gill Coleridge and Ursula Doyle of Picador; and in particular to Max Lowry, aged eighteen when I started this book, whose relish for rock music and bad videos prompted me to provide him and his generation with this pointer, to one of the oldest and best entertainments of all.

Index of Titles